# GOVERNMENT JOB FINDER

# DANIEL LAUBER

Published by

**PLANNING/COMMUNICATIONS**

**7215 Oak Avenue**
**River Forest, Illinois 60305-1935**
**708/366-5200**

Cover design by Salvatore Concialdi

For information on distribution or quantity discount rates, contact Planning/Communications. Distribution to the trade is by the National Book Network,
4720-A Boston Way, Lanham, MD 20706, 301/459-8696.

Disclaimer of All Warranties and Liabilities

The author and publisher make no warranties, either expressed or implied, with respect to the information contained herein. The information about periodicals and job services reported in this book is based on facts conveyed by their publishers and operators either in writing or by telephone interview. The author and publisher shall not be liable for any incidental or consequential damages in connection with, or arising out of, the use of materials in this book.

ISBN:  0-9622019-1-X
Library of Congress Catalog Card Number: 90-92307

# Table of Contents

## Chapter 4:
## Finding federal government jobs

## Chapter 5:
## Finding jobs in Canada and abroad

# Preface

All we've ever tried to do is fill a void in the job–search game. Back in 1976 when we first published the 16–page *Compleat Guide to Jobs in Planning* (1976, 1978), we did it because we discovered there were many more job sources for planners than your typical planner knew and they could use a reliable, one–stop shopping center for government job vacancies. Six years later we looked around and saw that nobody had done the same for public administration. The result was the 44–page *Compleat Guide to Jobs in Planning and Public Administration* (1982, 1984).

And in 1989 when we were running out of copies of that booklet, we looked around and realized that all the rest of government lacked a similar **one–stop shopping center for government job vacancies.** The result was the 183–page *Compleat Guide to Finding Jobs in Government* which is the immediate predecessor to this book that garnered the fine reviews quoted on the cover of this book.

This book is a vast expansion and updating of the 1989 volume. It has close to 33 percent more job sources as well as a greatly improved visual appearance. But it still achieves the goal of the 1989 volume: to give you enough reliable information about each source of local, state, and federal government job vacancies so you use them most effectively to find the government job where you want to live.

Today, with over 15,000 "Compleat Guides" in print, this new book covers the whole gamut of government positions—professional, trades, labor, technical, and office support—in local, state, and the federal government, both in the U.S. and abroad. In addition, we've added illustrations and cartoons to bring a little liveliness to a potentially dry subject. And we have continued our tradition of including dozens of references and puns on the musical and cultural "icons" of our day and age in both the sample resumes and cover letters. When we refer to other books that cover an area more thoroughly, we note if they are available from us in case you can't find them in your local bookstore.

We have continued another tradition that separates us from any other books that purport to do what this books does: **we verify our job sources** as thoroughly as is practical. Unlike some so-called job sourcebooks, we include only the latest and most thorough information about each source of government jobs. Unfortunately, some of these "sourcebooks" still list job sources that folded six years ago, hundreds of periodicals that no longer carry ads for government jobs, and placement services and on-line databases that ceased operating long ago.

This book could not have been prepared without the very kind cooperation of the people who publish and operate the job sources enumerated in these pages. I offer my deepest thanks to them for providing the information needed to determine if the job-quest aides they produce and operate would really help people seeking work in government.

Ronald Krannich of Impact Publications warrants my unending gratitude for his practical advice concerning the preparation and printing of this book and for his encouragement. He has been sort of a "fairy god-father" with his wise counsel.

I would particularly like to thank my research assistants— Christopher Lasch, Gerrold Macoy, Christopher M. Wienke, Matthew B. Wienke, and Quito Zuba—for a job well done. Little did they know that they would spend most of their summer vacation from college in libraries and on the phone eight hours a day tracking down leads and gathering information for inclusion in this book and its companion volumes: the *Professional's Job Finder* and the *Non-Profits' Job Finder.* Thanks also go to Edith Reposh and Nancy Raimondi who put in many hours of office support and without whose help this book would not have been written. And much appreciation is offered to cover designer Sam Concialdi for his patience and talent.

These companion volumes just mentioned grew out of the fact that when I started working on this book in November 1990, I noticed that there was no one-stop shopping center for private sector or non-profit sector jobs. As the research to update the *Compleat Guide* progressed, I decided to expand our work to include the private and non-profit sectors in these other two books. Since many job sources include a good number of positions in two or more sectors, there is a little bit of overlap between the three books. However, the vast majority of the job sources they provide are very different as explained in the catalog at the end of this book.

Most of all, I would like to thank my wife, Diana, for not only putting up with me during the 14 months it took to research and write this book (during which I did a fairly effective impersonation of an obsessed workaholic), but for also offering invaluable advice on the manuscript as well as moral support when the going got tough.

Finally, for those readers who have written or called during the last 15 years about the "misspelling" in the title of the three predecessor books: "compleat" in the title was not a mistake! That's just the old-fashioned way to spell "complete." I stumbled upon that spelling in a used-record bin where I spotted "The Compleat Tom Paxton." I thought this spelling might attract more attention than the conventional modern spelling. Obviously it did! However, I certainly do appreciate your well-intentioned concern.

But the title had to change with this edition. The editor of *Career Opportunities News* wrote about *The Compleat Guide to Finding Jobs in Government*: "An outstanding book, our only complaint is that the title is so passive it fails to reflect the terrific book which follows." The real nail on the coffin was a call I got from a fifth grade English teacher who asked how we can expect her to teach her pupils to spell correctly when we misspell "compleat." I guess her fifth graders are mighty precocious to look at job books at their age. Frankly, I just don't want to get those kinds of phone calls anymore.

While we have tried to make this book as inclusive as possible, we realize that some useful aides for the government job–search may have escaped our attention (and that we have, no doubt, made a few typographical errors). If you find any mistakes or know of any other sources of government job vacancies, please drop us a note so we can include them in the next edition. Let us know if you've encountered a job source that has moved, changed its phone number, or changed in any other relevant respect. There's a reader feedback form provided near the end of this book to help you send us such information.

Thanks for purchasing the *Government Job Finder*. If you follow the suggestions in Chapter 1 on how to use this book effectively, it will help you find the government job you want, in the locale in which you wish to live.

*Daniel Lauber*

Daniel Lauber
January, 1992

## Production notes for folks who really care about these things

This text of this book was prepared with WordStar 2000, Version 3.5. It was then imported into Ventura Publisher 3.0 and merged with the graphics and cartoons which were scanned in. Text is set in 11–point Palatine type to make reading easier, especially for the huge baby–boomer generation this is now discovering the joy of bifocals. Camera–ready copy was printed on a HP LaserJet III using HP Type Director.

## Dedication

The *Government Job Finder* is dedicated to the millions of often unappreciated men and women who work in all levels of government and who enable this country to function on a daily basis. Thank you for your hard work and dedication, especially when unnecessary bureaucracy and politics make it so difficult to perform your jobs.

# Chapter 1

# How to use the
# *Government Job Finder*

Hundreds of books tell us how to "get a job." Just as many purport to tell us to how to prepare for interviews and write dynamic resumes that will grab the eye of potential employers. Yet all this great advice—and much of it is mighty fine— is wasted if you can't find the job vacancies.

The *Government Job Finder* provides all you need to know to locate job openings in local, state, and the federal government— it's a **one–stop shopping center for job vacancies.** It also introduces you to the almost metaphysical exercise of applying for federal government jobs, and to the less onerous, but still mysterious task of applying for government jobs in Canada and overseas. Sources of government internships are also identified. In addition, the *Government Job Finder* offers solid, no–nonsense advice on writing effective cover letters and resumes as well as preparing for job interviews.

Once you have some idea of the type of government work you want, the *Government Job Finder* is the place to start your job search—and it is essential that you read this chapter before you go any further in this book so you will be able to find all the job sources that will help you. If you follow the suggestions this chapter presents for using the *Government Job Finder*, job openings at all levels of government will soon be at your fingertips in both the so-called "non-professional" technical, labor, trades, and office support (clerical, secretarial, etc.) fields, as well as in the following government professional specialities:

Accounting
Aerospace
Agriculture
Airport operations
Animal control
Aquariums
Architecture
Archival services
Arts
Code enforcement
Communications
Community development
Correctional services
Court administration
Court reporting
Data processing and computers
Economic development
Emergency management
Employee relations
Engineering
Environment
Finance
Fire protection
Fleet/facilities management
Forestry
Grounds management
Horticulture
Housing
Human services
Labor relations
Landscape architecture
Law enforcement
Legal services

Library services
Media
Mental health
Museum services
Parking
Parks and recreation
Personnel
Planning
Political industry
Port management
Property management
Public administration
Public health
Public safety
Public works
Purchasing
Real estate appraisal
Real estate management
Records management
Risk management/insurance
Sanitation services
Social services
Solid waste management
Tax assessment
Trades
Traffic engineering and parking
Transit management
Transportation planning
Urban design
Utilities management
Water/wastewater operations
Zoos

One of the most difficult parts of job hunting involves finding out what jobs are available in the geographic area in which you wish to ply your skills. Most people in government are aware of only one or two publications that advertise government positions in their field and maybe a job hotline with a tape recording that names job openings. Yet, every month, there are dozens and sometimes hundreds or even thousands of government jobs in the same field that are advertised in periodicals, job hotlines, or available from job–matching sevices that you never dreamed existed.

The *Government Job Finder* will lead you to the periodicals, job banks, and job hotlines that announce government job openings

## SYLVIA
by Nicole Hollander

in your specialty. Because it is often necessary to contact an agency directly to learn about job openings, this book identifies nearly 200 directories of local, state, and federal government officials, agencies, and departments to get you to the right person the first time you try.

In addition, this volume offers concise advice to help you prepare more effective cover letters and resumes. It also suggests techniques for preparing for a job interview so you can present the best possible portrait of yourself to the interviewer. Chapters two through five of this book also identify salary surveys that will enable you to be more effective when negotiating salary. Not only does this information clear up common misconceptions held by many entry-level job seekers, but it also serves as a refresher course for long-employed practitioners who have been out of the job market for years.

The *Government Job Finder* provides all the information you need to find and be hired for the government job you want, in the location you desire.

# Types of job sources

There are at least two basic ways to find job openings in government. One is the direct approach, in which you find actual job openings. The second is more circumspect, where you write, almost blindly, to possible employers to learn if there are any job openings, or if there are any expected in the near future. The *Government Job Finder* furnishes information for both techniques.

## Using the direct approach

### Periodicals

**Newspapers.** In some locales, the Sunday edition of the local newspaper may be the only accessible source for local government jobs openings. State and federal positions rarely make it into the local newspaper. In some states, a major newspaper is the best source for government job ads for locations throughout the state, and in areas like New England, throughout the region. The *Government Job Finder* identifies these newspapers in the state-by-state listings that appear in Chapter 3.

Be forewarned that it is sometimes a bit difficult to locate government job ads thanks to the unfathomable job categories used in the classified section. Many government jobs simply wind up under "Administration." Federal positions often appear in the business section. There is no national nor rational pattern. You'll have to rely on your wits to determine what categories to peruse.

**Specialty periodicals.** Most government positions, however, don't make it into the local newspaper. One of the best sources for government job openings is the specialty periodical that a professional association or private publisher produces. These appear in

Chapter 2 of the *Government Job Finder.*

Most state municipal leagues include ads for local government positions in their newsletters or magazines. Many of these periodicals devote a portion of their classified advertising to job ads or announcements. Some publish display ads for jobs, while still others print both types of ads. Some of these periodicals publish just one or two job ads an issue while others print a few hundred.

The vast majority of the specialty magazines are available to the general public, usually at higher subscription rates than for members. Some of these are available only to organization members. The *Government Job Finder* presents full information on these periodicals so you can focus on the ones most likely to carry ads for jobs for which you are qualified and in which you are interested.

**Job listing periodicals.** The best source of jobs in a particular government profession is usually a periodical devoted primarily or entirely to job ads or announcements. The number of job ads in a typical issue ranges from about a dozen to over 30,000.

Sometimes a periodical is available only to members of the organization that publishes it. Most, however, are available to nonmembers as well, although members often receive the job magazine for free as part of their membership package or for a reduced fee.

Since so many professional organizations publish job ads in their periodicals, the *Government Job Finder* also tells you about several directories of associations so you can track down any that might have escaped our attention. As your read this book, you'll find that some job listing periodicals are also published by private businesses rather than nonprofit professional or trade associations.

**State chapters of government professional or trade associations.** Many of the associations that publish periodicals with ads for government positions have state or regional chapters that also announce job openings in their chapter newsletters. Unfortunately, few of these national federations can provide information on which chapters publish job ads. You will have to contact an organization's national office to obtain the proper addresses and phone numbers to reach the chapter president or newsletter editor who can tell you if their newsletter features job openings. In

Chapter 2, the address and phone number given for a publication or job service issued by an association is almost always that for the association's headquarters.

**Positions wanted.** In addition to listing positions which are available, many of these periodicals let job seekers advertise themselves under a category like "Positions Wanted." Many of these are identified in the *Government Job Finder*. Before seeking to place a "Positions Sought" ad, you'd be prudent to first examine the periodical. Try to get a sample copy or examine one in a library. After you've identified the periodicals in which you want to advertise yourself, contact them directly to learn if they publish "Position Wanted" ads, any restrictions that limit such self-advertising to members only, the rates charged, and whether you can publish a "blind" ad without your name in it.

**Inspect periodicals first.** The *Government Job Finder's* descriptions of each periodical will give you a good idea whether it's worth subscribing to it. But in some cases you can't really decide without seeing a sample copy. Many publishers will be happy to send you a complimentary sample copy to help you decide if you want to subscribe. Others charge a few dollars for a single issue.

In addition, you can inspect many of the periodicals listed in the *Government Job Finder* at your local public library. Municipal reference libraries and university libraries are even better sources for the periodicals named here. The libraries of professional associations are also likely to carry relevant periodicals. However, it is usually worth the cost to subscribe to a periodical rather than rely on library copies since subscribers invariably receive their periodicals at least a few days before they are available at any library.

**Internships.** Throughout the next three chapters, you'll come upon some directories of internships and a few periodicals that carry internship announcements. The directories are more like the periodicals described here since they provide what amounts to job descriptions for the internships they list. Also be sure to consult the Index to find job sources that include internships.

## Listings for periodicals

For each periodical, the *Government Job Finder* provides the following information so you can make an informed decision whether or not to seek out the periodical:

- *Periodical's name.*
- *Address for subscriptions.*
- *Publisher's phone number. Toll-free "800" numbers are given when available.*

> If a publisher has moved and the forwarding order has expired, first check the telephone directory of the city in which you wrote to the publisher for a new address. Phone directories for cities across the country are usually available at public libraries. Another good source is a current directory of periodicals or associations which give publishers' addresses and phone numbers. These are also available at public libraries.

- *Frequency of publication.* To clear up the confusion, "biweekly" means every two weeks; "bimonthly" means every two months. Semimonthly is twice a month.
- *Subscription rates.* Both rates are given when a professional or trade association charges different rates for nonmembers and members. Contact the association for membership dues. Sometimes annual dues don't cost much more than the price of an annual subscription.

Prices given are for surface mail delivery to addresses in the United States and its possessions. Listings note when different rates are charged for Canada, Mexico, and/or other foreign countries. Most subscription rates are annual rates. Rates for shorter periods of time are noted. Contact the magazines if you wish to subscribe for more than 12 months since many offer discounts for two- or three-year subscriptions. Although prices are accurate of this printing, they are certainly subject to change without notice at any time.

- *Special information about the periodical.* If a periodical is regional in scope, the states within its region are noted. Also provided is any other pertinent information that will help you decide if the periodical is worth your time and money.
- *Heading under which job openings appear.* For the periodicals that contain articles as well as job listings, the heading under which job ads appear is given.
- *Number of job openings in a typical issue.* "Few job ads" means no more than two or three appear in the average issue.

## Job–matching services and job banks

Many trade and professional organizations, as well as state governments, operate a service in which the resumes of job candidates are matched with positions for which they qualify. These services can be quite effective for both government professionals and individuals seeking support, technical, trades, or labor positions in government.

Some services supply a form for the job candidate to complete, while others allow you to submit your regular resume. Most place the information you submit in a computer database while others operate manually. Some charge job candidates for their services, while others do not (they will usually charge employers a fee to access the candidates' database). The job–matching services operated by state Job Service Offices are free.

Listings of job banks or job–matching services provide the following information:

- *Name of service.*
- *Operator of service.*
- *Operator's address and phone number.*

- *Type of resume used.* Does the service require job seekers to fill out the service's own resume data form or do you submit your own regular resume?
- *How the service operates.* Is the service computer–based or manually operated?
- *Who contacts whom?* Does the job service tell the job candidate that an employer would like to contact her for an interview, or does the potential employer contact selected candidates directly?
- *Length of time resume is kept on file.*
- *Fees for applicants, if any.* Fees are accurate as of this printing. These fees, though, are no exception to the adage "things change."
- *Other pertinent information.* Some job services may be available only to members of the organization that operates the service. A few privately–operated job services attempt to compensate for past (and, to be candid, current) discrimination against minorities or women and, therefore, serve only members of the discriminated–against group.

### Job hotlines

Many professional and trade associations operate job hotlines which often offer tape recordings that describe available jobs. These hotlines have become much more sophisticated than just two years ago thanks to the wonders of the "automated attendant" device. You will almost certainly need a touch-tone phone to call these hotlines because the recorded voice at the other end will give you instructions that can be implemented only with a touch-tone phone. The most sophisticated job hotlines allow you to specify the geographic area(s) in which you are interested and the types of jobs about which you want to hear.

Some of the less high tech hotlines simply give you a recording that lists jobs. You have no control over what you hear. Often you will first hear a list of all the job titles available. If you want to hear a detailed description and how to apply for a particular position that was just listed, keep listening because that information is often conveyed next.

When you call a few of these hotlines, a live person will answer and read job openings to you. Other job hotlines can be accessed by computer (via a modem) to generate printed listings. Those that are accessible by computer modem are noted in chapters 2 and 3. Some of these job hotlines offer very extensive listings.

These are listed under the appropriate job specialty in Chapter 2 rather than under individual states in Chapter 3.

The main personnel offices of many federal departments operate tape recorded, 24-hour job hotlines. These phone numbers are listed by agency in Chapter 4.

Pay attention to the area code of the job hotline you are about to call. If the area code is "900," the call not only isn't free, but you will be charged an additional fee directly on your phone bill. When a "900" number is listed here, the charges are generally identified.

The *Government Job Finder* offers the following information on each of job hotlines it lists in chapters 2 and 3:

- *Name of job hotline.*
- *Name of the association or private business that operates the hotline.*
- *Operator's address and regular telephone number.*
- *Hotline's phone number.* A small, but growing number of hotline operators offer a "Telecommunications for the Deaf" number as well. These are identified as **TDD** phone numbers.
- *Hours the hotline operates.* Most of these recordings can be called 24-hours a day, eight days a week. But hours are listed if they are limited.
- *When job listings are changed.* So you don't waste time calling too often, most of the listings note when recordings are updated.
- *Types of jobs included.* Some job hotlines are for specific types of government jobs that may not be readily apparent from the name of the hotline. In addition, some operators of job hotlines like the State of California, have different hotline numbers for different types of state jobs.
- *Membership requirements, if any.* The description of a hotline notes when a hotline is available only to subscribers or to the sponsoring association's members.

# Using the indirect approach

Unfortunately, many public agencies are less than aggressive when announcing job openings. In a few extremely popular locales, like the San Francisco Bay Area, many agencies merely post announcements of open positions in obscure, albeit, legal places. Some governments don't advertise widely so they can keep the jobs in the "family." Others, like the City of Chicago, not only do not publicly advertise vacancies, but they post them only at the city personnel office and won't even let you apply for a job unless you already live in the city. Generally speaking, jurisdictions that do not allow nonresidents to apply are not good places to work. There is often a fear of fresh ideas that an "outsider" may bring in that could upset the apple–cart of the powers that be.

Many local and state government agencies and departments, will, upon request, place job candidates on a mailing list to receive announcements of certain types of job openings. Others will tell you about jobs available at the time you contact them. And in some instances, you just get lucky by contacting the right person at the right time.

## Using directories

*National directories.* The *Government Job Finder* includes close to 200 directories of officials and government departments to steer job seekers to the right person concerning possible job openings in a wide variety of government and government–related agencies. Speaking directly to the right person can give you a genuine competitive edge. It tells the hiring person that you've done your homework. Also, you can learn a lot more about the nature of vacant jobs and the character of the hiring agency by talking to someone in the know than just by reading job ads. As noted in Chapter 7 on interviewing, you would be most prudent to know something about the jurisdiction for which you are applying for a job when you step into that inteview.

## SYLVIA                                        by Nicole Hollander

Directories are also useful for networking purposes. They give you an opportunity to identify people who already work for the jurisdiction to which you want to apply. By knowing who they are when you meet them at professional gatherings, you can "network" with them and place yourself in a position to hear about vacancies even before they officially occur. For details on the networking game, see *Network Your Way to Job and Career Success* by Ron and Caryl Krannich ($11.95, 1989, 156 pages; for your convenience, it's available from Planning/Communications; see the catalog at the end of this book).

*State Directories.* Most state municipal leagues publish directories of municipal and county officials. A number of state governments publish directories as well. In addition, some state chapters of specialty associations publish directories of relevant local and state government departments and agencies. To learn if a state chapter publishes such a directory, contact the national organization to get the name, address, and phone number of the chapter president in each state in which you are interested.

*Libraries.* Some of the directories listed in the *Government Job Finder* are rather lengthy tomes that cost the proverbial arm and a leg. No rational individual would spend the hundreds of dollars some of these cost. Fortunately, most of them are available at well-stocked public libraries and can also be found through inter-library loan systems. Municipal reference libraries and libraries at colleges and universities are even more likely to carry the directories described in the next three chapters. The libraries of professional associations are also likely to carry relevant directories.

The following details are furnished for each of the directories of government agencies and/or officials:

- *Title*.
- *Publisher*.
- *Publisher's address and phone number*.
- *Price*. Members of an association that publishes a directory can often purchase it at a lower price than nonmembers or receive it free as part of their membership package. The price of the most recent edition is given. Subsequent editions may cost more. When a directory is available only to association members, this restriction is noted.
- *Frequency of publication*. Most of these directories are published annually or less frequently. The handful that are updated and republished several times a year are sold by subscription. The date of the most recent edition is usually given as is how often the directory is published.
- *Description of contents*. Information on the subjects a directory covers is provided when the directory's title doesn't adequately describe its contents. When it's helpful, indexing information is presented. The number of entries and pages is often provided, especially for the really large and expensive directories.

## Salary surveys

As Chapter 7 of the *Government Job Finder* explains, the more a job applicant knows about the wage scales in the locale or region for a particular position, the better he can negotiate salary and meet the employer's expectations in the job interview. In addition, knowing differences in salary between states and regions can help you decide where to look for a government job.

Consequently, the next three chapters include books, monographs, and articles that report the results of salary surveys. Many trade and professional associations collect salary data but do not publicize their findings very widely. To obtain salary information on the professions for which salary survey information is not listed, contact the appropriate professional or trade association directly. To find associations not mentioned in this book, see the directories of associations cited herein.

The descriptions of these salary survey books include:

- *Title.*
- *Publisher.*
- *Publisher's address and phone number.*
- *Price.*
- *Most recent publication date and frequency of publication.*
- *Survey coverage.* Descriptions often include details of how data is presented (by size of city, type of city, region, etc.).
- *Types of positions included.*

## How to use this book effectively

**Nationwide job–hunting helpers.** The periodicals, job hotlines, job–matching services, and directories described in the *Government Job Finder* can be divided into two classes based on the geographic area they cover. The periodicals and other job–hunting aides that feature job openings for the entire country are listed in Chapter 2. These are divided again into two groups based on the scope of their subject matter. Those that provide information on jobs for a broad range of government specialties are listed first. Next, those that focus on a particular field such as fire protection, social services, or utility management, are listed under the appropriate category of job specialties. When one or more specialities are closely related, a cross reference is provided to alert you to examine the job sources for the related specialities as well. When just one or two job sources listed under a different specialty is relevant, a cross reference to it is given.

**Local sources of state and local vacancies.** The other set of job–search aides present information on jobs available within a multi–state region or in just one state. Nearly all these job sources include the broad range of government job specialties. Chapter 3 identifies these periodicals, job hotlines, job–matching services, and directories.

**Federal jobs.** Chapter 4 guides you to the sources of federal job openings and through the unique maze job hunters encounter when seeking employment with the federal government. Also be sure to see the index listing for "Federal jobs" because it guides you to job sources in chapters 2 and 3 that also include federal positions in addition to the local and state positions on which they focus.

**Jobs in Canada and abroad.** Chapter 5 identifies periodicals, job-matching services, job hotlines, and directories that help job hopefuls find government positions in Canada and abroad. This chapter also presents general information on working, and finding work overseas.

**Cover letters, resumes, and interviews.** Chapter 6 presents succinct guidelines for writing cover letters and for preparing and designing resumes. Two sample cover letters and resumes are presented. Chapter 7 explains how to prepare for job interviews, what to wear, and how to perform at the interview. It addresses some of the many myths regarding interviews for government jobs.

# How to find technical, labor, trades, and support positions

## Local and state government jobs

Although they tend to concentrate on professional positions, many of the periodicals in the "Government Jobs in General" section of Chapter 2 carry advertisements for technical, trades, labor, and office support positions with local and state governments. Most of the periodicals and job hotlines listed under the categories of government specialties in Chapter 2 also list openings for these types of positions. Be sure to also look in the Index under "Trades" and other relevant entries.

**Local newspapers.** A fairly good source of advertisements for these types of state and local government positions is the classified advertising section in a local newspaper. Many libraries and newspaper vendors carry newspapers from around the country.

**Civil Service.** Many cities and states hire technical, trades, labor, and support personnel through their civil service systems. Contact local personnel departments directly to learn about job openings. Many of the directories of municipal officials described in Chapter 3 furnish the addresses and phone numbers of local government personnel departments. Each state–by–state listing explains how to find openings in that state's government.

**Job Service Offices.** One of your best bets is to examine the job sources available in the state–by–state listings in Chapter 3. These include Job Service or Employment Security offices which generally operate a computer–based system that matches applicants with the local and/or state government jobs for which they qualify. Since all government jobs are supposed to be listed with these services, you stand a very good chance of finding local and state positions at Job Service Offices. See the discussion of them in Chapter 3. For state government positions, read the specific sections on state jobs for each state in Chapter 3.

## Federal government jobs

Chapter 4 brings you descriptions of a number of periodicals that carry lists or announcements of jobs with the federal government. Unless otherwise indicated, these periodicals list job openings for technical, trades, labor, and support jobs, as well as for professional positions. Be sure to also look in the Index under ''Federal jobs'' for entries in other chapters that include federal positions.

Chapter 4 also explains how to find job openings directly from the federal government. It provides the telephone number for the main personnel office for over 200 federal departments and agencies as well as their job hotlines. In addition, it describes several guides to federal jobs including one specifically directed to technical, trades, support, and labor positions and one solely devoted to the U.S. Postal Service. For more details, see the discussion below on finding professional positions in the federal government.

**Federal Job Information Centers.** The Federal Job Information Centers (FJICs) located throughout the country are an excellent source of non-professional positions with the national government. These are discussed in detail in Chapter 4. Each center has information on federal jobs located in a specific geographic area. To find the FJIC closest to you, see the state-by-state listings in Chapter 3. Also note that many federal openings are listed in each state's Job Service Offices which are also identified in the state-by-state part of Chapter 3.

## Government jobs in Canada and abroad

While most of the periodicals listed in Chapter 5 won't help non-professionals very much, the directories will enable you to determine where to find job openings and to whom to apply for jobs with foreign governments. In addition, a number of the general books on overseas employment will be very helpful.

You should be aware, though, that many foreign governments hire only their own citizens. Before applying for a job with a foreign government, you would be prudent to first learn if it hires foreigners and learn the visa and work permit rules.

Since the United States government is one of the largest overseas employers, see Chapter 4 as well. The periodicals that list U.S. government jobs include both domestic and foreign positions for technical, trades, labor, and support employees. For more details, see the discussion below on overseas hiring for professional positions.

# How to find professional positions

## Local and state government jobs

Start with the nationwide job-quest aides identified in Chapter 2. First look under the heading "Government jobs in general" for the job sources that cover more than just one government job specialty. These job helpers are quite broad in coverage. Each issue of these periodicals is almost certain to include ads for professional positions in most, if not all, of the classifications into which job specialities are divided later in Chapter 2. The job sources in this section focus largely on local government jobs, although some state jobs and even federal positions creep in.

Next, turn to the section headed ''Jobs by specialty'' to find the job category or categories that are most related to the sort of work you seek. These categories are cross–referenced so periodicals, job–matching services, job hotlines, and directories that serve more than one discipline can be easily found. Virtually all of the job–search aides identified here are nationwide in scope. Regional and state job sources for a particular field are generally listed here with the nationwide job sources, rather than in the state–by–state listings of Chapter 3.

You'll find that the number of items presented in each category varies significantly. There are simply more job sources available for some specialties than for others. For those specialities with few nationwide job sources, you will have to rely more heavily on the job sources in the ''Government Jobs in General'' section of Chapter 2 and in the state–by–state listings in Chapter 3. *Be sure to also look in the Index.*

Finally, turn to Chapter 3 for job–search aides that cover multi–state regions and individual states. You'll first come upon a catalog of nationwide directories of local government officials and departments, followed by a list of nationwide directories of state agencies and officials. These can be used to contact the appropriate officials for local or state government jobs.

For job sources in a particular state, refer to the section headed ''Job sources: State–by–state.'' Be sure to read the material that precedes the state listings. Job sources identified include periodicals, usually state municipal league magazines, that carry local government job announcements; job–matching services; directories of local and/or state officials; and job hotlines. In addition, information specific to finding state jobs is provided. The state agency locator telephone number is provided for each state as is the address and phone of the pertinent Federal Job Information Center or centers.

# Federal government positions

Federal positions rarely appear in the periodicals, job hotlines, and job–matching services that handle state and local government jobs.

Chapter 4 walks you through the most effective ways to find jobs with the federal government. After explaining the federal hiring system, it presents the periodicals that list job openings in the federal government. Cross references are made to the relevant periodicals or job services listed earlier in Chapter 2. Be sure to also look in the Index under "Federal jobs" for entries in other chapters that include federal positions.

Next, you are introduced to the unique world of the federal government's own job sources. Using them is definitely not for the faint of heart. However, job seekers are often best off contacting an agency's personnel department directly to learn of job openings, obtain job announcements, and procure an application. You will be introduced to the directories that get you to the appropriate officials in each federal agency. An extensive list of job hotlines and main personnel office telephone numbers is furnished for selected federal departments.

The chapter ends with descriptions of several books that help you apply for a federal job. Some of these proffer detailed information on federal job classifications, which agencies hire which classifications, where the jobs are located, which jobs and departments and agencies are exempt from using the Office of Personnel Management's hiring procedures, and how to complete the dread SF–171 application form.

# Government jobs in Canada and abroad

Start with Chapter 5, which describes the periodicals, job services, and directories of foreign regimes and officials that guide you to government positions overseas and in Canada. Since job hunting outside the U.S. requires adapting to procedural and cultural differences, several books on the overseas job search game are included. You should also examine the entries in Chapter 2 because many of them include advertisements for jobs overseas. Look in the Index under "Foreign jobs" to find these. Those that frequently sport such announcements are so noted in their Chapter 2 listings. Chapter 5 also refers you directly to several periodicals in Chapter 2 that carry an extensive number of foreign job openings.

Just as only U.S. citizens can work for the United States government, many other countries also restrict government employment to their own citizens. Before applying for a position with a foreign government, be sure to find out if it hires aliens as well as its visa and work permit regulations.

Because the United State government is a major overseas employer, several of the job–hunting aides cited in Chapter 4 supply information on finding overseas employment with the federal government.

**Canada**. There are many fewer job services available in Canada than one might intuitively expect. Consequently, the listings for Canada are relatively slim. Job sources that serve a specific province are so identified.

Be sure to examine the periodicals listed in Chapter 2 because many of them contain job ads for positions in Canada. These are noted in the Index under "Canadian jobs." Those that have frequent announcements for government positions outside the U.S. are noted.

**Great Britain and New Zealand**. Several sources for government jobs in Great Britain and New Zealand are also presented. Information on government jobs was not forthcoming from other individual countries.

**Directories.** The directories presented in Chapter 5 furnish valuable information on foreign countries that is relevant to the job seeker. Use these directories to contact the relevant foreign professional associations not listed in this book to learn if they offer job–hunting services.

## Observations about patronage

Patronage continues to be the bane around the neck of cost–effective, fair local and state government. Hiring on the basis of whom you know rather than what you know has consistently led to wasteful, ineffective government employees. Bloated patronage armies continue to be one of the major reasons some state and local governments face a constant fiscal crisis.

Patronage is not limited to "non–professional" positions. By practicing "pin–stripe patronage," political bosses have been able to steer lucrative consulting contracts to favored law and accounting firms, suppliers, and consultants who contribute heavily come election time.

Fortunately, most government hiring in this country appears to be based on merit. But too much patronage remains. Rather than rant and rave further about the dimensions of the problem, let's give the last word on the subject to retired University of Pittsburgh public administration professor Christine Altenberger with the following article of hers from the November 1, 1990 issue of *PA Times*, published by the American Society for Public Administration. The article is reprinted with Ms. Altenberger's permission.

## Is patronage an ethical "No–No?"

Like other cities around the country, the City of Pittsburgh is in the process of drafting a Code of Ethics. It is fairly predictable that the debate over what, if anything, to say about patronage will be lively, and may generate more heat than light. It is a difficult area, but I hope that Code drafters will speak in a very restrictive way to patronage—for our purposes here, the awarding of public jobs to friends, relatives and political supporters. (I will beg the question of merit. Those practicing patronage almost always will assert the high qualifications of their appointees.)

What's wrong with patronage? The U.S. Supreme Court pondered that question in 1976 (*Elrod v. Burns*, 427 U.S. 347). Here, in the time–honored fashion, after local elections, the Republican sheriff of Cook County, Illinois, and other Republicans were replaced by Democrats. In a close decision, the Court held the dismissals unconstitutional: "The cost of the practice of patronage is the restraint it places on the freedoms of belief and association£. It breeds inefficiency, corruption and ineffective administration." The majority felt that accountability could be achieved by limiting patronage to policy–making positions—not the case in Cook County. In a stirring dissent, Justice Powell countered by saying, "The history and long prevailing practice across the country support the view that patronage hiring practices make a sufficiently substantial contribution to the practical functioning of our democratic system to support their relatively modest intrusion on first amendment interests...." The majority was not convinced.

The Court, in 1980, expanded and strengthened its holding in *Elrod*, saying that the ultimate inquiry is not whether the label "policy–maker" or "confidential" fits a particular position; rather, the question is whether the hiring authority can demonstrate that party affiliation is an appropriate requirement for effective performance of the public office involved. (*Branti v Finkel*, 445 U.S. 507.) The Court, then, in these two cases ... has placed significant restrictions on patronage practices. Nevertheless, there is still plenty of room for creative posturing and drafting of job descriptions.

But there is more to the ethical dimensions of patronage than has been addressed by the Court. There is more than questions of efficiency and good administration. There are larger issues and they have to do with the whole image of government and its ability to command the respect and trust of the people. This point is well illustrated in an article in the *New York Times*, March 27, 1986, headline: "The Power of Patronage."

> Federal indictments, in addition to listing extortion and bribery counts, charged that a city official and a former official used their ability to place people in city jobs as a tool to turn a city agency into a money–making machine. These officials controlled the City Parking Violations Bureau from the outside, because they used the power of political patronage to put their associates into key jobs.... They

turned the P.V.B. into their own private property, and it doesn't belong to them.

The very essence of a free government must be grounded in the belief that public offices are public trusts, bestowed for the good of the country and not for the benefit of friends, relatives, and political supporters of those in public office. The intricate web that is forged by patronage in governments across the country, in School Districts, and in authorities and special districts, is not only unfair, not only leads to corruption and inefficiency—it tears at the whole fabric of government. Is it wide-spread? You bet, if my clipping file is any indication. Is it an ethical "no-no?" Absolutely.

But wait. Is the answer really so easy and absolute? Consider the following case:

You are a member of a city council. There are two vacancies in your police department, and the city proceeds to hire two new officers. Under civil service the positions are publicly advertised, there is a competitive examination, and the top three names are certified to council. Your son takes the test and achieves the top score. He is hired by a unanimous vote of council.

Should there be a rule prohibiting relatives of elected officials from competing for city jobs?

❑ Yes     ❑ No

Should you have discouraged your son from applying for the police job in the first place?

❑ Yes     ❑ No

Should you have voted on his appointment?

❑ Yes     ❑ No

Interestingly, where this case has been "tossed out" for discussion with elected officials and others, there is strong disagreement, particularly with respect to the first two questions. A big concern is perception—how does this action look when it becomes public? How much should perception count in formulating a rule for the ethical code?

Since there is really not an easy answer to the patronage issue, is there help for those charged with pondering whether or not to restrict or prohibit its practice? Perhaps the best we can do is to keep before us a conceptual framework which provides the basis for evaluating every moral system. That framework has as its foundation the elements of human welfare, human dignity, and human justice. We are enjoined to:

- Serve the well-being of people: Do good, or at least do no harm. Ask what will provide the greatest good for the greatest number?
- Respect the rights and dignity of individuals. An individual's freedom should not be violated.
- Observe the canons of justice. Construct a political and legal system which will distribute fairly the burdens and benefits of life.

If one examines patronage within the context of this framework, does it give support to the proposition that it is ethically wrong? Going back to the illustration of the New York City Parking Violations Bureau, I think clearly it does. Here, the use of patronage did harm—to the bureau, the city, and the public. It would be hard to argue that a greater good was served. It would be hard to argue that it was fair. Public jobs belong to the public, not the friends, relatives and supporters of a few. What happened with the Parking Violations Bureau was also an affront to the dignity and freedom of all of us, and diminished the image and luster of government.

On the other hand, how about the second case—the son/police officer? It seems to me that the elements of human freedom and rights, and of fairness and justice look quite different.

In deciding the ethical dimensions of patronage, and what, if any, regulation might be appropriate, it becomes a question of balancing the interests exposed in the three elements above, and each of us might balance differently. For me, the ''greater good'' is overriding, and is not served by the traditional practice of patronage. The practice of patronage is government teaching a bad lesson about public service.

# Chapter 2

# Nationwide sources of local and state government jobs

This chapter presents the periodicals, job services (job hotlines and job–matching services), and directories that will help you find jobs in municipal, township, county, regional, and state government throughout the country. Aides that focus on a single state or a multi–state region appear in Chapter 3. Job sources solely for federal government positions are presented in Chapter 4.

In this chapter, the job–hunting aides that cover the wide gamut of government specialities are presented first. For additional job sources that focus on individual government specialties such as accounting, engineering, law enforcement, library services, planning, public administration, and waste water management—and their related technical, trades, labor, and support positions—see the "Job sources by specialty" entries in this chapter, where periodicals, job–matching services, job hotlines, and directories are identified for each of over 50 different government disciplines. Because so many of these specialities overlap, cross references are made to related fields and to specific periodicals, job services, and directories listed elsewhere in the *Government Job Finder*. For the government specialties which do not have helpful job aides that focus on them alone, job openings can be found in the periodicals and other job aides listed under "Government jobs in general'' as well as in the state–by–state listings in Chapter 3. Also, be sure to consult the Index for references to these specialties. However, some of these specialties really don't have many good sources for job vacancies that focus primarily on government positions. In those instances, you will be referred to one or both of the companion books to this volume, the *Professionals Job Finder* or the *Non-Profits' Job Finder*. The job sources in those books include the relatively few local and state government positions that get advertised.

Federal job seekers should be aware that federal positions sometimes appear in a number of the periodicals itemized in this chapter. The publication descriptions note when federal jobs are frequently listed. Also see ''Federal jobs'' in the Index.

Similarly, positions in Canada or abroad are included in some of the periodicals included in this chapter. A publication's description notes when ads for foreign positions appear in it on a regular basis. See ''Canadian jobs'' and ''Foreign jobs'' in the Index.

---

**Job sources are presented in groups under the labels: Job openings, Job services, Directories, and Salary surveys. Within each classification, sources are listed in this order: those with the broadest coverage that are the most helpful come first, followed by those with a more narrow focus.**

---

# Government Jobs in General

**How to procede.** The periodicals, job services (primarily job–matching placement services and job hotlines), and directories listed in this section will help government professionals find positions in virtually all of the fields itemized in the ''Jobs by specialty'' section that follows.

First, identify any items in this section that would help your job search. Then, be sure to check the applicable categories in the "Jobs by specialty" section. Many of the positions advertised in the periodicals detailed below may not appear in the more specialized periodicals, and vice versa. Ads for support jobs, labor, trades, and technical positions often appear in many of the periodicals listed by specialty. Be sure to also check the Index if you can't find your specialty with ease.

Few periodicals that present job openings in higher education are included here. See the *Non-Profits' Job Finder* for those job sources.

## Job openings

*Jobs Available: A Listing of Employment Opportunities in the Public Sector*

**Western Edition** (P.O. Box 1040, Modesto, CA 95353; phone: 209/571-2120) biweekly; $20/annual subscription plus 7.25 percent sales tax for California residents. Serves mainly the states from Colorado westward. A typical issue features 175 to 225 job openings in all facets of local government, including local school administration. The relatively few number of ads for state government positions are usually for positions in the smaller western states.

**Eastern/Midwest Edition** (P.O. Box 1222, Newton, IA 50208-1222; phone: 515/791-9019) biweekly, $17/annual subscription. Features 30 to 50 ads for mostly local government jobs from the Mountain Plains states to the Atlantic Ocean.

**If you didn't read Chapter 1 first, you will be unable to find all the job sources applicable to your job search. It explains how to use this book—exactly the sort of chapter nobody ever wants to read. But you will be lost without it—guaranteed!**

*Affirmative Action Register* (Warren H. Green, Inc., 8356 Olive Blvd., St. Louis, MO 63132; phones: 800/537-0655, 314/991-1335) monthly, individuals: $15/annual subscription, $8/six-month subscription; free to institutional and organizational minority, female, or disabled candidate sources. Dozens of positions in all phases of government appear throughout this publication.

*Careers and the disABLED* (Equal Opportunity Publications, 44 Broadway, Greenlawn, NY 11740; phone: 516/261-9080) three issues/year, $10/annual subscription. Over 60 display ads throughout this magazine feature positions in all areas of government (and the private sector) for college graduates from employers who certify they are equal opportunity employers who will hire people who have disabilities. Readers can submit their resume to the magazine which then forwards them to advertising employers the job seeker names—for free.

*Mainstream Magazine* (2973 Beech St., San Diego, CA 92102; phone: 619/234-3138) 10 issues/year, $20/annual subscription (U.S.), $32/Canada. More than five ads appear under "Classifieds—Employment" from employers who certify they are equal opportunity employers who will hire people who have disabilities.

*CareerWOMAN* (Equal Opportunity Publications, 44 Broadway, Greenlawn, NY 11740; phone: 516/261-8899) three issues/year, $13/annual subscription, free to female college graduates and female students within two years of graduation (request application form). Around a dozen or so job ads appear throughout the magazine, including federal positions. Readers can submit their resume to the magazine which then forwards them to advertising employers the job seeker names—for free.

*The Part-Time Professional* (Association of Part-Time Professionals, 7700 Leesburg Pike, Suite 216, Falls Church, VA 22043; phone: 703/734-7975) available only to members, included in dues. The typical issue includes about five positions under "Part-Time Job Leads Fed./State/Local Government."

*The National Directory of Internships* (National Society for Internships and Experiential Education, Suite 207, 3509 Haworth Dr., Raliegh, NC 27609; phone: 919/787-3263) biannual, $24/nonmember U.S., $20/member. Lists 28,000 internship opportunities in 72 different fields with chapters on the arts, business, clearinghouses, communications, consumer affairs, education, environment, government, health, human services, international affairs, musuems and history, public interest, sciences, women's issues, and resources for international internships.

*1992 Internships* (Petersons Guides, P.O. Box 2123, Princeton, NJ 08543-2123; phone: 800/338-3282) $27.95. Updated annually, this 300+ page book provides detailed descriptions and application instructions for 38,000 short-term job opportunities for 23 fields including all levels of government. It includes 6,400 overseas internship opportunities, geographic and alphabetical indexes, and details on regional and national internship clearinghouses.

*1992 Summer Employment Directory of the United States* (Petersons Guides, P.O. Box 2123, Princeton, NJ 08543-2123; phone: 800/338-3282) $14.95. Published annually in the autumn. Its 200+ pages list over 75,000 summer job openings at resorts, camps, amusement parks, national parks, and government.

## Job services

*Career Placement Registry* (Career Placement Registry, Inc., 302 Swann Ave., Alexandria, VA 22301; phones: 800/368-3093, 703/683-1085) registration fees: $15/students, others by salary sought: $25/through $20,000 salary, $35/$20,001-$40,000 salary, $45/$40,001+. Complete detailed data entry form. Resume information kept in database for six months. Database updated weekly. Maintains resume database that employers access through DIALOG Information Services computer network. Employers contact registrant directly. Over 11,000 governments and non-profit organizations—all potential employers—have access to CPR's database.

*CU Career Connection* (University of Colorado, Campus Box 133, Boulder, CO 80309-0133; phone: 303/492-4127) $20/two-month fee entitles you to a "passcode" which unlocks this job hotline. You need a touchtone phone to call and request the field in which you are interested and geographic area in which you want to hear job openings. One of the choices is a lengthy list of job vacancy hotline phone numbers. The hotline is turned off Monday through Friday, 2 to 4 p.m. for daily updating.

*JOBSource* (Computerized Employment Systems, Inc., 1720 W. Mulberry, Suite B9, Fort Collins, CO 80521; phones: 800/727-5627, 303/493-1779) There are three services available using an extensive database of over 700 positions, mostly in the environmental arena, but also including: administration, agricultural sciences, biological sciences, botany, camp personnel, chemistry, communication and the arts, computer science and mathematics, education, engineering, finance, fisheries, forestry, geology, health care, horticulture, hydrology/water quality, law, microbiology, natural resources, natural sciences, park and forest ranger and patrol, park administration, physical sciences, range sciences, recreation, social sciences, therapeutics, wildlife biology, and zoology.

For individuals, the most useful is JOBSource's in-house search program. Obtain a resume application form from JOBSource. Within two weeks of receiving your completed form, JOBSource will conduct a job search of its database for you. JOBSource guarantees from six to 25 matches per search. The cost is $30. If fewer than six matches are found, JOBSource will run a second search the next month for free. If the second run turns up fewer than six matches, there is a $5 charge for that second run.

However, if you have a computer and modem, you can download the entire database onto your computer for $20 plus your phone call. It takes 20 to 40 minutes to download the three files. To update, you need download just one file which takes about 20 minutes and costs $15. The database is updated every Thursday. A growing number of universities and colleges are subscribing to JOBSource. They receive the database and user programs around the 24th of each month and can conduct their own job searches. Subscriptions are available for a year ($495), the nine months of September through May ($375), or for the three months of January, April, and November ($189).

*Public Service Minority Résumé Bank* (ACCESS: Networking in the Public Interest, 50 Beacon St., Boston, MA 02108; phone: 617/720-5627). This service was still being designed at this writing. Contact for details.

*Computer Assisted Matching Program* (Air Force Association/Militran, 1501 Lee Highway, Arlington, VA 22209-1198; phones: 800/727-3337, 703/247-5800) available only to AFA members, free. Submit the completed resume form and this service will match you to available jobs in virtually any area of government.

## Directories

*National Trade and Professional Association of the United States* (Columbia Books, 1212 New York Ave., NW, Suite 300, Washington, DC 20005; phone: 202/898-0662) $55. With information on over 6,450 trade and professional associations, this annual volume enables you to identify any government professional associations beyond those included in this volume.

*Encyclopedia of Associations 1992* (Gale Research, Inc., 835 Penobscot Bldg., Detroit, MI 48226; phone: 800/877-4253) Volume 1: *National Organizations of the U.S.* $320/set of three parts, published July 1991, includes entries on over 22,000 associations including hundreds for government professionals. Usually available at public libraries. Volume 2: *Geographic and Executive Indexes*, $265, published July 1991, enable you to locate organizations in a particular city and state to identify association executives. Volume 3, $275, published in November 1991, provides full entries on associations not listed in Volume 1.

The *Encyclopedia of Associations* is available on the DIALOG online computer service (File number 114) on which records can be accessed by name, key word, description, publications, and other fields. For information on online subscriptions, contact DIALOG Information Services (3460 Hillview Ave., Palo Alto, CA 94304; phone: 800/334-2564)

The *Encyclopedia of Associations* is also available on CD-ROM as part of *Gale GlobalAccess: Associations* ($995/annual single-user subscription. Issued every June and December. Includes one updated replacement disc after six months.

## Salary surveys

*The American Alamanac of Jobs and Salaries* (Avon Books, 105 Madison Ave., New York, NY 10016) $15.95. 665 pages. This is a good general source on salaries. It covers a broad spectrum of careers. However, it is not nearly as thorough as the salary studies conducted by trade and professional organizations. Most recent 1990-1991 edition; expect a new edition by 1993.

*American Salaries and Wages Survey* (Gale Research, Inc., 835 Penobscot Bldg., Detroit, MI 48226; phone: 800/877–4253) $89.50, 1991, 1,125 pages. Covers more than 4,500 occupational classifications with salary ranges, entry level, highest paid. Figures are derived from more than 300 publications issued by federal, state, and local governments, and professional organizations.

*Governing* (Congressional Quarterly, Inc., 2300 N St., NW, Washington, DC 20037; phones: 800/829–9105, 202/867–8802) monthly, $48/annual subscription, $58/foreign. The December issue usually contains an annual survey the salaries of major city and county officials. *Note:* Sometimes several government job ads appear in the ''Bulletin Board'' section near the back of the magazine.

# Job sources by specialty

In this section, job–quest aides are presented by government specialty. To avoid unnecessary repetition, when a job–hunt aide provides job information for more than one discipline, a cross reference guides you to the page where a full description is given. When two specialties are very closely related, one category is cross referenced to the other where the job–search aides for both are described. When two disciplines are related, but not as closely, they are cross–referenced because many of the job–quest aides for one also encompasses the other discipline, although not as thoroughly.

## Accounting

*See listings under ''Finance/accounting.''*

## Agriculture

*Also see listings under ''Environment.''*

## Job openings

*Phytopathological News* (American Phytopathological Society, 3340 Pilot Knob Rd., St. Paul, MN 55121; phone: 612/454-7250) monthly, $15/annual nonmember subscription, free to members. About ten positions in plant pathology, genetics, or pesticides with the Department of Agriculture and extension services appear under "Classified."

*FMRA News* (American Society of Farm Managers and Rural Appraisers, Inc., Suite 500, 950 Cherry, Denver, CO 80222; phone: 303/758-3513) bimonthly, available only as part of membership package. Jobs listed under "Job Mart." Usually two to four job ads per issue, but some issues have no ads.

*Agronomy News* (American Society of Agronomy, 677 S. Segoe Rd., Madison, WI 53711; phone: 608/273-8080) monthly, $7/annual subscription, included in member-ship package. About 30 openings for agronomists and crop and soil scientists are described under "Personnel."

*Alternative Agriculture News* (Insti-tute for Alternative Agriculture, Suite 117, 9200 Edmonston Rd., Greenbelt, MD 20770; phone: 301/441-8777) monthly, $15/annual membership in-cludes subscription. Few ads in typical issue.

**Women in Agribusiness Bulletin** (WIA, P.O. Box 10241, Kansas City, MO 64111; phone: 816/361-5846) quarterly, annual subscrip-tions: $15/U.S., $20/elsewhere. Four or five jobs appear under "Classifieds."

*Farm Chemicals* (37841 Euclid Ave., Wiloughby, OH 44094; phone" 216/942-2000) monthly, free to qualified professionals. One to five display ads include jobs in agricultural chemicals, fertilizes, seed, and related regulatory and research positions.

## Job services

**Career Development and Placement Service** (American Society of Agronomy, 677 S. Segoe Rd., Madison, WI 53711; phone: 608/273-8080) $15/annual fee, free to members. Job seeker submits resume which is matched with jobs. The potential employer contacts the job seeker. Resume kept on file for 12 months; $7.50 fee to update resume during that time.

*APS Placement Service* (American Phytopathological Society, 3340 Pilot Knob Rd., St. Paul, MN 55121; phone: 612/454-7250) $35/non-members, free/members. This service sends all resumes to participating employers who then select whom they will interview. At the annual meeting, current resumes are placed in a bound volume for employers to examine. Positions are generally in plant pathology, genetics, or pesticides with the U.S. Department of Agriculture and extension services.

## Directory

*Accredited and General Membership Directory* (American Society of Farm Managers and Rural Appraisers, Inc., Suite 500, 950 Cherry, Denver, CO 80222; phone: 303/758-3513) write for price.

# Airport operations and aerospace

*Also see listings under "Engineering."*

## Job openings

*Air Jobs Digest* (P.O. Box 70127, Dept. JF, Washington, DC 20088; phone: 301/984-4172) monthly, $96/annual subscription (U.S. and Canada), $59/six-month subscription, $39/three-month subscription, $18/single issue, $140.04/foreign annual subscription (air mail). Among the 500 to 1,000 job vacancies described each issue are dozens of government positions in aviation and aerospace with the FAA, NASA, Defense Department, NOAA, and air traffic controllers and other federal positions including pilots, flight service station personnel, accident investigators, aviation safety instructors, avionics, technicians, engineers, and management and administration.

*Airport Highlights* (Airport Associations Council International, 1220 19th St., NW, Suite 200, Washington, DC 20036; phone: 202/293–8500) 24 issues/year, $110/nonmember annual subscription (U.S.), $150/elsewhere; included in membership package. About 10 positions are listed under ''Employment Opportunities.''

*Airport Report* (American Association of Airport Executives, 4212

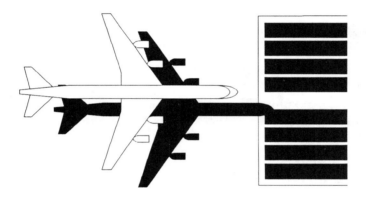

King St., Alexandria, VA 22302; phone: 703/824–0500) biweekly, available to members only, included in membership package. Jobs listed under ''Positions Open.'' Typical issue carries announcements of about 10 postions for airport managers, airport operations, and support staff (noise abatement, public affairs, engineers).

*Airport Report Express* (American Association of Airport Executives, 4212 King St., Alexandria, VA 22302; phone: 703/824–0500) biweekly, subscription price depends on size of subscribing airport. Entire issue consists of job openings for airport managers, airport operations, and support staff (noise abatement, public affairs, engineers). This newsletter, which usually features about 10 job openings, is delivered by fax rather than mail.

*Airport Executive* (Communication Channels, 6255 Barfield Rd., Atlanta, GA 30328; phones: 800/241–9834, 404/256–9800) monthly, $42/annual subscription. Among the ten ads under ''Employment Opportunities'' are usually one or two for government positions.

*Aviation Week & Space Technology* (McGraw Hill, 1221 Avenue of the Americas, New York, NY 10020; phones: 800/525–5003, 609/426–7070) 51 issues/year, $72/annual subscription. About six ads appear under "Classified–Recruitment."

*Plane and Pilot* (Warner Publications, 16000 Ventura Blvd., Suite 800, Enrico, CA 91436; phones: 800/283–4330, 818/986–8400) monthly, $18.95/annual subscription. Among the six ads under "Help Wanted" are aviation–related positions in law enforcement.

*Airport Services* (Johnson Hill Press, 1233 Janesville Ave., Fort Atkinson, WI 53538; phone: 414/563–6388) bimonthly, $24/annual subscription, free to qualified professionals. "Classified Advertising" features one or two government positions.

*National Defense* (American Defense Preparedness Association, 2101 Wilson Blvd., Suite 400, Arlington, VA 22201–3061; phone: 703/522–1820) monthly, $35/annual nonmember subscription, $30/members. Among the five or so positions for engineers, researchers, and management in the defense and aerospace industries listed under "Job Opportunities" are a few government positions.

*Air Traffic Control Journal* (Air Traffic Control Association, 2300 Clarendon Blvd., Suite 711, Arlington, VA 22201; phone: 703/522–5717) every three months, $36/nonmember annual subscription, included in membership package. A few positions are scattered throughout the magazine, although not in every issue, primarily for air traffic controllers in the U.S. and abroad, and for system engineers.

## Directories

*Who's Who in Airport Management* (American Association of Airport Executives, 4212 King St., Alexandria, VA 22302; phone: 703/824–0500) available to members only, included in membership package. Published annually.

**AOCI Member Directory** (Airport Associations Council International, 1220 19th St., NW, Suite 200, Washington, DC 20036; phone: 202/293–8500) available only to members for $35. Published annually.

# Animal control, aquariums, and zoos

## Job openings

**Shoptalk** (American Humane Association, 63 Inverness Dr. East, Englewood, CO 80112; phone:303/792–9900) bimonthly, $10/year annual subscription (U.S.), $25/elsewhere. As many as six jobs for animal care and control professionals (including administrative) appear in a typical issue under "Employment."

*Animal Keepers Forum* (American Association of Zoo Keepers, 635 Cage Blvd., Topeka, KS 60606; phone: 913/272–5821) available only to members, annual dues: $30/fulltime zoo keeper, $25/affiliates and associates, $20/libraries. Six to eight vacancies for animal keepers, veterinary technicians, and education specialists appear under "Opportunity Knocks."

*NACA News* (National Animal Control Association, P.O. Box 154, Indianola, WA 98342; phone: 800/828–6474) bimonthly, $15/nonmember annual subscription, included in membership package. Jobs listed under "Classified–Help Wanted." Four or five job ads for management and supervisory positions appear in the typical issue. For non–supervisory animal control officer positions, contact local government personnel offices and the state Job Service offices identified in Chapter 3.

*Communique Magazine* (American Association of Zoological Parks and Aquariums, Oglesbay Park, Route 88, Wheeling, WV 26003; phone: 304/242–2160) monthly, available only to members; annual dues range from $30 to $100; write for dues schedule. Jobs are listed under "Position Directory."

*Journal of the American Veterinary Medical Association* (American Veterinary Medical Association, 1931 N. Meacham Rd., Suite 100, Schaumburg, IL 60173; phone: 708/925–8070) biweekly, $70/annual nonmember subscription, included in dues. Among the 300 to 450 "Classifieds" are many positions for veterinarians and veterinary technicians.

*Veterinary Surgery* (J. B. Lippincott, P.O. Box 350, Hagerstown, MD 21741-9901; phones: 800/638-3030, 509/335-0711) bimonthly, $65/annual nonmember subscription, free to members of the American College of Veterinary Anesthesiologists. About two ads for government positions for veterinary surgeons and anesthesiologists appear in the "Classified Ad Section."

## Job services

*AVMA Job Placement Service* (American Veterinary Medical Association, 1931 N. Meacham Rd., Suite 100, Schaumburg, IL 60173; phone: 708/925-8070) available only to AVMA members, free. Complete a resume form and this service will match you with vacancies in government, clinical practice, or private industry.

## Directories

**Directory of Animal Care and Control Agencies** (American Humaine Association, 63 Inverness Dr. East, Englewood, CO

80112; phone:303/792-9900) $50 (or $2 per state listing) for non-profit agencies, $500 (or $10 per state listing) for individuals and profit-making organizations. This 200+ page directory of over 3,600 animal care and control agencies in the U.S. and Canada is maintained on computer and is published in a binder. Agencies are listed alphabetically by state and city. This directory is also available as cheshire or pressure sensitive labels.

*Zoological Parks and Aquariums in the Americas* (American Association of Zoological Parks and Aquariums, Oglesbay Park, Route 88, Wheeling, WV 26003; phone: 304/242-2160) $50/nonmembers, $25/members (add $3 shipping). Published in the summer of even-numbered years.

*ACVS Directory of Diplomates* (American College of Veterinary Surgeons, 4330 East West Highay, Suite 1117, Bethesda, MD 20814; phone: 301/718-6504) free. Published in late autumn of odd-numbered years.

# Architecture/Urban Design

*Also see listings under "Engineering" and "Planning." See the Professional's Job Finder for a larger collection of sources that sometimes have government job openings in them.*

## Job openings

*Progressive Architecture* (P.O. Box 95759, Cleveland, OH 44101; phone: 216/696–7000) monthly; annual subscription: $36/professional architects, designers, engeineers, and draftspersons, $45/others (U.S.), $75/Canada, $140/elsewhere. Jobs listed under "Job Mart." Very extensive list of job openings in good times. During recessions there are only about ten job openings listed plus "Situations wanted." Largely architecture and engineering positions. Some federal positions.

---

## If you can't find your specialty...

**You probably skipped Chapter 1, the chapter that tells you how to use this book most effectively—and the chapter nobody ever wants to read. *Please read it.* It explains how to use this chapter plus the Index to find job sources in your field, whether it be professional, trades, office support, labor, or technical.**

---

**AIA Referral Network Job Bulletin** (American Institute of Architects, 1735 New York Ave., NW, Washington, DC 20006; phone: 202/626–7300) weekly, available only to members and student members for $20 for 12 weeks. Lists jobs by category and geographic location. Can call the AIA Referral Network, 800/242-6381, for a computer printout of each job ($2 each).

*AIA Memo* (American Institute of Architects, 1735 New York Ave., NW, Washington, DC 20006; phone: 202/626–7300) monthly, $75/nonmember annual subscription, included in membership package. Typical issue has about five job announcements, although some issues have none.

## Job services

*AIA Referral Network* (American Institute of Architects, 1735 New York Ave., NW, Washington, DC 20006; phones: 800/242-6381, 202/626-7364) available only to AIA members and student members; call or write for fee structure and resume form to submit. Resume forms are on file for six months. Job seeker can call the network for a position search to get printout of positions that match her qualifications.

## Directories

*Profile* (American Institute of Architects, 1735 New York Ave., NW, Washington, DC 20006; phone: 800/242-4140) $175/nonmembers, $142/members). Lists architects and firms. Published annually.

# Archivists

*See listings under "Records management and archival services" and "Library services."*

# Code Administration and Enforcement

*Also see listings under "Engineering" and "Public Administration."*

## Job openings

*BOCA-The Building Official and Code Administrator Magazine* (BOCA, International, 4051 W. Flossmoor Rd., Country Club Hills, IL 60478; 708/799-2300) bimonthly, $18/nonmember annual subscription, add $3/year for postage outside U.S. Free to members. Jobs listed under "Classified Ads." Typical issue has about three to six job ads.

*BOCA Bulletin* (BOCA, International, 4051 W. Flossmoor Rd., Country Club Hills, IL 60478; 708/799-2300) bimonthly, available to members only. Write for membership information. Jobs listed under "Classified Ads." Typical issue sports about eight job ads.

*Building Standards Magazine* and *Building Standards Newsletter* (International Conference of Building Officials, 5360 S. Workman Mill Rd., Whittier, CA 90601; phone: 213/699-0541) published in alternating months, $21/nonmember annual subscription to the magazine, the newsletter is available only in the membership package. Jobs listed under "Job Opportunities." About 9 to 12 job ads appear in the usual issue.

*Southern Building* and *SBCCI Newsletter* (Southern Building Code Congress, International, 900 Montclair Rd., Birmingham, AL 35213-1206; phone: 205/591-1853) bimonthly in alternating months, $15/nonmember annual subscription to the pair, $12/member. Jobs listed under "Positions Available." Ranges from zero to ten jobs an issue. Includes architect and engineering positions.

## Directories

*BOCA Directory* (BOCA, International, 4051 W. Flossmoor Rd., Country Club Hills, IL 60478; phone: 708/799-2300) $40/nonmembers, $30/members. Published every two years.

**SBCCI Membership Directory** (Southern Building Code Congress, International, 900 Montclair Rd., Birmingham, AL 35213-1206; phone: 205/591-1853) $15. Published each January.

*Directory of Building Codes and Regulations* (National Conference of States on Building Codes and Standards, Suite 210, 505 Huntmar Dr., Herndon, VA 22001; phones: 800/362-2633, 703/481-2020) four-volume set: $200/nonmember, $130/member; *State Residential Codes*: $40/nonmember, $30/member; *City Residential Codes* (for 50 major cities): $40/nonmember, $30/member; *State Commercial Codes*: $75/nonmember, $50/member; *City Commercial Codes*(for 50 major cities): $75/nonmember, $50/member; add $5 for orders shipped outside the U.S. These directories help you decide where to seek a code enforcement position by identifying the codes each jurisdiction uses so you can match your experience with the jurisdiction. Also included are the names and addresses of state or city code officials.

*IAEI Membership Directory* (International Association of Electrical Inspectors, 901 Waterfall Way, Richardson, TX 75080) $25. Published annually.

# Communications

*See listings under "Media and the arts." Also see the* **Professional's** **Job Finder** *for a very extensive set of job sources which sometimes have government positions in addition to private sector jobs.*

# Community and economic development

*Also see listings under "Planning" and "Public administration."*

## Job openings

*Economic Developments* (National Council for Urban Economic Development, 1730 K St., NW, Suite 915, Washington, DC 20006; phone: 202/223–4735) 24 issues/year, available only to members; membership costs $275/year). Jobs listed under "Job Mart." Typical issue sports three to ten job ads.

**TRAVELS WITH FARLEY**

Reprinted by permission of Phil Frank. Copyright © 1982

*Council News* (American Economic Development Council, 9801 W. Higgins, Suite 540, Rosemont, IL 60018; phone: 708/692–9944) 10 issues/year, available to members only, annual membership: $265, plus $15 processing fee first year only; $140, plus $15 processing fee first year only, when another person in your office is already a member. Jobs listed under "Career Opportunities." About 10 job ads per issue.

*Resources for Community–Based Economic Development* (National Congress for Community Economic Development, Suite 523, 1875 Connecticut Ave., Washington, DC 20009; phone: 202/659–8411) quarterly, $39/annual subscription. Two to five jobs are listed under "The Checklist."

## Job services

*Resume Referral Service* (American Economic Development Council, 9801 W. Higgins, Suite 540, Rosemont, IL 60018; phone: 708/692–9944) $100/nonmembers for 12 months, free to members. Return form with 10 copies of your resume. AEDC lets you know when it matches your qualifications with a potential employer, but it is up to the employer to contact you for interview.

## Directories

*Private Sector Development Organizations: A Directory* (National Council for Urban Economic Development, 1730 K St., NW, Suite 915, Washington, DC 20006; phone: 202/223–4735) $20/nonmembers, $17.50/members. Profiles of organizations led, initated, and supported by community business and corporate leaders.

*CUED Directory* (National Council for Urban Economic Development, 1730 K St., NW, Suite 915, Washington, DC 20006; phone: 202/223–4735) $25/nonmembers, free/members. Published annually. Lists all private corporate members of National Council for Urban Economic Development.

*Who's Who in Economic Development* (American Economic Development Council, 9801 W. Higgins, Suite 540, Rosemont, IL 60018; phone: 708/692–9944) available only to members, included in dues. Published each August. Geographical and alphabetical listings of members throughout the world. Also includes lists geographical and alphabetical lists of certified industrial/economic developers.

*NCCED Membership Directory* (National Congress for Community Economic Development, Suite 523, 1875 Connecticut Ave., Washington, DC 20009; phone: 202/659–8411) $10. Published in odd–numbered years.

## Correctional services

*See listings under "Law enforcement" and "Public safety."*

## Court administration

*See listings under "Legal services and court administration."*

## Data processing and computers

### Job openings

*ASIS Jobline* (American Society for Information Science, Suite 501, 8720 Georgia Ave., Silver Springs, MD 20910–3602; phone: 301/495–0900) monthly, free. About 15 jobs appear in the typical issue.

*Computer* (IEEE Computer Society, 10662 Los Vaqueros Cr., Los Alamitos, CA 90720–1264; phone: 714/821–8380) avialable only to members. Two to 15 pages of "Career Opportunities" can be listed.

*Career Opportunity Update* (CRS Publications, 3621 S. Harbor Blvd., Santa Ana, CA 92704; phone: 714/556–1200) bimonthly, $72/annual subscription. About 50 job vacancies in computer science and engineering fill this newsletter.

*FEDfacts* (Federation of Government Information Processing Councils, c/o Virginia McCormick, 459 Carolwood Ln., Atlanta, GA 30342; 404/331–5106) free, quarterly. One to five job ads per issue.

*Journal of Systems Management* (Association of Systems Management, P.O. Box 38370, Cleveland, OH 44138; phone: 216/243–6900) monthly, $48/annual subscription, included in dues. About five positions are listed under "Joblink."

*Government Computer News* (Cahners Publishing, 8601 Georgia Ave., Suite 300, Silver Spring, MD 20910; phone: 301/650-2000) biweekly, $52.95/annual subscription, available only in U.S. Although "Career Opportunities" do not appear in every issue, when they do there are about ten positions for software engineers, programmers, and analysts, including federal positions

See also *APCO—Journal of Public-Safety Communications* listed under "Public safety."

See also *NELS* listed under "Law enforcement."

## Job services

*CU Career Connection* (University of Colorado, Campus Box 133, Boulder, CO 80309-0133; phone: 303/492-4127) $20/two-month fee entitles you to a "passcode" which unlocks this job hotline. You need a touchtone phone to call and request the field in which you are interested and geographic area in which you want to hear job openings. The hotline is turned off Monday through Friday, 2 to 4 p.m. for daily updating.

## Directory

*ASIS Handbook and Directory* (American Society for Information Science, Suite 501, 8720 Georgia Ave., Silver Springs, MD 20910-3602; phone: 301/495-0900) $100/nonmembers, free/members. Published each March.

## Salary surveys

*Computer Salary Survey and Career Planning Guide* (Source edp, P.O. Box 152109, Irving, TX 75015-9831; phones: 214/387-1600, 214/387-0795) free. Published annually by this computer recruiting firm.

*Profile of Systems Professional* (Association of Systems Management, P.O. Box 38370, Cleveland, OH 44138; phone: 216/243-6900) write for price, included in dues. Most recent edition, 1991.

## Economic development

*See listings under "Community and economic development" and listings in Chapter 5 on overseas employment.*

## Emergency management

*Also see listings under "Environment," "Public administration," and "Public health. See the listings in the state–by–state section of Chapter 3. See the information on state jobs sources in each state.*

### Job openings

*The NCCEM Bulletin* (National Coordinating Council on Emergency Management, Unit N, 7297 Lee Highway, Falls Church, VA 22042; phone: 703/533–7672) monthly, available only to members ($75/annual dues, membership open to anyone). Jobs listed under "Personnel Corner." About one job ad every three months.

See also *APCO—Journal of Public–Safety Communications* listed under "Public safety."

### Directory

*The NCCEM Membership Directory* (National Coordinating Council on Emergency Management, Unit N, 7297 Lee Highway, Falls Church, VA 22042; phone: 703/533–7672) $10. Published every January.

## Employee relations

*See listings under "Personnel/human resources."*

## Engineering

*Also see listings under "Architecture/urban design," "Planning," "Public safety," "Public works," "Sanitation/solid waste management," "Utilities management," and "Water/wastewater operations."*

## Job openings

*Civil Engineering–ASCE* (American Society of Civil Engineers, 345 E. 47th St., New York, NY 10017; phone: 212/705-7288 or 7276) monthly, $72/nonmember annual subscription, $101/foreign, included in membership package. Jobs listed under "Engineering Market Place." About 100 job ads in a typical issue.

*ASCE News* (American Society of Civil Engineers, 345 E. 47th St., New York, NY 10017; phone: 212/705-7288 or 7276) monthly, $33/nonmember annual subscription, $48/foreign, included in membership package. Jobs listed under "Engineering Market Place." About 100 job ads in a typical issue.

*NSBE Magazine* (National Society of Black Engineers, 344 Commerce St., Alexandria, VA 22314; phone: 703/549-2207) five issues/year; $10/nonmember annual subscription, included in membership package. From 35 to 75 engineering positions are advertised in every issue.

*Mechanical Engineering* (American Society of Mechanical Engineers, 345 E. 47th St., New York, NY 10017; phone: 212/705-7722) monthly, $45/nonmember annual subscription, $8/member annual subscription. Jobs listed under "Jobs Open." About 50 job ads appear in the average issue.

*Equal Opportunity* (Equal Opportunity Publications, 44 Broadway, Greenlawn, NY 11740; phone: 516/261-8899) three issues/year, $13/annual subscription, free to female engineering college graduates (or within two years of graduating) and women professional engineers. Over 25 display ads throughout this magazine feature positions in all areas of engineering. A readers can submit her resume to the magazine which then forwards it to advertising employers the job seeker names—for free.

*Woman Engineer* (Equal Opportunity Publications, 44 Broadway, Greenlawn, NY 11740; phone: 516/261-8899) quarterly, $17/annual subscription. Over 20 display ads throughout this magazine feature positions in all areas of engineering, including federal positions. A readers can submit her resume to the magazine which then forwards it to advertising employers the job seeker names—for free.

*Engineering Times* (National Society of Professional Engineers, 1420 King St., Alexandria, VA 22314; phone: 703/684–2800) monthly, $30/nonmember annual subscription, $48/foreign, $10/member annual subscription. Jobs listed under "Engineering Times Career Mart." A typical issue carries about ten to 15 job ads.

*Consulting–Specifying Engineer* (Cahners Publishing, 44 Cook St., Denver, CO 80206–5800; phone: 303/388–4511) 15 issues/year, $69.95/annual subscription, $80/Canada and Mexico, $100/elsewhere (surface mail), $150/elsewhere (air mail). Jobs listed under "Job Opportunities." Typical issue includes about three job ads.

*ENR—Engineering News Record* (McGraw–Hill, 1221 Avenue of the Americas, New York, NY 10020; phones: 800/257–9402, 212/512–3549) weekly; $51/annual subscription (U.S. and possessions), $59/Canada, $128/Europe, $144/elsewhere. Jobs listed under "Positions Vacant." Typical issue prints 50 to 100 job ads plus "Positions wanted.".

*Journal of the Air Pollution Control Association* (P.O. Box 2861, Pittsburgh, PA 15230; phone: 412/232–3444) monthly; annual subscription: $88/non–profit libraries and institutions, $150/others, add $10/Europe, add $15/Asia. Jobs listed under "Classified."

*The Diplomate* (American Academy of Environmental Engineers, Suite 100, 130 Holiday Ct., Annapolis, MD 21401; phone: 301/266–3311) quarterly, $20/annual subscription (U.S. and Canada), $30/elsewhere. Typical issue features two to four display ads for jobs.

*Graduating Engineer* (16030 Ventura Blvd., Suite 560, Encino, CA 91436; phone: 818/789–5293) monthly, $5/copy. About 30 or so display ads for all disciplines of engineers are in the typical issue.

See also *ITE Journal* listed under "Traffic engineering and parking."

See also *Airport Report* listed under "Airport services."

### Job services

*Professional Engineering Employment Registry* (Career Technologies Corp., Suite 6, 44 Nashua Rd., Londonderry, NH 03053; phone: 603/437–7337) Free service to members of American Society of Civil Engineers (345 E. 47th St., New York, NY 10017; phone: 202/705–7288 or 7276). ASCE members submit their resume (in their own format) to PEER which places it in its computer database which potential employers access via modem to identify job candidates to interview. Resumes are viewed without the job candidate's name, address, and phone, and are coded to prevent a current employer from ever seeing any portion of a current employee's resume. PEER never discloses a job candidate's identity. PEER contacts the job candidates employers wish to interview. Job candidates then can contact the employer directly.

*CU Career Connection* (University of Colorado, Campus Box 133, Boulder, CO 80309–0133; phone: 303/492–4127) $20/two–month fee entitles you to a "passcode" which unlocks this job hotline. You need a touchtone phone to call and request the field in which you are interested and geographic area in which you want to hear job openings. The hotline is turned off Monday through Friday, 2 to 4 p.m. for daily updating.

*SOLE Electronic Job Referral Service* (Society of Logistics Engineers, 8100 Professional Pl., Suite 211, New Carrollton, MD 20785; phones: 800/695–7653, 301/459–8446) free. Armed with a modem and communications software, use your computer to call 800/331–3808 (settings: 1200/2400 Baud, 8–N–1) and you'll be connected to a national bulletin board of job listings including federal and military positions. If you run into difficulty, call Dick Spinner at 301/584–3697 or SYSOP at 800/331–6026. A free printout of the job listings is available from Sam Hahn (9720 Redd Rambler Dr., Philadelphia, PA 19115; phone: 215/464–4442).

## Directories

*ASCE Membership Directory* (American Society of Civil Engineers, 345 E. 47th St., New York, NY 10017; phone: 212/705–7288 or 7276) $100/nonmembers, $25/members.

*SOLE Membership Directory and Handbook* (Society of Logistics Engineers, 8100 Professional Pl., Suite 211, New Carrollton, MD 20785; phones: 800/695–7653, 301/459–8446) free. Printed each April.

*Who's Who in Engineering* (American Association of Engineering Societies, 1111 19th St., NW, Suite 608, Washington, DC 20036–5703; phones: 800/658–8897, 202/296–2237) $200/nonmembers, $120/members. 900+ pages. Lists more than 14,000 engineers. Most recently published in September 1991.

*Directory of Engineering Societies and Related Organizations* (American Association of Engineering Societies, 1111 19th St., NW, Suite 608, Washington, DC 20036–5703; phones: 800/658–8897, 202/296–2237) $150/nonmembers, $90/members. 263 pages. Provides information on 350 organizations in the U.S. and 350 overseas. Last published in 1989.

*Directory of Engineering Societies and Related Organizations, 1990–1991 Supplement* (American Association of Engineering Societies, 1111 19th St., NW, Suite 608, Washington, DC 20036–5703; phones: 800/658–8897, 202/296–2237) $85/nonmembers, $48/members. Adds another 350 organizations to the 1989 edition. If purchasing both the 1989 edition and the supplement, the total cost is $200/nonmembers, $125/members.

*The Biotechnology Directory* (Stockton Press, 15 E. 26th St., New York, NY 10160–0077; phones: 800/221–2123 (outside New York state), 212/481–1334) $195 plus $3 shipping. Includes the ofetn hard–to–find government departments engaged in biotechnology as well as over 8,800 companies, research centers, and academic institutions involved in the field. The most recent edition was released in 1991.

## Salary surveys

*Professional Income of Engineers* (American Association of Engineering Societies, 1111 19th St., NW, Suite 608, Washington, DC 20036–5703; phones: 800/658–8897, 202/296–2237) $97/nonmembers, $59.50/members. 130+ pages. Includes data for federal, state, and local government engineers as well as broad industry groups. Published annually in July.

*Engineers' Salaries: Special Industry Report* (American Association of Engineering Societies, 1111 19th St., NW, Suite 608, Washington, DC 20036–5703; phones: 800/658–8897, 202/296–2237) $287.50/nonmembers, $169/members. 230 pages. Extremely detailed breakdown of engineering salaries according to industry type and geographic location, company size, years of experience, highest degree held, and supervisory status. Published each July.

## Environment

*Also see "Engineering," "Forestry and horticulture," "Parks and recreation," and "Planning." Additional job sources that occasionally include government positions appear in the **Professional's Job Finder** and the **Non-Profits' Job Finder**.*

### Job openings

Environmental Careers Bulletin (11693 San Vicente Blvd., Suite 327, Los Angeles, CA 90047; phone: 213/399-3533, no phone orders) monthly, free, but when you write for a subscription you must provide your job title, college major, college degree, and year received. From 150 to 200 display ads for environmental positions, largely private sector, appear in the typical issue. Details on this company's environmental job fairs held around the country are included.

*The Job Seeker* (Route 2, Box 16, Warrens, WI 54666; phone: 608/378-4290) biweekly, $60/annual subscription, $36/six-month subscription, $19.50/three-month subscription. Lists 200 environmental and natural resource vacancies in every aspect of these fields, including environmental education. A special supplement in one December issue features dozens of summer internships.

*Environmental Opportunities* (P.O. Box 4957, Arcata, CA 95521; phone: 707/839-4640) monthly, $47/annual subscription, $26/six-month subscription, $52/annual subscription (Canada), $60/annual subscription elsewhere. Over 125 jobs, internships, seasonal work, educational offerings, and conferences. Includes administrative positions, fisheries, wildlife, forestry, research, parks, outdoor recreation, and ecology. Write for free sample copy.

*Fisheries* (American Fisheries Society, 5410 Grosvenor Ln., Suite 110, Bethesda, MD 20814-2199; phone: 301/897-8616) bimonthly, $43.50/annual nonmember subscription, $47/Canada, $54/elsewhere, included in dues which, coincidentally are $43.50/U.S. and $47/foreign, $21.75/students. "Current Events and Announcements"

## TRAVELS WITH FARLEY

Reprinted by permission of Phil Frank. Copyright © 1982.

sports four or five ads including one or two for government positions, usually federal.

*Opportunities* (Natural Science for Youth Foundation, 130 Azalea Dr., Roswell, GA 30075; phones: 800/992–6793, 404/594–9367) bimonthly, $35/annual subscription, $10/single issue, included in membership package. ''Positions available '' lists details on 45 to 70 jobs for naturalists, curators, raptor rehabilitators, and administrative positions, largely at nature centers.

*EarthWorks* includes *Job Scan* (Student Conservation Association, P.O. Box 550, Charlestown, NH 03603; phone: 603/826–5206) monthly, $29.95/nonmember annual subscription, $25.95/member annual subscription. About 70 jobs in a typical issue plus 20 to 30 internships.

*The Caretaker Gazette* (P.O. Box 342, Carpentersville, IL 60110; phone: 708/658–6554, no phone orders) quarterly, $8/three issues, $14/six issues. Among its 60 job announcements are jobs and internships in forestry, fisheries, environment, and caretaking.

*Employment Opportunity Service* (National Association of Interpretation P.O. Box 1892, Ft. Collins, CO 80522; 303/491–6434) $3.00/week. This is a printout of the *Dial-a-Job* and *Dial-an-Internship* jobs listed by phone as described below under ''Job services.'' Be sure to indicate the week or weeks for which you want a printout.

*Environmental Science & Technology* (American Chemical Society, P.O. Box 3337, Columbus, OH 43210; phone: 614/447-3776) monthly, $73/nonmember annual subscription (individuals), $39/members. The "Classified Section" carries around 25 job vacancies, mostly in the private sector.

*The Wildlifer* (The Wildlife Society, 5410 Grosvenor Ln. Bethesda, MD 20814; phone: 301/897-9770) bimonthly, available only to members: $33/annual dues, $17/student dues. About 20 positions in conservation, wildlife, and natural resources appear under "Positions Available."

*Employment Announcements* (American Meteorological Society, 45 Beacon St., Boston, MA 02108-3693) monthly, $25/annual nonmember subscription, $12/members. About 25 jobs for weather forecasters and meteorologists grace these pages.

*Jobs Clearinghouse* (Association for Experiential Education, CU 249, Boulder, CO 80309; phone: 303/492-1547) monthly, $25/annual nonmember subscription, $15/members. Lists mostly internships and outdoor education instructorships, counselors, camp staff, program directors, and environmental educators, with an emphasis on wilderness experience, under "Job Openings." From 60 to 125 job vacancies per issue.

*Environmental Action* (Environmental Action, Inc., 1525 New Hampshire Ave., NW, Washington, DC 20036; phone: 202/745-4870) bimonthly; annual subscription: $35/institutions, $25/annual subscription for individuals. There are a few job vacancies listed under "Eco-Exchange."

*Journal of Soil and Water Conservation* (Soil and Water Conservation Society, 7515 NE Ankeny Rd., Ankeny, IA 50021-9764; phone: 515/289-2331) bimonthly, $35/annual subscription (U.S. and Canada), $40/elsewhere. Jobs listed under "Classified Advertising." About five job ads per issue.

*Journal of Air and Waste Management* (Air Pollution Control Association, P.O. Box 2861, Pittsburgh, PA 15230; phone: 412/232-3444) monthly, available only to members, free. About three vacancies are listed under "Manpower."

*Newsletter of the Ecological Society of America* (9650 Rockville Pike, Suite 2503, Rockville, MD 20814; phone: 301/530–7005) five issues/year, free. Ten to 15 ads for ecotoxicologists, plant ecologists, and ecologists appear under "Job Announcements." Most positions are with universities or other institutions. Some positions with the U.S. Department of the Interior appear.

*1992 Summer Employment Directory of the United States* (Petersons Guides, PO Box 2123, Princeton, NJ 08543–2123; phone: 800/338–3282) $14.95. Published annually in the autumn. Its 200+ pages list over 75,000 summer job openings at resorts, camps, amusement parks, national parks, and government.

See also *Journal of Environmental Health* listed under "Public safety."

## Job services

*JOBSource* (Computerized Employment Systems, Inc., 1720 W. Mulberry, Suite B9, Fort Collins, CO 80521; phones: 800/727–5627, 303/493–1779) There are three services available using an extensive database of over 700 positions, mostly in the environmental arena (fisheries, natural resources, wildlife, forestry, biology, recreation parks). For individuals, the most useful is JOBSource's in–house search program. Obtain a resume application form from JOBSource. Within two weeks of receiving your completed form, JOBSource will conduct a job search of its database for you. JOBSource guarantees from six to 25 matches per search. The cost is $30. If fewer than six matches are found, JOBSource will run a second search the next month for free. If the second run turns up fewer than six matches, there is a $5 charge for that second run.

However, if you have a computer and modem, you can download the entire database onto your computer for $20 plus your phone call. It takes 20 to 40 minutes to download the three files. To update, you need download just one file which takes about 20 minutes and costs $15. The database is updated every Thursday. A growing number of universities and colleges are subscribing to JOBSource. They receive the database and user programs around the 24th of each month and can conduct their own job searches. Subscriptions are available for a year ($495), the nine months of September through May ($375), or for the three months of January, April, and November ($189).

*Dial–a–Job* and *Dial–an–Internship* (National Association of Interpretation P.O. Box 1892, Ft. Collins, CO 80522; 303/491–6434) Call 301/491–7410 24 hours a day for a recording of full–time, seasonal, and temporary jobs in environmental education, interpretation, and related fields: naturalists, park rangers, outdoor education, biologists, historians, archaeologists, museum personnel, and publication designers. The tape runs from 10 to 30 minutes. Updated weekly. For internships, call 301/491–6784 24 hours a day. The tape runs from 5 to 20 minutes. Updated weekly.

*Environmental Career Hotline* (1224 Washington Ave., Suite 104, Golden, CO 80401; phone: 303/231–6144) $5/minute charged directly to your phone bill. Call this interactive hotline at 900/933–3393 from a touchtone phone, 24–hours a day, seven days a week, to hear job descriptions in air quality, water quality, waste management, industrial hygiene, and regulatory compliance. You are able to specify the specific field(s) that interest you. Updated weekly.

*Environmental Action Job Book* (Environmental Action, Inc., 1525 New Hampshire Ave., NW, Washington, DC 20036; phone: 202/745–4870) free. This up–to–date book of environmental jobs and internships can be seen only at the Environmental Action office.

## Directories

*World Directory of Environmental Organizations* (California Institute of Public Affairs, P.O. Box 189040, Sacramento, CA 95818; phone: 916/442–2472) $35 plus 7.25 percent sales tax for California residents, foreign: $38/surface mail, $48/air mail. 175 pages. Includes over government agencies, research institutes, and citizens' and professional associations in the U.S. and around the globe. Divided into 50 topics with index, glossary, and bibliography of related directories and databases. Most recent edition, published in 1989.

*Environmental Information Directory* (Gale Research, Inc., 835 Penobscot Bldg., Detroit, MI 48226; phone: 800/877–4253) $75, 1991. Divided into 20 chapters, this directory includes information on federal government and state agencies that deal with the environment in addition to private and non–profit players in the environmental field.

*NAI Membership Directory* (National Association of Interpretation P.O. Box 1892, Ft. Collins, CO 80522; 303/491–6434) available only to members, included in dues. Lists members and institutional members. Published each spring.

*Directory of Natural Science Centers* (Natural Science for Youth Foundation, 130 Azalea Dr., Roswell, GA 30075; phones: 800/992–6793, 404/594–9367) $78.50, $58.50/members. This 600 page tome gives details on over 1,350 nature centers. Last edition published in 1990. Next edition expected in 1994.

*Environmental Telephone Directory* (Government Institutes, 966 Hungerford Dr., Suite 24, Rockville, MD 20850; phone: 301/251–9250) $55. Detailed information on government agencies that deal with the environment, identifies the environmental aides of U.S. Senators and Representatives. Published in odd–numbered years.

*Directory of Environmental Information Sources* (Government Institutes, 966 Hungerford Dr., Suite 24, Rockville, MD 20850; phone: 301/251–9250) $69. Includes federal and state government resources, professional, scientific, and trade organizations; newsletters, magazines, and databases. Published in September of even–numbered years.

*The Wildlife Society Membership Directory and Certification Registry* (The Wildlife Society, 5410 Grosvenor Ln. Bethesda, MD 20814; phone: 301/897–9770) $3/nonmembers, included in dues. Published each September.

*The Northeast Directory of Programs* (Association for Experiential Education, CU 249, Boulder, CO 80309; phone: 303/492–1547) $5/nonmembers, $7.50/members; add $3.50 shipping. This 35-page index lists over 100 experiential education programs and agencies in the northeast.

*The Northwest Directory of Experiential Programs* (Association for Experiential Education, CU 249, Boulder, CO 80309; phone: 303/492–1547) $5/nonmembers, $7.50/members; add $3.50 shipping. This directory lists 36 programs in seven states and British Columbia.

*New Careers: A Directory of Jobs and Internships in Technology and Society* (Student Pugwash USA, 1638 R St., NW, Suite 32, Washington, DC 20009; phone: 202/328–6555) $18, $10/students (add $3 shipping). Offers full details on where and how to apply for internships and entry–level jobs with non–profits in the environment and energy, development, communications, peace/security, health, law, and general science. Published in even–numbered years.

*The Intermountain Referral Service Guide to Western States Indoot/Outdoor Summer Employment with the United States Federal Government* (Intermountain Publishing, 703 S. Broadway, Suite 100–B0, Denver, CO 80209; phone: 303/988–6707) $9, $5/subscribers to any edition of the *Rocky Mountain Employment Newsletter* described under "Job sources for multi–state regions" in Chapter 3. This four–page guide is chock full of tiny type explaining how to find and apply for summer positions with the Forest Service, Department of Energy, Bureau of Mines, Bureau of Land Management, Geological Survey, Fish and Wildlife Service, and the National Park Service.

# Films—motion pictures and television

*See listings under "Media." Also see the* **Professional's Job Finder** *for a very extensive set of job sources which sometimes have government positions in addition to private sector jobs.*

# Finance/accounting

*Also see listings under "Public Administration."*

## Job openings

*GFOA Newsletter* (Government Finance Officers Association, Suite 800, 180 N. Michigan Ave., Chicago, IL 60601–7476; phone: 312/977–9700) biweekly; $50/annual nonmember subscription to both *GFOA Newsletter* and *Government Finance Review* (does not include job ads), included in membership package. Jobs listed under "Employment Opportunities." Very extensive listing of finance/accounting positions.

*The Employment Flash* (Association of Government Accountants, 2200 Mt. Vernon Ave., Alexandria, VA 22301; phone: 703/684–6931) biweekly, $15/six–month subscription. AGA sends the *Flash* to its chapters which reproduce its contents in their chapter newsletters. However, subscribers to the *Flash* see the job notices before they appear in chapter newsletters. About 24 jobs appear in a typical issue.

*Position Report* (David J. White & Associates, Suite 200, 809 Ridge Rd., Wilmette, IL 60091; phone: 708/256–8826) weekly, $42.50/four week subscription, $115/12 weeks, $220/24 weeks, $440/48 weeks. This is a collection of 500+ job ads in finance and accounting taken from over 100 newspapers and periodicals nationwide, including government and institutional positions.

*Internal Auditor* (Institute of Internal Auditors, 249 Maitland Ave., Altamonte Springs, FL 32701–4201; phone: 407/830–7600) bi-monthly, $36/nonmember annual subscription (U.S.), $56/else-where (air mail), $42/elsewhere (surface mail), included in membership package. Typical issue features four to eight job ads plus ads from recruitment agencies. Includes ads for positions overseas.

*In Search Of* (American Academy of Actuaries, 1720 I St., NW, Washington, DC 20006; phone: 202/223–8196) monthly, available only to members, included in dues. From three to five state and federal positions for actuaries fill this one to two page newsletter.

*The Insight* (Society of Financial Examiners, 4101 Lake Boone Trail, Raleigh, NC 27607; phone: 919/787-5181) monthly, available only to members. The few job ads that appear under "Classifieds" are for government regulatory agencies.

## Job services

*PRESORT* (Association of Government Accountants, 2200 Mt. Vernon Ave., Alexandria, VA 22301; phone: 703/684-6931) This is a pay-by-the-minute job-matching hotline for accountants, auditors, tax specialists, and other financial positions, largely in government. Using a touch-tone phone, you call 900/773-7678. You'll be asked to indentify the part of the country in which you'd like to work, the salary range you seek, and the type of financial position you want. The computer will then match your requirements with some of the 500+ jobs in its database and then give you details on those you match. The charge is $1.95 for the first minute and 95¢ a minute thereafter. Reportedly, a typical call takes about six minutes. The database is growing and expanding to include private sector positions as well.

*Job Hotline* (American Association for Budget and Program Analysis, P.O. Box 1157, Falls Church, VA 22041; phone: 703/941-4300) free. Call 703/941-4300 between 9 a.m. and 5 p.m. *only on Thursdays.* Tell the operator the location(s) in which you are interested and the type of position. She will read to you one-line listings with the job title, location, series, grade level (if federal), closing date, and, upon request, where to apply. Nearly all the 75 jobs on the usual list are federal positions, including military; some local and state positions occasionally show up.

## Directories

*American Academy of Actuaries Yearbook* (American Academy of Actuaries, 1720 I St., NW, Washington, DC 20006; phone: 202/223-8196) $50/nonmembers, included in dues. Published each January.

*American Bankruptcy Institute Membership Directory* (American Bankruptcy Institute , 51 C St., NE, Washington, DC 20002; phone: 202/543-1234) available only to members. Includes bankruptcy judges and clerks. Published annually.

*AWSCPA Roster* (American Women's Society of Certified Public Accountants, 111 E. Wacker Dr., Chicago, IL 60601; phone: 312/644-6610) available only to members, included in dues. Published annually.

## Fire protection

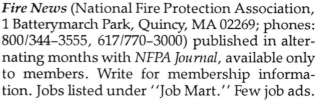

*Also see listings under "Public safety."*

### Job openings

*NFPA Journal* (National Fire Protection Association, 1 Batterymarch Park, Quincy, MA 02269; phones: 800/344-3555, 617/770-3000) published in alternating months with *Fire News*, available only to members. Write for membership information. Jobs listed under "Classifieds." About ten ads appear in a typical issue.

*Fire News* (National Fire Protection Association, 1 Batterymarch Park, Quincy, MA 02269; phones: 800/344-3555, 617/770-3000) published in alternating months with *NFPA Journal*, available only to members. Write for membership information. Jobs listed under "Job Mart." Few job ads.

**Fire Chief** (Communication Channels, P.O. Box 1147, Skokie, IL 60076, phones: 800/421-9778, 708/647-7124) monthly, $49/annual subscription (U.S.), $69/North America, $119/overseas air mail. The classifieds section usually contains ads for five or more fire chief, deputy chief, and fire department administrator positions.

*IAFC On Scene* (International Association of Fire Chiefs, 1329 18th St., NW, Washington, DC 20036; phone: 202/833-3420) biweekly, $60/nonmember annual subscription. Jobs listed under "Classifieds." Generally two to four job ads per issue.

*The Voice* (International Society of Fire Service Instructors, 30 Main St., Ashland, MA 01721; phone: 508/881–5800) monthly, $72/nonmember annual subscription, included in membership package (dues: $60/year). Jobs listed under "Classifieds." From one to five job ads in the typical issue.

See also *APCO—Journal of Public–Safety Communications* listed under "Public safety."

See also *Law Enforcement News* listed under "Law enforcement."

## Directories

**Fire and Emergency Services Leadership Directory** (International Association of Fire Chiefs, 1329 18th St., NW, Washington, DC 20036; phone: 202/833–3420) $50/nonmembers, free to members. Published each winter.

## Salary surveys

*Fire Personnel Salaries* (International City Management Association, 777 N. Capitol St., NE, Washington, DC 20002; phone: 202/289–4262) $29.95 (add $4.30 shipping and handling if not prepaid). State–by–state listings of minimum and maximum salaries each jurisdiction pays to firefighters, paramedics, engineers, arson investigators, medical technicians, fire captains, fire lieutenants, fire prevention officers, fire code inspectors, deputy chiefs, assistant chiefs, fire chiefs, and fire commissioners. Published 1990.

*Police, Fire, and Refuse Collection, 1989* (International City Management Association, 777 N. Capitol St., NE, Washington, DC 20002; phone: 202/289–4262) $16.50 (add $4.30 shipping and handling if not prepaid). A comparative study depicting trends in salary and expenditures data from police, fire, and refuse collection and disposal services.

# Fleet/facilities management

## Job openings

*Automotive Fleet* (Bobit Publishing, 2512 Artesia Blvd., Redondo Beach, CA 90278; phone: 213/376–8788) 13 issues/year, $24/annual subscription. Jobs listed under "Classifieds." About three to six job ads in typical issue. Many more "Postitions Wanted" ads appear in each issue.

*NAFA Newsletter* (National Association of Fleet Managers, 120 Wood Ave. South, Iselin, NJ 08830; phone: 908/494–8100) monthly, $48/nonmember annual subscription to both *Newsletter* and *The NAFA Fleet Executive* (which does not contain job ads), both included in membership package. Jobs listed under "Jobs Available." About five job ads in the typical issue. Many more "Positions Wanted" ads are run.

*IFMA News* (International Facility Management Association, 1 E. Greenway Place, 11th Floor, Houston, TX 77046–0194; phone: 713/623–4362) monthly, available only to members. Two or three positions in facilities management appear under "FM Jobs."

Also see *Community Transportation Reporter* listed under "Transit management."

## Directories

*State Fleet Managers* (The Council of State Governments, Iron Works Pike, P.O. Box 11910, Lexington, KY 40578; phones: 800/800–1910, 606/231–1939) $20. Published in odd–numbered years. Compilation of state fleet administrators and the types of vehicles each state uses.

*IFMA Membership Directory* (International Facility Management Association, 1 E. Greenway Place, 11th Floor, Houston, TX 77046–0194; phone: 713/623–4362) available only to members, include in dues. Published each August.

# Forestry and horticulture

*Also see listings under "Environment" and "Parks and recreation."*

## Job openings

*Journal of Forestry* (Society of American Foresters, 5400 Grosvernor Lane, Bethesda, MD 20814–2198; phone: 301/897–8720) monthly; $50/nonmember individuals annual subscription (U.S. and Canada), $65/individuals elsewhere (surface mail), subscription included in membership package. Jobs listed under "Classifieds." About 12 job ads per issue.

*City Trees* (Society of Municipal Arborists, c/o Leonard Phillips, Editor, P.O. Box 364, Wellesley Hills, MA 02181; phone: 617/235–7600, ext. 330) bimonthly, $20/annual subscription, included in $40 annual dues. Typical issue has one or two ads for arborists, horticulturalists, or urban foresters.

*American Forestry* (American Forestry Association, P.O. Box 2000, Washington, DC 20013; phones: 800/368–5748, 202/667–3300) bimonthly, $24/annual subscription. Jobs as foresters, resource managers, arborists, and environmental policy directors appear under "The Green Pages."

*AABGA Newsletter* (American Association of Botanical Gardens and Arboreta, 786 Church Rd., Wayne, PA 19087; phone: 215/688–1120) monthly, available only to members. About 15 positions in public horticulture ranging from gardener to director appear under "Positions Available." Annual dues: $50, $25/students.

*Forest Products Journal* (Forest Product Reseach Society, 2801 Marshall Ct., Madison, WI 53705; 608/231–1361) 10 issues/year, $115/annual nonmember subscription, included in dues. Three to six positions are listed under "Employement Referral Service."

*Internship Directory* (American Association of Botanical Gardens and Arboreta, 786 Church Rd., Wayne, PA 19087; phone: 215/688–1120) $4/nonmember, $3/member. This is a very extensive state-by-state listing of summer internships available in public horticulture and private estates. Published each October.

*Association of Zoological Horticulture Newsletter* (Jim Martin, Riverbanks Zoo, P.O. Box 1060, Columbia, SC 29202–1060; phone: 803/779–8717) quarterly, available only to members, $25/annual professional dues, $15/annual student dues. A few positions for zoo horticulturists and gardeners are listed under "Positions available." "Positions wanted" listings included.

*Journal of the National Technical Association* (Black Collegiate Services, Inc., 1240 S. Broad St., New Orleans, LA 70125; phone: 504/821–5694) quarterly, $30/annual subscription, $35/foreign. Among the 10 or so positions in display ads and listed under "Job Opportunities Bulletin," are a handful of government jobs, sometimes with the U.S. Department of Agriculture's Forest Service. Most positions, though, are for health physicists, biologists, and environmental scientists.

## Job services

*Jobs Hotline* (American Association of Botanical Gardens and Arboreta, 786 Church Rd., Wayne, PA 19087; phone: 215/688–1120) free. Call 215/688–9127 weekdays 5 p.m. to 8 a.m. (eastern time) and 24 hours on weekends for a tape recording listing four to eight jobs in public horticulture.

*Florapersonnel* (2180 W. State Rd. 434, Suite 6152, Longwood, FL 32779–5008; phone: 407/682–5151) free. The job seeker completes Florapersonnel's form and submits it along with her resume. Resumes are kept on file indefinitely. When a match is made, Florapersonnel contacts the job seeker and, if the job seeker gives the okay, Florapersonnel gives her name and resume to the potential employer who then contacts the employer. (Normally, we don't list "headhunters" in this book, but the horticulture field has so few job sources that it seems essential to include this listing.) Jobs range from greenhouse growers to directors. Includes nursery, landscape, and irrigation.

## Directories

*AABGA Membership Directory* (American Association of Botanical Gardens and Arboreta, 786 Church Rd., Wayne, PA 19087; phone: 215/688–1120) available to members only in membership package. Lists institutional members of AABGA. Annual dues: $50, $25/students.

*The FPRS Membership Directory* (Forest Product Reseach Society, 2801 Marshall Ct., Madison, WI 53705; 608/231–1361) available only to members, free. Published annually.

## Housing

*See also listings under "Community and Economic Development," "Planning," and "Public Administration."*

### Job openings

*NAHRO Monitor* (National Association of Housing and Redevelopment Officials, 1320 18th St., NW, Washington, DC 20036–1803; phone: 202/429–2960) biweekly; available only to members. Jobs listed under "Jobs Available." Typical issue features ten or more job openings generally in housing administration, planning, and community or neighborhood development.

*Journal of Housing* (National Association of Housing and Redevelopment Officials, 1320 18th St., NW, Washington, DC 20036–1803; phone: 202/429–2960) 11 issues/annual; $33/annual subscription. Jobs listed under "Classifieds." Few job ads. Professionals can place job wanted ads.

*Trends in Housing* (Trends, Inc., 1629 K St., NW, Suite 802, Washington, DC 20006; phone: 202/833–4456) bimonthly, $18/annual subscription. A few ads appear under "Job Opportunities Available in Housing."

### Directories

*NAHRO Directory of Local Agencies* (National Association of Housing and Redevelopment Officials, 1320 18th St., NW, Washington, DC 20036–1803; phone: 202/429–2960) $55. Includes national listings on housing authorities and community development and redevelopment departments. Published in September 1991 and every three years thereafter.

*Directory of State Housing Finance Agencies* (National Council of State Housing Agencies, Suite 412, 444 North Capitol St., NW, Washington, DC 20001; phone: 202/624–7710) $150/nonmembers, $5/member Housing Finance Authorities, $10/affiliates. 40 pages. Published each February. Provides names, addresses, and phone numbers for key staff and affiliated individuals.

Travels with Farley reprinted by permission of Phil Frank.
Copyright © 1978. All rights reserved.

*State Housing Finance Agency Program Catalog* (National Council of State Housing Agencies, Suite 412, 444 North Capitol St., NW, Washington, DC 20001; phone: 202/624–7710) contact for prices, published in late 1991. This five–volume tome gives excruciating detail on over 600 programs operated by the nation's state housing finance agencies. It will be available as individual volumes: 1–Homeownership Programs, 2–Rental Housing Programs, 3–Special Needs Programs, 4–Economic Devvelopment Programs, and 5–Technical/Financial Assistance Initiatives and Financing Tools.

*Directory of Housing Attorneys (Low and Moderate Income Housing and Community Development)* (American Bar Association, Order Fulfillment 1391–5720, 750 N. Lake Shore Dr., Chicago, IL 60611; phone: 312/988–5000) $20 + $3.95 shipping, most recent edition: 1990–91. Extensive listing of lawyers who practice in the housing field.

# Human services

*See listings under "Public administration" and "Social services."*

# Labor relations

*See listings under "Personnel" and under "Public administration."*

# Landscape architecture

*Also see listings under "Parks and recreation" and "Planning."*

## Job openings

*Landscape Architecture* (American Society of Landscape Architects, 4401 Connecticut Ave., NW, Washington, DC 20008-2302; phone: 202/686-2752) bimonthly; $38/annual subscription, $28/students (U.S.), elsewhere: $65/surface mail, $117/air mail. Jobs listed under "Buyers Guide." Few job ads.

See also the *Employment Referral Service* of the Golf Course Superintendents Association of America listed under "Parks and recreation."

## Directory

*ASLA Membership Handbook* (American Society of Landscape Architects, 4401 Connecticut Ave., NW, Washington, DC 20008-2302; phone: 202/686-2752) $29.95/individuals, $40/institutions, $12.50/libraries, included in membership package. Includes national listing of landscape architecture firms. Published annually.

# Law enforcement

*Also see listings under "Public administration" and "Public safety." Sources of positions in the private sector security industry appear in the Professional's Job Finder.*

*NELS—National Employment Listing Service* (Criminal Justice Center, Sam Houston State University, Huntsville, TX 77341–2296; phone: 409/294–1692, 1690) monthly, individuals: $30/annual subscription, $37.50/foreign, $17.50/six–month subscription; institutions and agencies: $65/annual subscription (U.S.), $85/foreign; Texas residents must include 8.25 percent sales tax; tax–exempt institutions must include proof of tax exempt status. Each issue describes 100 to 200+ positions in five categories: Law enforcement and security (police officers, document examiners, print examiners, criminalists, public service aides, jailers); Community services and corrections (correctional trainees, psychologists, social workers, physicians, speech pathologists, communications, clerical, counselors, probation officers); Courts (pretrial service officers); Institutional corrections (correctional officers, psychologists, nurses, chaplains, cooks, therapists, pharamcists, trades and laborers); and Academics and research.

*Police Career Digest and Express Jobs Newsletter* (PCCD, P.O. Box 1672, Eaton Park, FL 33801; phones: 800/359–6260, ext. 25, 813/666–3184) published in alternating months, $32/annual subscription, $23/six–month subscription. Jobs listed in *Police Career Digest* under "Law Enforcement Opportunities." *Express Jobs Newsletter* is all job announcements. Forty to 50 ads for police personnel are in the typical issue of *Police Career Digest* while *Express Jobs Newsletter* has half as many.

*PSIC Listing* (Protective Services Information Center, P.O. Box 1562, Decatur, IL 62525) monthly, $57.95/annual subscription, $16.95/three–month subscription. Includes entry–level through supervisory positions in law enforcement and private security.

*The Police Chief* (International Association of Chiefs of Police, Inc., Suite 200, 1110 N. Glebe Rd., Alrington, VA 22201; phone: 703/243–6500) monthly, $25/nonmember annual subscription, included in membership package. About eight police chief and public safety director jobs under "Classified" and advertised in display ads throughout the magazine.

*NPA Advocate* (National Black Police Association, 3251 Mt. Pleasant St., NW, Washington, DC 20010–2103; phone: 202/986–2070) quarterly, free. Two or three openings appear under "Positions Available."

*American Jails* (American Jail Association, Suite 100, 1000 Day Rd., Hagerstown, MD 21740; phone: 301/790–3930) bimonthly, $4.50/annual subscription, included in membership package ($20/annual dues). Five to eight job ads in typical issue.

*Law Enforcement News* (Criminal Justice Center of John Jay College of Criminal Justice, Suite 438, 899 Tenth Ave., New York, NY 10019; phone: 212/237–8442) bimonthly, $18/annual subscription (U.S.) $28/foreign countries. Jobs listed under "Jobs."

*Law and Order* (Hendon, Inc., 1000 Skokie Blvd., Wilmette, IL 60091; phone: 708/256–8555) monthly, $20/annual subscription. Jobs listed under "Classified Ads." About five job ads per issue.

*The ASLET Journal* (American Society of Law Enforcement Trainers, 9611 400th Ave., P.O. Box 1003, Twin Lakes, WI 53181; phone: 414/279–5700) bimonthly, available only as part of membership package. Few job ads; job ads not in every issue.

*NARC Officer* (International Narcotic Enforcement Officers Association, Inc., Suite 1200, 112 State St., Albany, NY 12207; phone: 518/463–6232) monthly; annual subscription: $35/nonmembers, $30/members (add $35 for surface mail to foreign countries; add $40 for air mail to Canada/Mexico, $45 to the Caribbean, $60 to Europe, $85 to Asia). Publishes a limited number of job ads and position wanted ads (no charge).

*Food Service Director* (633 Third Ave., New York, NY 10017; phone: 212/984–2299) monthly, $35/annual subscription, free to qualified food service personnel. Among the eight job ads under "Classifieds" is often a prison system food service management or cook position.

*The Criminologist* (American Society of Criminology, 1314 Kinnear Rd., Suite 212, Columbus, OH, 43212; phone: 614/292–9207) bimonthly, $7.50/annual nonmember subscription, included in dues. Eight to 28 jobs for probation officers, police, and faculty are listed under "Positions Announcements."

*Employment Bulletin* (American Sociological Association, 1722 N St., NW, Washington, DC 20036; phone: 202/833-3410) monthly, $21/nonmember annual subscription, $7/members. The entire newletter features about 20 positions, half of which are not academic and which often include jobs in the criminal justice system.

*Forum Newsletter* (Criminal Justice Statistics Association, 444 N. Capitol St., NW, Suite 606, Washington, DC 20001) quarterly, $25/annual nonmember subscription, free to members. One or two jobs for analysts, programmers, researchers, and administrative positions in criminal justice statistics appear in the typical issue.

*Laboratory Medicine* (American Society of Pathologists, 2100 W. Harrison St., Chicago, IL 60612; phone: 312/738-1336) monthly, $40/annual nonmember subscription (U.S.), $55/foreign, included in membership package. About 45 openings for pathologists, technicians, and other laboratory-related positions are listed under "Professional Exchange."

*American Journal of Pathology* (J. B. Lippincott Company, Downville Pike, Route 3, Box 20-B, Hagerstown, MD 21740; phones: 800/638-3030, 215/238-4206) monthly, $145/annual subscription (U.S.), $205/foreign. Ten to 12 "Classifieds" appear for pathologists in government and private practice.

### Job services

*Law Enforcement and Security Hot Line* (National Association of Chiefs of Police, 3801 Biscayne Blvd., Miami, FL 33137; phone: 305/573-0202) $15/year. Calls are accepted weekdays from 9 a.m. to 4 p.m. The list of positions as peace officers, correctional staff, private security in government agencies, and private firms is updated monthly. When you call you get a live person, not a recording. Vacancies are available by geographical area and qualifications.

*Employment Hotline* (American Federation of Police, 3801 Biscayne Blvd., Miami, FL 33137; phone: 305/571-0700) free, but available only to "active" members, $30/annual active membership. Member calls the hotline number (available from the federation) and hears brief job descriptions of 20 to 30 police positions.

Member contacts hiring agency directly.

*ACAnet* (American Correctional Association, 8025 Laurel Lakes Ct., Laurel, MD 20707–5075; phone: 301/206–5050) $60/nonmember one–time sign–up fee, $40/members. To use this computer bulletin board, you need a modem and telecommunications software. Usage charges are 45¢ per minute for nonmembers, 35¢/members.

*Job Advisory Service* (American Correctional Association, 8025 Laurel Lakes Ct., Laurel, MD 20707–5075; phone: 301/206–5050) $5/request; available only to members. The job seeker identified three specialties and is sent a list of job vacancies for those specialties. Dozens of jobs are on file at any one time.

## Directories

*National Directory of Law Enforcement* (National Police Chiefs & Sheriffs Information Bureau, P.O. Box 365, Stevens Point, WI 54481–0365; phone: 715/345–2772) $49; 600 pages. This annual directory includes chiefs of police; sheriffs; county and district prosecutors; state police and high patrols; state criminal investigation units; state correctional agencies; college and university security and police departments; 57 federal agencies; U.S. military; airport, harbor, and railroad police departments; and more. It is also available on computer disks and as mailing labels.

*International Association of Chiefs of Police Membership Directory* (International Association of Chiefs of Police, Inc., Suite 200, 1110 N. Glebe Rd., Alrington, VA 22201; phone: 703/243–6500) $75/nonmembers, included in dues. Published each October.

*Directory of Juvenile and Adult Correctional Institutions and Agencies* (American Correctional Association, 8025 Laurel Lakes Ct., Laurel, MD 20707–5075; phone: 301/206–5050) $70. Published each January.

*American Society of Criminology Membership Directory* (American Society of Criminology, 1314 Kinnear Rd., Suite 212, Columbus, OH, 43212; phone: 614/292–9207) available only to members, included in dues. Most recent edition published 1991.

## Salary surveys

*Police Personnel Salaries* (International City Management Association, 777 N. Capitol St., NE, Washington, DC 20002; phone: 202/289–4262) $29.75 plus $4.30 shipping and handling if not prepaid. Last published in 1990, this report gives state–by–state data on minimum and maximum salaries that jurisdictions pay to: police private, motorcycle officer, police corporal, detective, serfeant, lieutenant, captain, inspector, deputy chief, assistant chief, police chief, and police commissioner.

*Police, Fire, and Refuse Collection, 1989* (International City Management Association, 777 N. Capitol St., NE, Washington, DC 20002; phone: 202/289–4262) $16.50 plus $4.30 shipping and handling if not prepaid. A comparative study depicting trends in salary and expenditures data from police, fire, and refuse collection and disposal services.

# Legal services and court administration

*Also see listings under ''Library services.'' Extensive listings of positions in the private sector appear in the* **Professional's Job Finder***.*

*National and Federal Legal Employment Report* (Federal Reports, Inc., Suite 408, 1010 Vermont Ave., NW, Washington, DC 20005; phone: 202/393–3311) monthly. Subscription rates for individuals: $32/three–month, $55/six–month, $99/annual subscription; rates for institutions: $40, $75, $130, respectively. Typical issues contains descriptions of 500 to 600 attorney and law–related positions primarily in the federal government, state and local government, and private employers in government–related fields, including legal aid offices. Includes legal positions outside the U.S.

*Opportunities in Public Interest Law* (ACCESS: Networking in the Public Interest, 50 Beacon St., Boston, MA 02108; phone: 617/720–5627) quarterly, $175/annual subscription. With over 3,000 jobs from 600+ employers, this national job register includes the following all sorts of government positions, encompassing the federal government, congressional committees, state agencies and legislatures, state attorney general offices, district attorney, and city solicitor offices.

*Job Announcements* (National Center for State Courts, Publications Coordinator, 300 Newport Ave., Williamsburg, VA 23187; phone: 804/253-2000) biweekly, $24/annual subscription, $12/six-month subscription. Thirty to 50 announcements for all levels of employment appear in a typical issue.

*Lawyers Job Bulletin Board* (Federal Bar Association, Suite 408, 1815 H St., NW, Washington, DC 20006; phone: 202/638-0252) monthly, $30/nonmember annual subscription, $20/members, $20/students. Typical issue features 25 job openings primarily with the federal government, although about 10 percent of the ads are for positions with District of Columbia area courts, private firms, and non-profits.

---

### "We never do anything illegal without checking with county counsel first." —Anon Y. Mous, planning commissioner,

quoted in *California Planner*, May 1982

---

*Municipal Attorney* (National Institute of Municipal Law Officers, Suite 92, 1000 Connecticut Ave., NW, Washington, DC 20036; phone: 202/466-5424) bimonthly, available only as part of membership package. Runs only ten to 20 announcements a year for municipal attorney positions.

*Clearinghouse Review* (National Clearinghouse for Legal Services, 407 S. Dearborn, Chicago, IL 60605; phones: 800/621-3256 [outside Illinois], 312/939-3830) monthly, $75/annual subscription (U.S.), $95/foreign. About 25 ads for attorneys, paralegals, and faculty appear under "Job Market."

*Job Market Preview* (National Clearinghouse for Legal Services, 407 S. Dearborn, Chicago, IL 60605; phones: 800/621-3256(outside Illinois), 312/939-3830) monthly, $35/annual subscription, $20/six-month subscription. About 30 jobs ads fill this newsletter, often the same jobs that appear in *Clearinghouse Review.*

*Position Report* (David J. White & Associates, Suite 200, 809 Ridge Rd., Wilmette, IL 60091; phone: 708/256-8826) weekly, $42.50/four week subscription, $115/12 weeks, $220/24 weeks, $440/48 weeks. This is a collection of 500+ job ads for attorneys taken from over

100 newspapers and periodicals nationwide, including government and institutional positions.

*Legal Times* (1730 M St., NW, Washington, DC 20036; phone: 202/457-0686) weekly, $175/annual subscription. The classifieds section contains job vacancies largely in the DC area, but also nationally, under these headings: "Attorney Employment, Government," about 5 jobs; "Employment" has about ten jobs for paralegals and legal assistants and four for legal secretaries.

*The NLADA Cornerstone* (National Legal Aid and Defender Association, 8th Floor, 1625 K St., NW, Washington, DC 20006; phone: 202/452-0620) quarterly, $20/nonmember subscription, included in membership package. "Job Listings" usually includes 15 to 20 job announcements.

*Food and Drug Law Institute Update* (Food and Drug Law Institute, 1000 Vermont Ave., NW, Suite 1200, Washington, DC 20005; phone: 202/371-1420) bimonthly, available only to members, included in dues. Three or four jobs and internships appear under "Positions Available."

*NCRA Employment Referral Service Bulletin* (National Court Reporters Association, 8224 Old Courthouse Rd., Vienna, VA 22182; phone: 703/281-4677) biweekly, $24/nonmember annual subscription, $12/members. Typical issue features 20 to 30 job announcements for both freelance and more formal court reporter positions.

*See also Law Enforcement News* listed under "Law enforcement" and *Public Interest Employment Report* in Chapter 3 listed under California.

*Summer Legal Employment Guide* (Federal Reports, Inc., Suite 408, 1010 Vermont Ave., NW, Washington, DC 20005; phone: 202/393-3311) $15 plus $2 shipping, published annually. Describes federal summer legal intern  and clerkship programs for law students. Since these internships go quickly, contact Federal Reports about a copy by mid-autumn of the year before you want a summer internship. 35 pages.

## Job services

*NCRA Employment Referral Service* (National Court Reporters Association, 8224 Old Courthouse Rd., Vienna, VA 22182; phone: 703/281–4677) $6/six–month nonmember registration, free to members. Obtain Employment Referral Data Sheet. Completed data sheets kept on file for six–month period. Copy of data sheet furnished to potential employers. NCRA recommends that you also contact your state court reporters association to see if it has a referral service. Contact NCRA for the address and phone of the association in your state.

*CU Career Connection* (University of Colorado, Campus Box 133, Boulder, CO 80309–0133; phone: 303/492–4127) $20/two–month fee entitles you to a ''passcode'' which unlocks this job hotline. You need a touchtone phone to call and request the field in which you are interested and geographic area in which you want to hear job openings. The hotline is turned off Monday through Friday, 2 to 4 p.m. for daily updating.

*Local Women's Bar Associations.* A number of these operate job services. Contact the National Conference of Women's Bar Associations (P.O. Box 77, Edenton, NC 27932–0077; phone: 919/482–8202) for information.

## Directories

*Directory of Legal Aid and Defender Offices in the U.S. and Territories* (National Legal Aid and Defender Association, 8th Floor, 1625 K St., NW, Washington, DC 20006; phone: 202/452–0620) $30/nonmember, $15/member. Published annually.

*NDAA Membership Directory* (National District Attorneys Association, 1033 Fairfax St., Suite 200, Alexandria, VA 22314; phone: 703/549–9222) $15/nonmembers, $10/members. Lists all district attorney offices across the country. Published in 1989 and every three years thereafter.

*Federal Careers for Attorneys* (Federal Reports, Inc., Suite 408, 1010 Vermont Ave., NW, Washington, DC 20005; phone: 202/393–3311) $21.95 plus $2 shipping. Comprehensive guide to legal careers with over 300 U.S. government general counsel and other federal legal offices throughout the country and abroad. Each entry specifies attorney hiring procedures, special recruitment programs, where to apply, and type of legal work. Includes Subject Matter Index with over 80 major areas of government legal practice and Geographic Index of about 400 cities in the U.S. and abroad. 170 pages. Most recent edition published in March 1991.

*Federal Law–Related Careers* (Federal Reports, Inc., Suite 408, 1010 Vermont Ave., NW, Washington, DC 20005; phone: 202/393–3311) $14.95 plus $2 shipping. Describes over 80 law–related careers and identifies the primary federal agency employer in each field. Includes addresses for over 1,000 federal recruiting offices. 86 pages.

*Paralegal's Guide to U.S. Government Jobs* (Federal Reports, Inc., Suite 408, 1010 Vermont Ave., NW, Washington, DC 20005; phone: 202/393–3311) $14.00 plus $2 shipping. Designed for both entry-level and experienced paralegals, this book explains federal hiring procedures, describes 70 law–related careers for which paralegals qualify, outlines special hiring programs, and includes a directory of over 1,000 federal agency personnel offices that hire the most paralegal talent.

*Federal Legal Directory* (Federal Reports, Inc., Suite 408, 1010 Vermont Ave., NW, Washington, DC 20005; phone: 202/393–3311) $140 plus $2 shipping. This 568–page volume, plus free six–month supplement, includes details on hundreds of federal legal offices and the phone numbers of over 7,000 personnel.

*FDL Directory* (Food and Drug Law Institute, 1000 Vermont Ave., NW, Suite 1200, Washington, DC 20005; phone: 202/371–1420) free. Most recent edition published in 1991.

*Judicial Staff Directory* (Staff Directories, Ltd., P.O. Box 62, Mt. Vernon, VA 22121; phone: 703/739–0900) $59. Over 11,000 individuals listed for the 207 federal courts, 13,000 cities and their courts, court administration, U.S. marshalls, U.S. attorneys, and the U.S. Department of Justice. Includes 1,800 biographies. 865+ pages. Published every October.

## Library services

*Also see listings under "Records management and archival services" and see the **Non–Profits' Job Finder** listings under "Museums and library services." Nearly all of the job sources listed below include positions in private sector libraries as well as public sector.*

# Nationwide job sources

### Job openings

*American Libraries* (American Library Association, 50 E. Huron St., Chicago, IL 60611; phones: 800/545–2433 (outside Illinois), 800/545–2444 (Illinois only), 800/545–2455 (Canada only), 312/280–4211) 11 issues/year; $50/annual subscription for libraries, subscription included in membership package. Jobs listed under "Career Leads." Typical issues features 75 to 100 job ads.

Job notices can be obtained three weeks prior to publication in *American Libraries* in *Career Leads Express* which is a copy of the uncorrected galleys of job notices that will appear in the next issue of *American Libraries*. *Career Leads Express* is available to nonmembers and members alike for $1/issue, prepaid only. With your check, send a self–addressed stamped (two ounces postage) #10 envelope to AL Leads Express, 50 E. Huron, Chicago, IL 60611." Typical issue includes 75 or more positions.

*Library Journal* (Bowker Magazine Group, P.O. Box 1977, Marion, OH 43305–1077; phones: 800/669–1002, 614/382–3322) 20 issues/year, $74/annual subscription (U.S.), $99/Canada, $130/elsewhere (air mail). Jobs listed under "Classified Advertising." Fifty to 70 ads for librarian positions grace the pages of a typical issue.

*Information Today* (Learned Information, Inc., 143 Old Marlton Pike, Medford, NJ 08055; phone: 609/654–6266) 11 issues/year, $34.95/annual subscription. About five ads for library positions appear under "Classified Today."

*Wilson Library Bulletin* (The H. H. Wilson Company, 950 University Ave., Bronx, NY 10452; phones: 800/367–6770 ext. 2245, 212/588–2245) 10 issues/year, $46/annual subscription. Typically, about two ads for librarians, information brokers, or library consultants appear under "Library Services Directory."

*School Library Journal* (Cahners Publishing, P.O. Box 1978, Marion. OH 43305; phones: 800/842–1669, 614/382–3322) monthly, $63/annual subscription (U.S.), $80/Canada, $104/elsewhere. About 15 librarian positions with public libraries and university, elementary, and secondary school libraries appear under "Classifieds."

*Journal of Academic Librarianship* (Mountainside Publishing Co., 321 S. Main St., Suite 300, Ann Arbor, MI 48107; phone: 313/662–3925) bimonthly, $27/annual subscription (individuals), $49/institutions. Two or three ads for university librarians appear appear under "Classified Ads."

*Institutional Library Mail Jobline* (c/o S. Carlson, Rhode Island Department of State Library Services, 300 Richmond St., Providence, RI 02903; phone: 401/277–2726) monthly, free. Send self-addressed stamped envelope for copy. Lists institutional library positions in U.S. and its territories.

*Jobline* (American Society for Information Science, 8720 Georgia Ave., Suite 501, Silver Spring, MD 20910–3602; phone: 301/495–0900) monthly, available to nonmembers upon request, included in membership package.

*Rural Libraries Jobline* (Center for the Study of Rural Librarianship, Department of Library Science, Clarion University of Pennsylvania, Clarion, PA 16214; phone: 814/226–2383) monthly, $1/issue.

*Specialist* (Special Libraries Association, 1700 18th St., NW, Washington, DC 20009; 202/234–4700) monthly, $48/annual subscription, $58/foreign. From five to ten jobs are listed under "Positions Open."

*Canadian Association of Special Libraries and Information Services, Ottawa Chapter Jobline* (Job Bank Coordinator, CASLIS, 54 Mason Terrace, Ottawa, Ontario K1S 0K9 Canada) Call 613/237–3688 for recording of job openings.

*Newsletter* (American Association of Law Libraries, Suite 940, 53 W. Jackson, Chicago, IL 60604; phone: 312/939–4764) 10 issues/year, $50/nonmember annual subscription, free to members. Jobs listed under "Career Hotline." Over 20 job ads appear in the typical issue. Advance copies of job ads are available for $2.50/month prepaid. The advance copies include job ads two to four weeks before they are published in the *Newsletter* and ads not published in the *Newsletter*.

*Job Database* (American Association of Law Libraries, Dept. 77–6021, Chicago, IL 60678–6021; phone: 312/939–4764) monthly, $25/annual subscription. This is a monthly compilation of all jobs listed on the AALA's *Job Database Service* and *Career Hotline described later under "Job services." Expect to see 25 to 35 positions in an issue.*

*MLA News* (Medical Library Association, 6 N. Michigan Ave., Suite 300, Chicago, IL 60602; phone: 312/419–9094) 10 issues/year, $50/nonmember annual subscription, included in dues. From 15 to 20 ads appear in the "Classifieds" for librarian posts in the health sciences.

*Veterans Administration Librarian Register.* For printed job list, write to: Diane Wiesenthal (Library Division (143B)), Virginia Control Office, 810 Vermont Ave., NW, Washington, DC 20420, Atten: Vacancy List; phone: 202/233–2820) Most listings are for medical librarian positions with the Department of Veterans Affairs. Only for persons eligible for inclusion on Veterans Administration Licensed Register of Professional Librarians.

## Job services

*Grapevine Job Database* (American Library Association, 50 E. Huron St., Chicago, IL 60611; phones: 800/545–2433 (outside Illinois), 800/545–2444 (Illinois only), 800/545–2455 (Canada only), 312/280–4214). Contact Deputy *Grapevine* System Manager for details on how to use this computer database of jobs that is updated every Monday. Includes some jobs that do not appear in *Career Leads Express* or *American Libraries*.

*Resume Referral Service* (Special Libraries Association, 1700 18th St., NW, Washington, DC 20009; 202/234–4700) fee for six-month listing: $75/nonmember $50/members, $25/student members. Exclusively for library/information professionals seeking positions in the U.S. or Canada, this service has the job seeker submit ten copies of his resume and a completed application form detailing your job, salary, and geographical preferences. When a match is found, your resume is forwarded to the potential employer who chooses whom to interview.

*Career Hotline* (American Association of Law Libraries, Suite 940, 53 W. Jackson, Chicago, IL 60604) Call 312/939–7877 for a tape of job listings for law libraries. Recording is changed every two weeks. Five or more jobs on each recording.

*SpeciaLine Employment Clearinghouse Job Hotline* (Special Libraries Association, 1700 18th St., NW, Washington, DC 20009; 202/234–4700) Call 202/234–3632 for 24–hour tape recording of jobs with special libraries.

*American Library Association Job Hotline* (American Library Association, 50 E. Huron St., Chicago, IL 60611; phones: 800/545–2433 (outside Illinois), 800/545–2444 (Illinois only), 800/545–2455 (Canada only), 312/280–4211). If you want to work for the ALA, call 312/280–2464 to hear a recording of job openings at the ALA. 24–hours, seven days a week.

*Career Hotline/Job Database Service* (American Association of Law Libraries, Suite 940, 53 W. Jackson, Chicago, IL 60604; phone: 312/939–4764). Call the 24–hour Career Hotline, 312/939–7877, for a recording of brief job descriptions of law librarian positions and where to apply. This is the index to the AALL's *Job Database Service* which is updated weekly by Friday noon. AALL members can request a free printout of all job listings by calling 312/939–4764 or faxing a request to 312/431–1097. Nonmembers can obtain a printout for $5 (send to: AALL, Dept. 77-602, Chicago, IL 60678–6021). There are typically 10 to 15 jobs listed at any one time.

*See also ASIS Jobline* listed under "Data processing and computers."

## Directories

*AALL Directory and Handbook* (American Association of Law Libraries, Suite 940, 53 W. Jackson, Chicago, IL 60604; phone: 312/939–4764). This annual directory of government and private law libraries is available only to members.

*COSLA Directory* (The Council of State Governments, Iron Works Pike, P.O. Box 11910, Lexington, KY 40578; phone: 606/231–1939) $12.50. Lists information on state library agencies, consultants and administrative staff. Includes ALANET numbers, electronic mail letters and FAX numbers. Published each spring.

*American Library Directory* (R. R. Bowker, P.O. Box 31, New Providence, NJ 07974–9904; phone: 800/521–8110) $199.95 plus 5 percent shipping and handling, two volumes, published each July. Provides information on over 38,000 public, government, academic, and special libraries and library–related organizations in the U.S. and Canada.

*World Guide to Libraries* (R. R. Bowker, P.O. Box 31, New Providence, NJ 07974–9904; phone: 800/521–8110) $325 plus 5 percent shipping and handling, published each July. 1,275 pages. Provides information on over 40,000 libraries worldwide.

*Who's Who in Special Libraries* (Special Libraries Association, 1700 18th St., NW, Washington, DC 20009; 202/234–4700) $25/nonmembers, included in membership package. Includes alphabetical and geographical lists of special libraries. Published annually in the autumn.

*Directory of Special Libraries and Information Centers* (Gale Research, Inc., 835 Penobscot Bldg., Detroit, MI 48226; phone: 800/877–4253) $380, in two parts, 1991. Provides comprehensive information on 18,600 information centers, archives, and special and research libraries in the U.S., Canada, and elsewhere. Includes subject index.

*Subject Directory of Special Libraries* (Gale Research, Inc., 835 Penobscot Bldg., Detroit, MI 48226; phone: 800/877–4253) $675/three volumes, 1990. These volumes contain the same material as the *Directory of Special Libraries and Information Centers*, but rearranged into 14 subject areas in three volumes, available invidually: Business, Government, and Law Libraries, $250; Computers, Engineering, and Science Libraries, $250; Health Sciences Libraries, $250.

*New Special Libraries* (Gale Research, Inc., 835 Penobscot Bldg., Detroit, MI 48226; phone: 800/877–4253) $335, 1990. Furnishes comprehensive information on special libraries in the U.S., Canada, and elsewhere.

*Directory of Federal Libraries* (Oryx Press, 4041 N. Central, Phoenix, AZ 85012–3397; phone: 800/279–6799) $75, April 1992, 256 pages. Includes close to 3,000 special and general libraries, presidential and national libraries, as well as federal libraries in technical centers, hospitals, and penal institutions. Includes each library's administrator and selected staff.

*Directory of the Medical Library Association* (MLA, 6 N. Michigan Ave., Suite 300, Chicago, IL 60602; phone: 312/419–9094) $42.75/nonmembers, included in dues. Published each October.

# Regional job sources

## Job openings

*MPLA Newsletter* (Mountain Plains Library Association, I.D. Weeks Library, University of South Dakota, Vermillion, SD 57069; phone: 605/677–6082) bimonthly, $17/nonmember annual subscription (U.S.), $20/foreign, included in membership package. States covered: Arizona, Colorado, Kansas, Montana, Nebraska, Nevada, North Dakota, Oklahoma, South Dakota, Utah, and Wyoming. Jobs listed under "Joblist." Three or four job ads per issue.

## Job services

*Drexel University College of Information Studies Jobline* (c/o Placement Office Assistant, College of Information Studies, Drexel University, Philadelphia, PA 19104; phone: 215/895–2478) Call 215/895–1672 for recording of job openings. States included: Delaware, New Jersey, Pennsylvania.

*Jobline* (Mountain Plains Library Association, I.D. Weeks Library, University of South Dakota, Vermillion, SD 57069; phone: 605/677–6082) 24–hour tape recording of open public and private library positions in Arizona, Colorado, Kansas, Montana, Nebraska, Nevada, North Dakota, Oklahoma, South Dakota, Utah, and Wyoming. Updated each Friday. Job hotline numbers: 605/677–5757, 800/356–7820 (from only within states listed).

*Job Hotline* (Midwest Federation of Library Associations, Room 305, 1100 W. 42nd St., Indianapolis, IN 46208; phone: 317/926–6561) 24–hour Job Hotline recording updated on Mondays: 317/926–8770. Covers job openings in Illinois, Indiana, Michigan, Minnesota, Ohio, and Wisconsin. This regional association has been pretty transient. If the hotline number has been disconnected, contact another state library association in the region for the new number.

*New England Library Jobline* (GSLIS, New England Library Jobline, Simmons College, 300 The Fenway, Boston, MA 02115) Call 617/738-3148 for available jobs.

*Pacific Northwest Library Association Jobline* (PNLA Jobline, c/o Graduate School of Library and Information Sciences, FM-30, University of Washington, Seattle, WA 98195) Call 206/543-2890 for recording of available positions.

*Jobline* (Drexel University College of Information Studies, Placement Office Assistant, Philadelphia, PA 19104; phone: 215/895-2478). Call 215/895-1672 for a recording with job vacancies in Delaware, New Jersey, and Pennsylvania.

# State job sources

## Job services and newsletters

Many state library associations publish newsletters with job announcements in them or operate 24-hour job hotlines with tape recorded job announcements. *American Libraries,* the first periodical listed under ''Library Services,'' frequently publishes a list of all the state library association job hotlines (if a job hotline has been disconnected, contact the American Library Association to get the new phone number or address). The following state library associations operate a job hotline or publish a periodical with job ads or announcements:

*Arizona Job Hotline* (Research Division, Room 300, Arizona Department of Library, Archives, and Public Records, 1700 W. Washington, Phoenix, AZ 85007). Call 602/275-2325 for taped job announcements.

*British Columbia Library Association Jobline* (BCLA, #110—6545 Bonsor Ave., Buraby, British Columbia V5H 1H3, Canada; phone: 604/430-9633). Call 604/430-6411 for a recording of positions in British Columbia.

*California Library Association Jobline* (CLA, Suite 300, 717 K St., Sacramento, CA 95814-3477; phone: 916/447-8541) Call 916/443-1222 or 818/797-4602 for tape recording of job openings.

*California Media and Library Educators Association Job Hotline* (CMLEA, Suite 142, 1499 Old Bayshore Highway, Burlingame, CA 94010; phone: 415/692-2350) Call 415/697-8832 for taped job announcements.

*San Andreas–San Francisco Bay Special Libraries Association Job Hotline* (phone: 415/620-4919) For a tape recording of job openings call, 408/252-7248, 415/391-7441, or use these electronic mail services: Dialmail or Ontyme.

*Southern California Chapter, Special Libraries Association Job Hotline* (c/o Paul Morton, Southern California Edison, 2244 Walnut Grove Rd., Rosemead, CA 91770; phone: 818/302-8966). Call 818/795-2145 for tape recording of job openings.

*Colorado State Library Jobline* (Jobline, 201 E. Colfax, Denver, CO 80203; phone: 303/866-6910) Call 303/866-6741 for job openings.

## If you can't find your specialty...

**You probably skipped Chapter 1, the chapter that tells you how to use this book most effectively—and the chapter nobody ever wants to read.** *Please read it!* **It explains how to use this chapter and the Index to find job sources in your field, whether it be professional, trades, office support, labor, or technical.**

*Connecticut Library Association Jobline* (CLA Jobline, Connecticut State Library, 638 Prospect Ave., Hartford, CT 06105). Call 203/645-8090 for a 24-hour recording updated weekly.

*Metropolitan Washington (D.C.) Library Jobline* (Metropolitan Washington Library Council, Suite 200, 1875 I St. NW, Washington, DC 20006; phone: 202/223-6800, extension 458) Call 202/962-3712 to hear the Jobline recording.

*Delaware Library Association Jobline* Call 302/739-4748 extension 69 (800/282-8696 only within Delaware) for job openings. Delaware positions are also listed on the New Jersey, Pennsylvania, and Maryland joblines.

*Florida Jobline* (State Library of Florida, R.A. Gray Building, Tallahassee, FL 32301; phone: 904/487-2651) Call 904/488-5232 for job openings.

*Illinois Library Jobline* (Illinois Library Association, Suite 301, 33 W. Grand Ave., Chicago, IL 60610; phone: 312/644-1896) Call 312/828-0930 for recording. Includes positions with special libraries.

*Indiana Statewide Library Jobline* (1100 W. 42nd St., Indianapolis, IN 46208; phone: 317/926-6561) Call or write for printout of of job openings. Direct access to the Jobline is available through the RBSS Computer Bulletin Board, 317/924-9584.

*Iowa Library Joblist* (Annette Van Cles, Editor, State Library of Iowa, Historical Building, Des Moines, IA 50319; phone: 515/281-4350) monthly. Contact for rates.

*Maryland Library Association Jobline* (MLA, 115 W. Franklin St., Baltimore, MD 21201; phone: 301/685-5760, Mondays and Fridays only) Call 301/685-5760 for job listings.

*Michigan Library Association* (1000 Long Blvd., Lansing, MI 48911; phone: 517/694-6615) 24-hour Job Hotline recording changed on Monday afternoons: 517/694-7440

*Missouri Library Association Jobline* (Parkade Plaza, Suite 9, Columbia, MO 65201). Job Hotline recording changed every other Friday: 314/442-6590

*Nebraska Job Hotline* (Nebraska Library Commission, 1420 P St., Lincoln, NE 68508) Call 402/471-2045 for recording of job openings. In Nebraska only, call 800/742-7691.

*New Jersey Library Association Job Hotline* (P.O. Box 1534, Trenton, NJ 08607) Call 609/695-2121 for 24-hour recording of job openings.

*New York Library Association Jobline* (252 Hudson Ave., Albany, NY 12210) Call 518/432-6952 for job opening recording; in New York only call 800/232-6952.

*New York Chapter Special Libraries Association Hotline* (c/o Nan Schubel, Ernst & Young, Office of the General Counsel, 380 Madison Ave., New York, NY 10017). Call 212/808-5450 for jobs recording.

*North Carolina Jobline* (Association's phone: 919/733–2570) Call 919/733–6410 for recording or use Western Union's EASYLINK, NCJOBS for computer viewing of job openings.

*Jobline* (Cleveland Area Metropolitan Library System, 3645 Warrenville Center Rd., Suite 116, Shaker Heights, OH 44122). For jobs only in northeast Ohio, call 216/921–4702 24 hours a day.

*Oklahoma Department of Libraries Jobline* (Department phone: 405/521–2502) Call 405/521–4202 for recording of jobs 5 p.m. to 8 a.m. on weekends and holidays only. Updated on the 1st and 15th each month.

*Oregon Library/Media Jobline* (Oregon State Library, State Library Bldg., Salem OR 97310; phone: 503/378–4243) Call 503/585–2232 for job recording.

*Pennsylvania Cooperative Job Hotline* (Agency phone: 717/233–3113) Call 717/234–4646 for job openings.

*RILA Bulletin* (Rhode Island Library Association, R. Stoddard, Government Publications Office, University Library, University of Rhode Island, Kingstown, RI 02881) monthly. For copies, send self–addressed, stamped envelopes. Jobs listed under ''Jobline.''

*University of South Carolina College of Library and Information Science Jobline* (Admissions and Placement Coordinator, CLIS, University of South Carolina, Columbia, SC 29208). Call 803/777–8443 for job openings.

*Texas State Library Jobline* (Kay Easter, Texas State Library, 1200 Brazos, P.O. Box 12927, Austin, TX 7811; phone: 512/463–5447). Call 512/463–5470 for 24–hour recording of job openings, which is changed weekly.

*Virginia Library Jobline* (Virginia Library Association, 80 S. Early St., Alexandria, VA 22314) Call 703/370–7267 for job recording.

*West Virginia.* Call the Pennsylvania Cooperative Job Hotline.

## Media and the arts

*For an extensive list of job sources for the media and the arts that include some government jobs as well as private and non–profit sector positions, also see the* **Professional's Job Finder** *and the* **Non–Profits' Job Finder***.*

## Job openings

*Job Information Letter* (National Association of Government Communicators, 669 S. Washington St., Alexandria, VA 22314; phone: 703/519–3902) biweekly, $50/nonmember annual subscription (no subscription fee to members) plus send NAGC 26 self-addressed stamped #10 envelopes (2 ounce postage) for NAGC to mail the issues to you; in membership package. Typical issue lists about 30 to 35 federal government positions plus photocopies of 50 or more classified ads for editorial and art positions for several metropolitan areas. Also identifies over a dozen job hotlines and referral services.

See also *APCO—Journal of Public–Safety Communications* listed under ''Public safety.''

See also *FEDfacts* listed under ''Data processing and computers.''

*WESTAF's National Arts Jobbank* (236 Montezume Ave., Santa Fe, NM 87501; phone: 505/988–1166) biweekly, U.S.: $36/annual subscription, $24/six–month subscription, $15/three–month subscription; foreign: $45/annual subscription, $27/six–month subscription, $17/three–month subscription. Generally a number of government positions are included in the 100+ job vacancies in arts administration, performance, production/technical, and academia.

*Government and Military Video* (PSN Publications, 2 Park Ave., Suite 1920, New York, NY 10016; phone: 212/779–1919) monthly, free to qualified professionals. The ''Classifieds'' section usually has three or four positions in broadcase engineering.

*Also see PD News* listed under ''Data processing and computers'' which includes jobs for technical writers.

## Job Services

*Jobphone* (Editorial Freelance Association, 36 E. 23rd St., 9th floor, New York, NY 10110; phone: 212/677-3357). Anybody can call the "Jobphone," 212/260-6470, to hear a recording that briefly describes about 40 freelance writing, editing, proofreading, and translating opportunities. Listings are updated weekly. Only EFA members who subscribe to this service can call another phone number to get details (such as pay and whom to contact) on the listed jobs. Members can subscribe to "Jobphone" for $20/year. Write for membership rates (they're a little complicated to explain).

*CU Career Connection* (University of Colorado, Campus Box 133, Boulder, CO 80309-0133; phone: 303/492-4127) $20/two-month fee entitles you to a "passcode" which unlocks this job hotline. You need a touchtone phone to call and request the field in which you are interested and geographic area in which you want to hear job openings. The hotline is turned off Monday through Friday, 2 to 4 p.m. for daily updating.

## Directories

*Locations* (Association of Film Commissioners International, 159 W. Main St., Suite 344, Webster, NY 14580-2967; phone: 716/671-6727) semiannual, free. Includes names, addresses, and phone numbers for municipal and state film commissioners as well as filmcommissioners abroad.

*Madison Avenue Handbook: The Image Makers Source* (Peter Glenn Publications, 17 E. 48th St., 6th floor, New York, NY 10017; phone: 212/688-7940) $45, published every April. Includes directory of state and local film commissions for the U.S. and possessions as well as for Canada and other foreign countries.

*New Careers: A Directory of Jobs and Internships in Technology and Society* (Student Pugwash USA, 1638 R St., NW, Suite 32, Washington, DC 20009; phone: 202/328-6555) $18, $10/students (add $3 shipping). Offers full details on where and how to apply for internships and entry-level jobs in communications. Published in even-numbered years.

*On Location Annual Directory* (On Location Publishing, P.O. Box 2810, Hollywood, CA 90028; phone: 213/541-4363) $99. Includes directory of government film commissions among its 1,000 + pages listing goods and services necessary for filming on location throughout the U.S. and other English speaking countries. Published each October.

## Mental health

*Also see listings under "Public administration," "Public health and health care," and "Social services." Also see the* **Non-Profits' Job Finder.**

### Job openings

*The APA Monitor* (American Psychological Association, 1200 17th St., NW, Washington, DC 20036; phone: 202/955-7690) $25/nonmember annual subscription, included in membership package. Jobs listed under "Position Openings." From 400 to 800 job ads grace the pages of a typical issue.

*Psychiatric News* (American Psychiatric Association, 1400 K St., NW, Washington, DC 20005; phone: 202/682-6000) bimonthly, $40/nonmember annual subscription (U.S.), $60/foreign, included in membership package. Jobs listed under "Classified Notices." Over 390 job ads in the typical issue.

*Archives of General Psychiatry* (American Medical Association, Circulation Dept., 515 N. State St., Chicago, IL 60610; phone: 312/464-0183) monthly, $58/annual subscription, $73 foreign (surface mail), special rates for residents and medical students. About 20 positions, including Veterans Administration, are listed under "Classified Advertising."

*National Council News* (National Council of Community Mental Health Centers, Suite 320, 12300 Twinbrook Pkwy, Rockville, MD 20852; phone: 301/984-6200) 11 issues/year, $21/nonmember annual subscription, included in dues. Jobs listed under "JOBank." Typical issue features 20 to 30 job ads for social workers and counselors, psychiatrists, psychologists, clinical workers, and administrative positions.

*AMHCA Advocate* (American Mental Health Counselors' Association, 5999 Stevenson Ave., Alexandria, VA 22304; phones: 800/326–2642, 703/823–9800) bimonthly, $25/nonmember annual subscription, included in membership package. Jobs listed under "Classifieds." About four job ads in the usual issue.

## Job services

*Psychiatric Placement Service* (American Psychiatric Association, 1400 K St., NW, Washington, DC 20005; phone: 202/682–6000) free. Obtain an application form and submit it with your resume. After being matched with a vacancy, both the job seeker and the potential employer are notified. Resumes are kept on file indefinitely.

## Directories

*Mental Health Directory* (Superintendent of Documents, Government Printing Office, Washington, DC 20402; phone: 202/783–3238) $23. Stock number.017–024–01419–2. Prepared by the National Institute of Mental Health, this directory included hospitals, group homes, and halfway houses by city and state.

*APA Membership Directory* (American Psychological Association, 1200 17th St., NW, Washington, DC 20036; phone: 202/955–7690) $35/nonmembers, $22.50/members. Published every four years. Most recent edition, 1991.

*National Registry of Community Mental Health Services* (National Council of Community Mental Health Centers, Suite 320, 12300 Twinbrook Pkwy, Rockville, MD 20852; phone: 301/317–8912) $59/nonmembers, $29/members. This directory contains information on over 1,900 agencies in the U.S. and possessions. Published every four years; most recent edition published in December 1991.

*AMHA Membership Directory* (Association of Mental Health Admnistrators, 60 Revere, Suite 500, Northbrook, IL 60062; phone: 708/480–9626) contact them for price. This directories of mental health adminstrators was first published in August 1991.

*American Association of State Psychology Boards Membership Roster* (American Association of State Psychology Boards, P.O. Box 4389, Montgomery, AL 36103; phone: 205/832–4580) $4. Lists information on state and provincial psychology licensing boards in the U.S. and Canada.

## Salary survey

*Survey of Salary Benefits and Staffing Pattersn of Community Mental Health Providers* (National Council of Community Mental Health Centers, Suite 320, 12300 Twinbrook Pkwy, Rockville, MD 20852; phone: 301/317–8912) $69/nonmembers, $49/members. Based on a sample of over 500 community mental health providers, this survey gives salary and fringe benefit figures by region, service area type, and nationally. Published in December of odd–numbered years.

# Parks and recreation

*Also see listings under "Environment" and "Forestry and horticulture."*

## Job openings

*Park and Recreation Opportunities Job Bulletin* (National Recreation and Park Association, 3101 Park Center Dr., Alexandria, VA 22302; phone: 703/820-4940) 22 issues/year, individual copies available to nonmembers and members for $5 prepaid; annual subscription available only to members, $30. Typical issue includes 40 to 60 jobs by geographic area in the U.S. and foreign positions.

*Opportunities* (Natural Science for Youth Foundation, 130 Azalea Dr., Roswell, GA 30075; phones: 800/992–6793, 404/594–9367) bimonthly, $35/annual subscription, $10/single issue, included in membership package. "Positions available " lists details on 45 to 70 jobs for naturalists, curators, raptor rehabilitators, and administrative positions, largely at nature centers.

*Park Maintenance* (P.O. Box 1936, Appleton, WI 54913; phone: 414/733–2301) monthly, $16/annual subscription (U.S.), $20/Canada, $24/elsewhere. Two or three ads for administrators of large outdoor grounds such as parks, golf courses, and campuses appear under "Classifieds."

*1992 Summer Employment Directory of the United States* (Petersons Guides, PO Box 2123, Princeton, NJ 08543–2123; phone: 800/338–3282) $14.95. Published annually in the autumn. Its 200+ pages list over 75,000 summer job openings at resorts, campls, amusement parks, national parks, and government.

*Golf Course Management* (Golf Course Superintendents Association of America, 1421 Research Park Dr., Lawrence, KS 66049–3859; phones: 800/422–6383, 913/832–4466) monthly; $30/annual subscription, included in dues. Jobs listed under "Classifieds." About eight ads including municipal golf courses, appear in a typical issue.

*Employment Referral Service* (Golf Course Superintendents Association of America, 1421 Research Park Dr., Lawrence, KS 66049–3859; phones: 800/422–6383, 913/832–4466) Available only to members for $10/six months. Typical issue lists ten job openings in golf course management and landscape architecture.

*Parks and Grounds Management* (P.O. Box 1936, Appleton, WI 54913–1936; phone: 414/733–2301) monthly, $16/annual subscription. A handful of ads in management of public parks and college campuses appear under "Classified."

*Marine Technology Society Currents* (Marine Technology Society, 1825 K St., NW, Suite 218, Washington, DC 20006; phone: 202/775-5966) bi-monthly, $10/annual subscription, included in dues. Two or three ads for such positions as fish hatchery managers appear near the back of the newsletter.

## Job services

*JOBSource* (Computerized Employment Systems, Inc., 1720 W. Mulberry, Suite B9, Fort Collins, CO 80521; phones: 800/727-5627, 303/493-1779) There are three services available using an extensive database of over 700 positions, mostly in the environmental arena (fisheries, natural resources, wildlife, forestry, biology, and especially parks and recreation). For individuals, the most useful is JOBSource's in-house search program. Obtain a resume application form from JOBSource. Within two weeks of receiving your completed form, JOBSource will conduct a job search of its database for you. JOBSource guarantees from six to 25 matches per search. The cost is $30. If fewer than six matches are found, JOBSource will run a second search the next month for free. If the second run turns up fewer than six matches, there is a $5 charge for that second run.

However, if you have a computer and modem, you can download the entire database onto your computer for $20 plus your phone call. It takes 20 to 40 minutes to download the three files. To update, you need download just one file which takes about 20 minutes and costs $15. The database is updated every Thursday. A growing number of universities and colleges are subscribing to JOBSource. They receive the database and user programs around the 24th of each month and can conduct their own job searches. Subscriptions are available for a year ($495), the nine months of September through May ($375), or for the three months of January, April, and November ($189).

*NRPA/SCHOLE Network* (National Recreation and Park Association, 3101 Park Center Dr., Alexandria, VA 22302; phone: 703/820–4940) $75/annual subscription for nonmember individuals, $225/nonmember agenices, $50/member individuals, $150/member agencies. This computer information and communications network includes NRPA's *Park and Recreation Opportunities Job Bulletin. Updated biweekly.*

## Directories

The National Association of State Park Directors recommends that job applicants contact the state park agency for the state in which they are interested. For a list of state park directors, write to the National Association of State Park Directors (c/o Ney Landrum, Executive Director, 126 Mill Branch Rd., Tallahassee, FL 32312) or see *The National Directory of State Agencies, State Administrative Officials Classified by Function* in Chapter 3.

*Compendium of Special Recreation* (Special Recreation, Inc., 362 Koser Ave., Iowa City, IA 52246–3038; phone: 219/337–7578) $49.95/nonmembers. Lists organizations that deal with recreation for people who have disabilities. Published new edition expected in 1992.

*Directory of Natural Science Centers* (Natural Science for Youth Foundation, 130 Azalea Dr., Roswell, GA 30075; phones: 800/992–6793, 404/594–9367) $78.50, $58.50/members. This 600 page tome gives details on over 1,350 nature centers. Last edition published in 1990. Next edition expected in 1994.

*Society of Municipal Arborists Membership List* (Society of Municipal Arborists, c/o Office of the City Forester, 6801 Delmar Blvd., University City, MO 63130; phone: 314/862–1711) available only to members, included in $40 annual dues. Published every March.

*Who's Who in Golf Course Management* (Golf Course Superintendents Association of America, 1421 Research Park Dr., Lawrence, KS 66049–3859; phones: 800/422–6383, 913/832–4466) available only to members, included in dues. This directory of members includes salary data for golf course superintendents. Published each March.

# Personnel/human resources

*Also see listings under "Public Administration."*

## Job openings

*HR News* (Society for Human Resource Management, 606 N. Washington St., Alexandria, VA 22314; phone: 703/548-3440) monthly, $39/nonmember subscription, included in membership package. Jobs listed under " HR News Employment Service." Contains 30 to 35 job ads in a typical issue.

*Recruiter Service* (International Personnel Management Association, 1617 Duke St., Alexandria, VA 22314; phone: 703/549-7100) monthly $21/nonmember annual subscription, included in dues. Four to six public agency personnel positions appear in the typical issue.

*Personnel Journal* (A. C. Croft, Inc., Suite B-2, 245 Fischer Ave., Costa Mesa, CA 92626; phone: 714/751-1883) monthly; $50/annual subscription. Jobs listed under "Classified." Typical issue features five to 12 jobs ads, mostly in the private sector.

*IPMA News* (International Personnel Management Association, 1617 Duke St., Alexandria, VA 22314; phone: 703/549-7100) monthly, $21/nonmember annual subscription, included in membership package. Jobs listed under "Recruiter Service." Typical issue carries about 12 job ads for personnel, public administration, fire and police chiefs.

*National Public Employer Labor Relations Newsletter* (National Public Employer Labor Relations Association, 1620 I St. NW, Washington, DC 20006; phone: 202/296-2230) monthly, available only as part of membership package; membership limited to labor-manager and personnel professionals in local and state government. Jobs listed under "Positions Available." Few job ads.

## Job services

*CU Career Connection* (University of Colorado, Campus Box 133, Boulder, CO 80309-0133; phone: 303/492-4127) $20/two-month fee entitles you to a "passcode" which unlocks this job hotline. You need a touchtone phone to call and request the field in which you are interested and geographic area in which you want to hear job openings. The hotline is turned off Monday through Friday, 2 to 4 p.m. for daily updating.

## Directories

*Who's Who in Human Resources* (Society for Human Resource Management, 606 N. Washington St., Alexandria, VA 22314; phone: 703/548–3440) available only to members, included in dues. Published annually.

*IPMA Membership Directory* (International Personnel Management Association, 1617 Duke St., Alexandria, VA 22314; phone: 703/549–7100) $150/nonmembers, included free in membership. Published annually.

*State Personnel Offices: Roles and Functions* (The Council of State Governments, Iron Works Pike, P.O. Box 11910, Lexington, KY 40578–1910; phone: 606/231–1939) Write for price. Published in odd–numbered years. Includes roster of state personnel officials.

*NPELRA Membership Directory* (National Public Employer Labor Relations Association, 1620 I St., NW, Washington, DC 20006; phone: 202/296–2230) Available only as part of membership package. Membership limited to labor–manager and personnel professionals in local and state government.

# Planning

*Also see listings under "Community and economic development," "Housing," and "Public administration."*

## Job openings

*JobMart* (American Planning Association, 1313 E. 60th St., Chicago, IL 60637; phone: 312/955–9100) 22 issues/year, annual subscription rates: $25/first class mail, $35/Canada, $65/elsewhere, $15/bulk rate (U.S. only); available only to members; also available as part of reduced–cost package deal with *Planners Referral Service* discussed below under "Job services." Write to APA for salary–based dues structure. Spring issues include job ads for summer internships. With over 1,200 public agency and consulting firm jobs listed annually, the typical issue features from 25 to 50 ads itemized by state.

*Planning* (American Planning Association, 1313 E. 60th St., Chicago, IL 60637; phone: 312/955-9100) monthly, $40/annual subscription (U.S.), $50/elsewhere, included free in membership package. Write for salary-based dues schedule. Growing number of display ads featuring job announcements, usually for higher-level positions in public agencies—generally three to eight ads per issue. Note that most of APA's state chapters publish newsletters that include timely job announcements. Many of these chapters allow nonmember subscriptions or chapter-only membership which includes the chapter newsletter. Many chapters also publish rosters of planners within their state. Contact APA for names, addresses, and phone numbers of the presidents of the state chapters you wish to contact.

*Regional Reporter* (National Association of Regional Councils, Suite 1300, 1700 K St., NW, Washington, DC 20006; phone: 202/457-0710) monthly, available only to members. Jobs listed under "Job Opportunities." Four job ads in typical issue.

*Preservation News* (National Trust for Historic Preservation, 1785 Massachusetts Ave., NW, Washington, DC 20036; phone: 202/673-4075) available to members only; membership is $15/year.

*URISA Marketplace* (Urban and Regional Information Systems Association, 900 Second St., NE, Suite 304, Washington, DC 20002; phone: 202/289-1685) monthly, available to members only, included in dues. Typical issue includes about 15 positions, largely in geographic information system management, operation, and design.

*GIS World* (2629 Redwing Rd., Suite 280, Fort Collins, CO 80526; phone: 303/223-4848) 9 issues/year, $60/annual subscription, $39/government employees. Under "Classified Ads—Positions Available" appear seven to 11 job vacancies for geographic information system operators,managers, and engineers.

*ACSM Bulletin* (American Congress on Surveying and Mapping, 5410 Grosvenor Ln., Bethesda, MD 20814; phone: 301/493-0200) bimonthly, $70/annual nonmember subscription (U.S.), $80/foreign, free to members. About six openings for land surveyors, cartographers, and geographic information system specialists appear under "Professional Directory."

HERMAN copyright 1983 by Jim Unger.
Reprinted with permission of Universal
Press Syndicate. All rights reserved.

*Photogrammetric Engineering & Remote Sensing* (American Society for Photogrammetry & Remote Sensing, 5410 Grosvenor Ln., Suite 210, Bethesda, MD 20814-2160; phone: 301/493-0290) monthly, $120/annual nonmember subscription, $65/members. Job openings for GIS/LIS specialists, computer specialists, and engineers and scientists in the surveying and mapping sciences appear under "Classified."

*AAG Newsletter* (Association of American Geographers, 1710 16th St., NW, Washington, DC 20009; phone: 202/234-1450) 10 issues/year, available only to members. From 25 to 50 positions, primarily academic, are listed under "Jobs in Geography."

*Bulletin* (Society of Government Economists, P.O. Box 9622 Friendship Station NW, Washington, DC 20016; phone: 202/272-2610) 11 issues/year, available only to members; $25/annual dues. Jobs listed under "Job Announcements." About half of the five or six job announcements are for federal positions.

*Job Openings for Economists* (American Economic Association, 2014 Broadway, Suite 305, Nashville, TN 37203; phone: 615/322-2595) bimonthly, $25/annual nonmember subscription (U.S.), $32.50/foreign, $15/AEA regular members, $7.50/AEA junior members. Among the 150 plus jobs in a typical issue are just four or five government positions, primarily federal.

*Job Placement Bulletin* (National Economics Association, School of Business, University of Michigan, Ann Arbor, MI 48109-1234; phone: 313/763-0121) available only to members. About eight jobs for economists appear in typical issue.

*Practicing Anthropology* (Society for Applied Anthropology, P.O. Box 24083, Oklahoma City, OK 73124; phone: 405/843-5113) quarterly, $14/nonmember annual subscription (U.S.), $40/foreign; included in dues. Two or three display ads for anthropologists and sociologists including planning positions are in the typical issue.

*Bulletin of the SAA* (Society for American Archaeology, 808 17th St., NW, Suite 200, Washington, DC 20006; phone: 202/223-9774) five or six issues/year, $15/annual nonmember subscription, included in dues. About six ads for archaeologists and anthropologists are listed under "Positions Open."

*Population Today* (Population Reference Bureau, Inc., 777 14th St., NW, Suite 800, Washington, DC 20005; phone: 202/639-8040) available to members; annual dues: $45/U.S., $56/foreign, $25/U.S. student, $28/foreign student. A few job ads appear under "Population Positions."

## Job services

*Planners' Referral Service* (American Planning Association, 1313 E. 60th St., Chicago, IL 60637; phone: 312/955-9100) $25/annual registration fee; available only to members; also available in reduced-cost package deal with *JobMart* discussed above under "Job ads:" get both for $40/*JobMart* sent via first class mail (U.S.), $50/Canada, $80/elsewhere, $32/*JobMart* sent by bulk rate mail (U.S. only). Resumes are kept in computer file for one year. Six-month renewals are available. An employer requests APA to search its computer file for qualified applicants. Employers contact applicants directly to arrange interviews.

*National Association of County Planners Job Exchange Program* (c/o Phil Sieber, Director, Arapahoe County Planning Department, 5334 S. Prince St., Littleton, CO 80166; phone: 303/795-4450) $25/nonmembers, free to members. This clearinghouse service enables city, county, and regional planners, and consultants, to temporarily trade jobs and abodes for a year. Participants must have a letter from their chief executive officer indicating a willingness to participate if a match can be found. Your permanent employer still pays your salary and benefits. Write or call for application form.

*National Registry for Economists* (c/o Illinois Department Employment Security, 29 E. Congress, Chicago, IL 60605; phone: 312/793-4904; operated in conjunction with the Allied Social Science Association) free. Request application form. Completed forms kept on file for one year. The Registry submits forms of qualified registrants to employers seeking economists. Employers then contact registrants directly.

## Directories

*American Planning Association Membership Directory* (American Planning Association, 1313 E. 60th St., Chicago, IL 60637; phone: 312/955-9100) $31.95 plus $3.95 shipping. Alphabetical listing of 26,000 professional planners and planning commissioners plus geographical index and specialty index. First published in 1990, there may be a new edition in 1992.

*AICP Roster* (American Institute of Certified Planners, c/o American Planning Association, 1776 Massachusetts Ave., NW, Washington, DC 20036; phone: 202/872-0611) $30/nonmember, $20/APA member, included in AICP membership package. AICP is an institute within the American Planning Association. This directory lists the 7,000+ AICP members alphabetically and by city within state. Although AICP membership is achieved by passing a demanding test, it does not indicate that AICP members are better qualified or more competent than other professional planners. Since titles are listed, this is a good source to identify directors of municipal and county planning departments and related departments. Published in even-numbered years.

*MPO Directory* (National Association of Regional Councils, Suite 1300, 1700 K St., NW, Washington, DC 20006; phone: 202/457-0710) $50/nonmembers, $25/members. New edition expected in 1992. Lists metropolitan planning agencies and organizations.

*Directory of Regional Councils* (National Association of Regional Councils, Suite 1300, 1700 K St., NW, Washington, DC 20006; phone: 202/457-0710) $100/nonmembers, free to members.

*Directory, National Association of County Planners* (c/o National Association of Counties, 440 First St., NW, Washington, DC 20001; phone: 202/393-6226) free. Lists about 100 county planners around the country.

*Directory of Black Economists* (National Economoc Association, School of Business, University of Michigan, Ann Arbor, MI 48109–1234; phone: 313/763–0121) $25/nonmembers, included in dues. New edition scheduled for 1992 and even–numbered years thereafter.

*ACSM Membership Directory* (American Congress on Surveying and Mapping, 5410 Grosvenor Ln., Bethesda, MD 20814; phone: 301/493–0200) available only to members for $31. Most recent edition published in 1991.

*ASPRS Directory of Mapping Sciences* (American Society for Photogrammetry & Remote Sensing, 5410 Grosvenor Ln., Suite 210, Bethesda, MD 20814–2160; phone: 301/493–0290) available only to members. Published each June.

## Salary surveys

*Planners' Salaries and Employment Trends, 1991* (American Planning Association, 1313 E. 60th St., Chicago, IL 60637; phone: 312/955–9100) $20/general public and APA members, $10/subscribers to APA's Planning Advisory Service. Published in December of odd–numbered years.

*NAPRC Salary Survey* (National Association of Regional Councils, Suite 1300, 1700 K St., NW, Washington, DC 20006; phone: 202/457–0710) $110/nonmembers, included in dues. Published annually. Covers top salaries and benefits of top positions with regional councils.

# Political industry

*Note: Jobs in political campaigns and with campaign consultants usually are found via word of mouth. The magazines and job service listed here represent nascent attempts to move beyond networking. This is one field in which directories are an extremely valuable job–quest aid.*

## Job openings

*Roll Call* (Levitt Communications, 900 Second St., NE, Washington, DC 20002; phone: 202/289–4900) twice weekly, $175/annual subscription. Among the 15 or so job ads under "Roll Call Classifieds—Employment," are positions with political campaigns (during the campaign season) and jobs with non–profit organizations, political organizations, and private industry that require a knowledge of politics and Capitol Hill: lobbbyists, government affairs/relations directors, legislative assistants, press directors, etc. The "Hill Climbers" column announces when legislative staff leave their jobs. It's a good source to learn about pending vacancies.

*Campaign Magazine* (Artistotle Industries, 205 Pennsylvania Ave., SE, Washington, DC 20003–1164; phones: 800/243–4401, 202/543–8345) monthly, $24//annual subscription. Two to ten positions in political campaigns appear under "Classified."

*Campaigns and Elections Magazine* (1835 K St., NW, Suite 403, Washington, DC 20006; phone: 800/237–7842) bimonthly, $29.95 annual subscription. One to three campaign positions occasionally appear "Job Bank." The February issue includes the "Political Pages," a thorough directory of all facets of the political industry.

## Job services

*Democratic Job Bank and Talent Pool* (Democratic National Committee, 430 S. Capitol St., SE, Washington, DC 20003; phone: 202/863–8115) free. Submit completed application form to DNC. This service matches job candidates with Democratic Senate and Congressional campaigns around the country. There is no comparable service for any other political party.

## Directories

*Political Resource Directory* (Political Resources, Inc., P.O. Box 4278, Burlington, VT 05406; phone: 800/423–2677) $95 plus $3.50 postage if not prepaid. Published each January, this 400 page book is the official directory of the American Association of Political Consultants on this $2 billion industry. Over 4,100 individuals and 2,800 organizations are listed with party affiliation and a description of services. Entries are listed by alphabetically with a specialization index and principals index. Also listed are federal and state boards of election and state Republication and Democratic party offices which are also potential employers.

*Political Resource Directory* (Gale Research, Inc., 835 Penobscot Bldg., Detroit, MI 48226; phones: 800/877-4253, 313/961-2242) $95, 1991. Includes 2,400 companies and 3,400 key executives including all members of the American Association of Political Consultants. Also listed are federal and state boards of election and state Republication and Democratic party offices which are also potential employers.

*American Lobbyists Directory* Gale Research, Inc., 835 Penobscot Bldg., Detroit, MI 48226; phones: 800/877-4253, 313/961-2242) $175, 1989. Includes about 4,000 federal lobbyists representing 8,000 organizations; the 57,000 lobbyists who represent 26,000 organizations at the state level, and a list of state and federal agencies that regulate lobbyists.

# Port management

## Job openings

The Advisory (American Association of Port Authorities, 1010 Duke St., Alexandria, VA 22314; phone: 703/684-5700) weekly, available only to members (membership fee: $500/year). Jobs listed under "Help Wanted." Few jobs ads; job ads not in every issue.

## Directories

*Traffic Management Buyers Guide Issue* (Cahners Pubishing, 44 Cook St., Denver, CO 80206-5800; phone: 800/622-7776) monthly, $59.95/annual subscription (U.S.), $89.95/Canada and Mexico, $95/elsewhere (surface), $135/air mail). Buyers Guide published as the March issue; available for $25/U.S., $35/foreign. Includes directory of major North American port authorities, shippers associations, and agents.

*Mini-Directory to U.S. Port Authorities* (American Association of Port Authorities, 1010 Duke St., Alexandria, VA 22314; phone: 703/684-5700) free.

*Seaports of the Western Hemisphere* (K–III Press, Inc., 424 W. 33rd St., New York, NY 10001; phone: 212/714–3100) $60/general public, free to members of American Association of Port Authorities.

# Public administration

*Also see listings under "Library services" and "Planning."*

## Job openings

*ICMA Newsletter* (International City Management Association, 777 N. Capitol St., NE, Washington, DC 20002; phone: 202/289–4262) biweekly; $95/nonmember annual subscription; included in ICMA membership package. Jobs listed under "Placement and Support Services." The typical issue features about 25 to 40 job listings in all phases of local government, particularly public administration.

*J.O.B The Job Opportunities Bulletin for Minorities and Women in Local Government* (International City Management Association, 777 N. Capitol St., NE, Washington, DC 20002; phone: 202/289–4262) currently every three weeks, will change to biweekly in 1992, $25/nonmember annual subscription, $15/members. Thirty to 50 ads for all phases of local and regional government appear throughout this newsletter.

*Public Administration Times* (American Society for Public Administration, Suite 500, 1120 G St., NW, Washington, DC 20005; phone: 202/393–7878) 12 issues/year, $40/nonmember annual subscription for first class mail (U.S.), $25/nonmember annual subscription for third class mail (U.S.), $70/foreign air mail, $35/foreign surface mail. Jobs listed under "The Recruiter." Typical issue features about 20–25 ads for government jobs plus additional ads for university positions.

*News Digest* (International Institute of Municipal Clerks, 160 N. Altadena Dr., Pasadena, CA 91107; phone: 818/795–6153) monthly, $15/nonmember annual subscription, included in membership package. Jobs listed under "Positions Available." About four job ads for municipal clerk and assistant clerk positions appear in the typical issue, but it has gone two or three consecutive issues without any job ads at all.

## Job services

*Job Opportunities Notices* (International Institute of Municipal Clerks, 160 N. Altadena Dr., Pasadena, CA 91107; phone: 818/795–6153) free. Sends notices of job vacancies for municipal clerks and assistant clerks to individuals who request to be sent them. Available to members and nonmembers alike.

*CU Career Connection* (University of Colorado, Campus Box 133, Boulder, CO 80309–0133; phone: 303/492–4127) $20/two–month fee entitles you to a "passcode" which unlocks this job hotline. You need a touchtone phone to call and request the field in which you are interested and geographic area in which you want to hear job openings. The hotline is turned off Monday through Friday, 2 to 4 p.m. for daily updating.

## Directories

*The Municipal Yearbook* (International City Management Association, 777 N. Capitol St., NE, Washington, DC 20002; phone: 202/289–4262) $77.50 plus $4.30 shipping if not prepaid). (The price is expected to rise with each new edition. Contact ICMA for the price of the new edition published each May.)

Includes the following directories: officials in U.S. municipalities which features the form of government, manager/administrator, city clerk, finance officer, fire chief, police chief, and public works director; county officials in U.S. counties which lists county board chairperson, county executive or appointed administrator, clerk, chief financial officer, personnel director, and chief law enforcement officer; state municipal leagues, state agencies for community affairs; state, provincial (Canadian), and international municipal management associations; state associations of counties; provincial (Canadian) and territorial associations; provincial and territorial agencies for local affairs in Canada; directors of councils of governments recognized by ICMA; local government chief administrators in other countries; and professional,

special assistance, and educational organizations serving local and state governments.

*Who's Who in Local Government Management* (International City Management Association, 777 N. Capitol St., NE, Washington, DC 20002; phone: 202/289–4262) free, available *only* to ICMA members (not available to student members). Annual directory of ICMA members and ICMA–recognized governments.

## Salary survey

**Compensation 90: An Annual Report on Local Government Executive Salaries and Fringe Benefits** (International City Management Association, 777 N. Capitol St., NE, Washington, DC 20002; phone: 202/289–4262) $180/nonmembers, $125 members (add $4.30 shipping and handling if not prepaid). Presents salary and fringe benefit information on city and county managers, councils of governments directors, assistant managers, police and fire chiefs, finance directors, parks and recreation directors, and public works directors. Includes average salaries by state, region, and jurisdiction size. Published annually.

# Public health and health care

*Also see listings under "Public administration," "Public safety," and "Social services."*

## Job openings

*The Nation's Health* (American Public Health Association, 1015 15th St., NW, Washington, DC 20005; phone: 202/789–5600) 11 issues/year, $15/annual subscription (U.S.), $33/foreign. Jobs listed under "Job Openings" in the "Classified Advertising" section. Typical issue announces about 75 job openings.

*American Journal of Public Health* (American Public Health Association, 1015 15th St., NW, Washington, DC 20005; phone: 202/789-5600) monthly, $160/annual subscription (U.S.), $240/foreign. Jobs listed under "Job Opportunities." The typical issue features about 40 job ads.

*Emergency Medical Services* (Creative Age Publications, 7628 Densmore Ave., Van Nuys, CA 91406-2088) monthly, $18.95/annual subscription (U.S.), $29/foreign. About four positions for paramedics and emergency physicians appear under "Employment Opportunities."

**Charlie**

...THIS IS THE POLICE - WE FOUND YOUR STOLEN CAR IN AN APPLE ORCHARD UP IN PLAINVILLE, BUT SOME MIGRANT WORKERS ARE LIVING IN IT AND THE BOARD OF HEALTH HAS GIVEN YOU 48 HOURS TO INSTALL PLUMBING AND ELECTRICITY IN IT OR IT'S THREE MONTHS IN THE COUNTY JAIL !!!

*Journal of the American Dietetic Association* (ADA, 216 W. Jackson Blvd., Chicago, IL 60606; phone: 312/899-0040) monthly, $90/nonmember annual subscription, included in dues. About 40 ads for dieticians appear under "Classified Advertising" each issue.

*Nationwide Jobs in Dietetics* (P.O. Box 3537, Santa Monica, CA 90408-3537; phone: 213/453-5375) monthly, $72/annual subscription, $36/four-month subscription, $24/two-month subscription. Around 10 percent of the 300 dietician and nutritionist jobs in a typical issue fall under the moniker "Public Health & Community Nutrition." Your first issue will include a sheet that names additional sources of government and private sector positions.

*Journal of Perentology* (25 Van Zant St., East Norwalk, CT 06855; phone: 203/838-4400) quarterly, $60/annual subscription (U.S.), $80/foreign. The "Classified" section has around ten positions for nutritionists, perentologists (prenatal), and nurses.

*California Jobs in Dietetics* (P.O. Box 3537, Santa Monica, CA 90408–3537; phone: 213/453–5375) biweekly, $48/six–issue subscription. Almost 10 percent of the 230 dietician and nutritionist jobs in a typical issue are listed under "Public Health & Community Nutrition." Your first issue will include a sheet that names additional sources of government and private sector positions in Calfornia and nationally.

*Indian Health Service* (Chief, Nutrition and Dietetics Section, Indian Health Service, 5600 Fishers Ln., Rockville, MD 20857; phone: 301/443–1114) free. Contact for a list of openings available nationally to work in the Indian community as a dietician as an employee of a tribe, Civil Service, or the U.S. Public Health Service.

*U.S. Public Health Service* (Division of Maternal Child Health, Bureau of Health Care Delivery and Assistance, HRSA/PHS/HHS, Room 7A–23, Rockville, MD 20857; phone: 301/443–2370). Contact the Chief Nutritionist for information on available dietician positions with the U.S. Public Health Service.

*U.S. Army Reserve* (AMEDD Personnel Counselor/SP, Captain Deborah Stetts, U.S. Army Medical Department, 1020 Milwaukee Ave., Suite 320, Deerfield, IL 60015–3555; phone: 708/541–3360 or 3365). Write or call collect for information on clinical and adminstrative dietician positions in the army reserve medical units throughout the world.

*Paid Internship Opportunities—U.S. Army Reserve* (AMEDD Personnel Counselor/SP, Captain Deborah Stetts, U.S. Army Medical Department, 1020 Milwaukee Ave., Suite 320, Deerfield, IL 60015–3555; phone: 708/541–3360 or 3365). Write or call collect for information on paid dietician internships in the U.S. army and reserves.

*Journal of Nuclear Medicine* (Society of Nuclear Medicine, 136 Madison Ave., New York, NY 10016; phone: 212/889–0717) monthly, $120/annual nonmember subscription, $130/Canada, $160/elsewhere; included in membership package. Among the 20 to 25 positions for physicians, technologists, and radiologists are a number of positions in Veterans Administration hospitals.

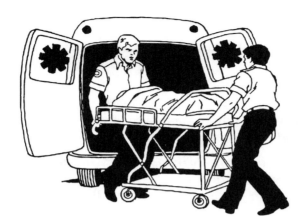

*Journal of Environmental Health* (National Environmental Health Association, Suite 970, South Tower, 720 S. Colorado Blvd., Denver, CO 80222; phone: 303/756-9090) bimonthly, $40/nonmember annual subscription, included in dues ($50/year, $15/students). Jobs listed under ''Opportunities.'' Five to ten job ads appear in the typical issue for sanitarians, toxicologists, health planners, and related positions.

*NACHO News* (National Association of County Health Officials, 440 First St., NW, Washington, DC 20001; phone: 202/783-5550) bimonthly, write for new subscription rates. Job ads do not appear in every issue.

*Local Health Officers News* (U.S. Conference of Local Health Officers, 1620 I St., NW, Washington, DC 20006; phone: 202/293-7330) bimonthly, $35/nonmember annual subscription, free to members. When job ads appear—which is not every issue—they are listed under ''Employment Opportunities.

*Career Mart* (American College of Healthcare Executives, 840 N. Lake Shore Dr., Chicago, IL 60611; phone: 312/943-0544) monthly, available only to members, $30/member six-month subscription. Typical issue includes more than 40 upper-level healthcare management positions listed under ''Career Mart.''

*Healthcare Forum Journal* (The Healthcare Forum, 830 Market St., San Francisco, CA 94102; phone: 415/421-8810) bimonthly, $35/annual subscription (U.S.), $38/Canada and Mexico, $55/elsewhere. Jobs listed under ''Classified.'' Four or five job ads per issue.

*Modern Healthcare* (Crain Communications, 740 N. Rush St., Chicago, IL 60611; phone: 312/649-5350) weekly, $110/year. Jobs listed under "People/Career Opportunities." Five or six job ads per issue.

*Rural Health Care* (National Rural Health Care Association, 301 E. Armour Blvd., Kansas City, MO 64111; phone: 816/756-3140) monthly, available only to members, included in dues. About 15 physician and nursing positions appear under "Classified."

*New England Journal of Medicine* (Massachusetts Medical Society, 10 Shattuck St., Boston, MA 02115-6094; phone: 617/893-3800) weekly, $89/annual subscription. From 300 to 500 physician positions are advertised in the "Classifieds" section and in display ads throughout the magazine. A handful of government positions are included.

*Annals of Internal Medicine* (American College of Physicians, Independence Mall West, 6th St. at Race, Philadelphia, PA 19106; phone: 800/523-1546) $75/annual nonmember subscription, $120/Canada, $138/elsewhere; $56.25/nonmember physicians, $37.50/nonmember medical students, included in membership package. From 250 to 400 vacancies for physicians in internal medicine appear under "Classified." A handful of government positions are included.

*JAMA: The Journal of the American Medical Association* (American Medical Association, Subscription Dept. 515 N. State St., Chicago, IL 60610; phone: 312/464-0183) weekly, $69/annual nonmember subscription, $86/nonmember foreign (surface mail), $126/foreign (air mail), included in membership package. "Classified Advertising" offers openings for 275 to 325 physicians of all types. A handful of government positions are included.

*New Careers: A Directory of Jobs and Internships in Technology and Society* (Student Pugwash USA, 1638 R St., NW, Suite 32, Washington, DC 20009; phone: 202/328-6555) $18, $10/students (add $3 shipping). Offers full details on where and how to apply for internships and entry-level jobs in health care and related fields. Published in even-numbered years.

*See also NELS* under "Law enforcement."

*See also Journal Water Pollution Control Federation* under "Water/wastewater operations."

## Job services

*Safety and Industrial Hygiene Recruiting* (Safety Recruiting Specialist, Southern Management Registry, P.O. Box 35036, Charlotte, NC 28235; phone: 704/372-7640) free. Submit resume to this nationwide executive search firm. The firm contacts registrant when an employer is interested. Resumes kept on file as long as applicant requests. Includes junior level through top level professional positions.

*CU Career Connection* (University of Colorado, Campus Box 133, Boulder, CO 80309-0133; phone: 303/492-4127) $20/two-month fee entitles you to a "passcode" which unlocks this job hotline. You need a touchtone phone to call and request the field in which you are interested and geographic area in which you want to hear job openings. The hotline is turned off Monday through Friday, 2 to 4 p.m. for daily updating.

*National Physicians Register* (295 Cambridge St., Suite 422, Dept. JF, Boston, MA 02114; phone: 800/342-1007) free. A physician submits a copy of her resume and gives her geographic preference and type of position sought. NPR creates a synopsis of the resume and assigns a code number to it. These synopses are published with code numbers rather than the physician's name in a bulletin sent bimonthly to 7,500 hospitals, clinics, group practices, and health maintenance organizations—including Veterans Administration hospitals. The potential employer tells NPR which doctors interest it and NPR sends the full resume to the employer. However, if the physician tells NPR that he doesn't want his name given out, NPR sends the job seeker a letter telling him a particular facility is interested in him and that he should contact the potential employer directly. About 300 physicians are registered at any one time, although that number is growing. Serves both M.D. and osteopathic physicians.

*Toll-Free Instant RSVP Nursing Career Directory* (Springhouse Corp, 1111 Bethlehem Pike, Springhouse, PA 19477; phone: 215/646-8700) free. Published each January, this directory lists over 600 hospitals and health centers that are looking for nursing professionals. Job openings are listed under "Nurse Recruitment." You can be put directly in touch with a facility's nurse recruiter by calling 800/633-2648 (in Pennsylvania, call 800/633-

2649) and giving your qualifications and specialty interests or sending in the reader service card from the directory. The RSVP line calls the nurse recruiter at the facilities of your choice. The nurse recruiter sends you an application form.

*Jobs for Dieticians Job Advice Hotline* (P.O. Box 3537, Santa Monica, CA 90408–3537; phone: 213/453–5375) available only to subscribers to either the national or California edition of *Jobs for Dieticians* described above under "Job openings." Hotline number is given in the newsletter.

*New England Technologists Section Job Hotline* (Society of Nuclear Medicine, 136 Madison Ave., New York, NY 10016; phone: 212/889–0717) free. Medical technologists can call 800/562–6387 to register. They are sent a list of vacancies from Tom Starno who operates this service which is funded by the Tech Physicians of New England. To reach Tom Starno for more information, call 207/945–7186. Vacancies are kept on the list for three months.

## Directories

*Hospital Phone Book* (U.S. Directory Service, 655 NW 128th St., Miami, FL 33168; phone: 305/769–1700) $47.95 plus $4 shipping. Information on over 7,940 government and private hospitals in the U.S. Most recent edition, 1991.

*U.S. Medical Directory* (U.S. Directory Service, 655 NW 128th St., Miami, FL 33168; phone: 305/769–1700) $150 plus $5 shipping. Over 1,000 pages of information on doctors, hospitals, nursing facilities, medical laboratories, and medical libraries. Most recent edition, 1990.

*National Association of County Health Officials Sustaining Membership Directory* (National Association of County Health Officials, 440 First St., NW, Washington, DC 20001; phone: 202/783–5550) free. Published each July.

*American College of Healthcare Executives Directory* (American Association of Healthcare Executives, 840 N. Lake Shore Dr., Chicago, IL 60611; phone: 312/943–0544) $100/nonmembers, $75/members. Published in the spring of even–numbered years. Lists over 16,000 health care executives in public and private sectors.

*Nationwide Jobs in Dietetics* (P.O. Box 3537, Santa Monica, CA 90408–3537; phone: 213/453–5375) monthly, $72/annual subscription, $36/four–month subscription, $24/two–month subscription. The first issue includes an insert with a list of the directors of state departments of health, public health nutrition or the WIC program—agencies that employ dieticians.

*Membership Directory for the Society of Nuclear Medicine* (Society of Nuclear Medicine, 136 Madison Ave., New York, NY 10016; phone: 212/889–0717) $50/nonmembers, included in dues. Last published in September 1991. New edition expected in 1993.

# Public safety

*Also see listings under "Engineering," "Fire protection," "Law enforcement," "Public administration," and "Public health."*

## Job openings

*JobLine Bulletin* (American Society of Safety Engineers, 1800 E. Oakton St., Des Plaines, IL 60018–2187; phone: 708/692–4121, ext. 33) monthly, $80/nonmembers for six–month subscription, $25/members, free/unemployed members. Special issues are published occasionally upon employer request. About 30 safety and health job openings in government, construction, communications, insurance, manufacturing, utilities, and transportation appear throughout the typical issue.

*Professional Safety* (American Society of Safety Engineers, 1800 E. Oakton St., Des Plaines, IL 60018–2187; phone: 708/692–4121, ext. 13) monthly, $43/nonmember annual subscription (U.S., Canada, and Mexico), $50/elsewhere surface mail, $102/elsewhere by air mail; included in membership package. About 25 safety and health job openings in government, construction, communications, insurance, manufacturing, utilities, transportation, and petrochemical industries as well as university faculty opportunities are listed under "Personnel Center."

*Applied Occupational and Environmental Hygiene* (American Conference of Governmental Industrial Hygienists, 6500 Glenway Ave,. Bldg. D-7, Cincinnati, OH 45211; phone: 513/661-7881) monthly, $70/nonmember annual subscription, $35/members. About five positions for occupational safety and health inspectors and industrial hygienists appear in "Classified Advertising."

*APCO Bulletin—Journal of Public–Safety Communications* (Associated Public–Safety Communications Officers, Inc., 2040 S. Ridgewood Ave., South Daytona, FL 32119-2257; phone: 904/322-2500) $30/annual subscription (U.S.), $40/Canada, $50/elsewhere. Jobs listed under "Public Safety Job Opportunities."

# Public works

*See also listings under "Engineering," "Public administration," "Sanitation/solid waste management," "Utilities management," and "Water/wastewater operations."*

## Job openings

*APWA Reporter* (American Public Works Association, 1313 E. 60th St., Chicago, IL 60637; phone: 312/667-2200) monthly; available only to members as part of membership package. Annual membership: $60/professionals, libraries, $10/full–time students. APWA will move in 1992 or 1993 to Kansas City, Missouri. Jobs listed under "Positions." Thirty or more ads per issue.

*Public Works* (Public Works Journal Corp., 200 S. Broad St., Ridgewood, NJ 07451; phone: 201/445-5800) monthly; $30/annual subscription (U.S.), $60/elsewhere). Jobs listed under "Classified Advertisements/Public Works Careers." Typical issue features 25 to 30 job ads.

*American City & County* (Communication Channels, 6225 Barfield Rd., Atlanta, GA 30328; phones: 800/241-9834, 404/256-9800) monthly; $48/annual subscription (U.S.), $68/foreign (surface mail), $118/foreign (air mail). Jobs listed under "Job Search & Classified." Ads are mostly for engineers, public works, and public administration.

*See also APCO Bulletin—Journal of Public-Safety Communications* under "Public safety."

## Directory

***American Public Works Association Directory*** (American Public Works Association, 1313 E. 60th St., Chicago, IL 60637; phone: 312/667-2200) $50/nonmembers, $40/members. Lists individual members (geographic and alphabetic), public agency members, public utility members. Published in even-numbered years.

## Purchasing

*Also see listings under "Public Administration."*

## Job openings

***Employment Opportunity Listing*** (National Association of Purchasing Management, 2055 E. Centennial Cr., Tempe, AZ 85282; phone: 602/752-6276) monthly, distributed to NARMS 168 affiliate offices. Twenty to 25 purchasing and materials management positions are in the usual issue.

***Contract Management*** (National Contract Managers Association, 1912 Woodford Rd., Vienna, VA 22182; phones: 800/344-8096, 703/448-9231) monthly, $72/nonmember annual subscription, included in dues. Typical issue has about 14 ads for contract managers, procurement, materials management, contractor negotiators, administrators, buyers, attorneys, and certified public accountants listed under "Job Watch" and in display ads in the "CM Final Edition" supplement. The vast majority of positions are private sector.

***Purchasing World*** (29100 Aurora Rd., Solon, OH 44139; phone: 216/248-1125) monthly $65/annual subscription, $70/Canada, $120/elsewhere, free to qualified purchasing professionals. The "Marketplace" lists 20 vacancies.

***NIGP Technical Bulletin*** (National Institute of Governmental Purchasing, Suite 201, 115 Hillwood Ave., Falls Church, VA 22046; phones: 800/367-6447, 703/533-7300) bimonthly, $30/nonmember annual subscription, included in membership package. The few jobs that are advertised are either listed under "Employment Opportunities" or appear on inserted sheets.

**NIGP Letter Service Bulletin** (National Institute of Governmental Purchasing, Suite 201, 115 Hillwood Ave., Falls Church, VA 22046; phones: 800/367–6447, 703/533–7300) quarterly, available only as part of membership package.The few jobs that are advertised are either listed under "Employment Opportunities" or appear on inserted sheets.

## Job services

**NAPM Services, Inc.—Employment Services** (National Association of Purchasing Management, 2055 E. Centennial Cr., Tempe, AZ 85282; phone: 602/752–6276) free, available only to members. The job seeker submit a copy of her resume with an informal cover letter that outlines her salary requirements, geographical prefer- ence, and three major areas of commodities expertise. When a match is found, the Employment Service contacts the job seeker to confirm her interest in the position and then sends the job seeker's resume to the employer who is responsible for contacting the potential employee for an interview.

**Job Matching Service** (American Purchasing Society, 11910 Oak Trail Way, Port Richey, FL 34668; phone: 813/862–7998) free. Send your resume to APS with a request that it be kept on file for job openings. When an employer submits a request for job candi- dates, APS sends a copy of the resume of qualified persons to the employer who is responsible for contacting candidates for inter- views. APS also sends a letter to each candidate when her resume has been sent to an employer to tell her the employer's name and address, and suggest that she contact the employer for more information about the job. Resumes are kept on file for three years.

**NCMA's Job Referral Service** (National Contract Managers Asso- ciation, 1912 Woodford Rd., Vienna, VA 22182; phones: 800/344– 8096, 703/448–9231) free. Complete the service's resume form and submit it with ten copies of your resume. The service forwards the resumes of qualified applicants to employers who are respon- sible for contacting the job hopeful. Resumes are kept on file for six months. The vast majority of positions are private sector.

*Employment Opportunities Register* (National Institute of Governmental Purchasing, Suite 201, 115 Hillwood Ave., Falls Church, VA 22046; phones: 800/367-6447, 703/533-7300) In this very informal service, NIGP keeps resumes of members on file and sends job notices to them which include the jobs advertised in the *NIGP Technical Bulletin* and *NIPC Letter Service Bulletin* described above under "Job openings."

# Real estate appraisal and tax

## Job openings

*Appraiser News* (Appraisal Institute, 875 N. Michigan Ave., Suite 2400, Chicago, IL 60611; phone: 312/819-2466) semimonthly, $15/annual nonmember subscription, included in dues. The "Job Search" section features 20 to 30 positions including a number of local and state government positions.

*Real Estate Appraisal Newsletter* (National Association of Real Estate Appraisers, 8383 E. Evans Rd., Scottsdale, AZ 85260-3614; phone: 602/948-8000) quarterly, available only as part of membership package. Jobs listed under "Appraiser Job Mart." Four to ten positions in typical issue.

## If you can't find your specialty...

**Yo, dude! You probably skipped Chapter 1, the chapter that tells you how to use this book most effectively—and the chapter nobody ever wants to read. *Please read it!* It's a most excellent chapter that explains how to use this chapter and the Index to find job sources in your field, whether it be professional, trades, office support, labor, or technical.**

*IAAO Update* (International Association of Assessing Officers, 1313 E. 60th St., Chicago, IL 60637; phone: 312/947–2048) monthly, available only to members. Write for membership information. Lists jobs under ''Opportunities.'' Two to seven job ads per issue.

*Appraiser–Gram* (National Association of Independent Fee Appraisers, 7501 Murdoch, St. Louis, MO 63119; phone: 314/781–6688) monthly, $20/annual nonmember subscription, included in dues. Jobs listed under ''Career Opportunities.'' Few job ads.

*FMRA News* (American Society of Farm Managers and Rural Appraisers, Inc., Suite 500, 950 Cherry, Denver, CO 80222; phone: 303/758–3513) bimonthly, available only as part of membership package. Jobs listed under ''Job Mart.'' Usually two to four job ads per issue, but some issues have no ads.

*Tax Administrators News* (Federation of Tax Administrators, 444 North Capitol St., NW, Washington, DC 20001; phone: 202/624–5890) monthly; $30/annual subscription. Jobs listed under ''Positions Open.'' Very few job ads. Most issues have no ads.

## Job services

*NAREA Job Referral Service* (National Association of Real Estate Appraisers, 8383 E. Evans Rd., Scottsdale, AZ 85260–3614; phone: 602/948–8000) free, available only to members. This is a very informal member service where the NAREA puts job candidates in touch with potential employers.

*NAMA Member Referral Program* (National Association of Master Appraisers, 303 W. Cypress, San Antonio, TX 78212; phones: 800/531–5333, 512/225–2897) free, available only to members. Your resume is placed on file. Employers request resumes of qualified candidates. Employer contacts candidate directly.

*NAMA Internship Program* (National Association of Master Appraisers, 303 W. Cypress, San Antonio, TX 78212; phones: 800/531–5333, 512/225–2897) free, available only to members. New appraisers can request free list of agencies and firms that offer internships. Candidate is responsible for contacting possible internship employers.

## Directories

*Appraisal Institute Directory of Members* (Appraisal Institute, 875 N. Michigan Ave., Suite 2400, Chicago, IL 60611; phone: 312/819–2466) free. Contains business information on 13,000 members. Published each spring.

*NAMA Membership Directory* (National Association of Master Appraisers, 303 W. Cypress, San Antonio, TX 78212; phones: 800/531-5333, 512/225-2897) free. Published each February.

*IAAO Membership Directory* (International Association of Assessing Officers, 1313 E. 60th St., Chicago, IL 60637; phone: 312/947–2069) $25/nonmembers, included in membership package. Published annually. Lists member real estate assessors and appraisers.

*Accredited and General Membership Directory* (American Society of Farm Managers and Rural Appraisers, Inc., Suite 500, 950 Cherry, Denver, CO 80222; phone: 303/758-3513) write for price.

*A Guide to Appraising for Federal Agencies* (Appraisal Institute, 875 N. Michigan Ave., Suite 2400, Chicago, IL 60611; phone: 312/819-2466) $5. Last published in 1987. Lists national, regional, and district offices of 17 federal agencies that utilize the services of real estate appraisers. Explains how to get on their panels. 130 pages.

# Real estate/property management

*Also see listings under "Housing" and "Public administration."*

## Job openings

*CPM® Aspects* (Institute of Real Estate Management, 430 N. Michigan Ave., Chicago, IL 60611; phone: 312/329-6000) 7 issues/year, available only to members. Write or call for membership information. Jobs listed under "JOBSBulletin." About 65 job ads for property managers appear in the typical issue. Also lists "Positions Wanted" ads from members seeking employment.

*ARM® News* (Institute of Real Estate Management, 430 N. Michigan Ave., Chicago, IL 60611; phone: 312/329–6000) 8 issues/year, available only to members, included in dues. About ten positions for property mangers and site managers of residential real estate are included under "Jobs Bulletin." ARM® program participants may place "Position Wanted" ads.

*FMRA News* (American Society of Farm Managers and Rural Appraisers, Inc., Suite 500, 950 Cherry, Denver, CO 80222; phone: 303/758–3513) bimonthly, available only as part of membership package. Jobs listed under "Job Mart." Usually two to four job ads per issue, but some issues have no ads.

See also *Economic Developments* under "Community and economic development."

## Directories

*Accredited Management Oganization® Directory* (Institute of Real Estate Management, 430 N. Michigan Ave., Chicago, IL 60611; phone: 312/329–6000) nonmembers: submit written request for a copy, included in membership package. This geographical listing of accredited management organization® firms is published every April.

*IREM Membership Directory* (Institute of Real Estate Management, 430 N. Michigan Ave., Chicago, IL 60611; phone: 312/329–6000) nonmembers: submit written request for a copy, included in membership package. This geographical listing of certified property managers® and accredited management organizations® in the U.S., Canada, and overseas, is published each April.

*Accredited Residential Manager Directory* (Institute of Real Estate Management, 430 N. Michigan Ave., Chicago, IL 60611; phone: 312/329–6000) nonmembers: submit written request for a copy, included in membership package. This geographical listing of accredited residential managers in the U.S. and Canada is published in every April.

*Accredited and General Membership Directory* (American Society of Farm Managers and Rural Appraisers, Inc., Suite 500, 950 Cherry, Denver, CO 80222; phone: 303/758–3513) write for price.

## Salary surveys

*CPM® Profile and Compensation Study* (Institute of Real Estate Management, 430 N. Michigan Ave., Chicago, IL 60611; phone: 312/329–6000) $17.95/nonmembers, $16.16/members. Published in 1989 and every three years thereafter.

*Accredited Residential Manager® Profile and Compensation Study* (Institute of Real Estate Management, 430 N. Michigan Ave., Chicago, IL 60611; phone: 312/329–6000) $18.95/nonmembers, $17.06/members. Published in 1990 and every three years thereafter.

# Records management and archival

## Job openings

*News Notes and Quotes* (Association of Records Managers and Administrators, Suite 215, 4200 Somerset Dr., Prairie Village, KS 66208; phone: 913/341–3808) bimonthly, available only as part of membership package. Jobs listed under "Job Opportunities." About six to 12 job ads per issue.

*SAA Newsletter* (Society of American Archivists, Suite 504, 600 S. Federal, Chicago, IL 60605; phone: 312/922–0140) published in alternating months with *SAA Employment Bulletin*, available only to members. Jobs listed under "Employment Opportunities." About 25 job ads per issue.

*SAA Employment Bulletin* (Society of American Archivists, Suite 504, 600 S. Federal, Chicago, IL 60605; phone: 312/922–0140) published in alternating months with *SAA Newsletter*, available to members for $24/year; nonmembers can purchase individual issues for $6. Lists only jobs. About 25 jobs ads per issue.

*AIC Newsletter* (American Institute for Conservation of Historic and Artistic Works,, Suite 340, 1400 16th St., NW, Washington, DC 20036; phone: 202/232–6636) bimonthly, available to members only. Jobs listed under "Positions Available." Around 20 job ads per issue, largely for conservators.

See also *FEDfacts* listed under "Data processing and computers."

*OAH Newsletter* (Organization of American Historians, 112 N. Bryan St., Bloomington, IN 47408; phone: 812/855-7311) quarterly, available only to members, included in dues. About 12 positions for government, public, and U.S. historians; archivists; and university faculty appear under "Professional Opportunities." OAH also runs a job registry at its annual national meeting.

## Job services

*Career Placement Service* (Association of Records Managers and Administrators, Suite 215, 4200 Somerset Dr., Prairie Village, KS 66208; phone: 913/341-3808) $25/available to members only. Places candidate's resume in the Career Placement Registry on DIALOGUE.

## Directories

*AIC Directory* (American Institute for Conservation of Historic and Artistic Works,, Suite 340, 1400 16th St., NW, Washington, DC 20036; phone: 202/232-6636) $43/nonmembers, included in dues. Members listed alphabetically, geographically, and by specialty. Published each August.

*NAGARA Directory* (The Council of State Governments, Iron Works Pike, P.O. Box 11910, Lexington, KY 40578-1910; phone: 606/231-1939) $10/non-members, $7/members. Lists state government record management and archival programs. Published every spring.

# Risk Management/Insurance

*Also see listings under "Public administration" and "Public safety."*

## Job openings

*Business Insurance* (Crain Communications, 740 N. Rush St., Chicago, IL 60611; phone: 800/992-9970) weekly, $80/annual subscription (U.S.), $118/Canada (surface mail), $185/Canada (air mail, $118/elsewhere (surface mail). About 20 job ads appear in the typical issue, including municipal and state positions.

*PARMAFacts* (Public Agency Risk Managers Association, c/o Teri Marie Pacioni, Suite 200, 1407 Oakland Blvd., Walnut Creek, CA 94596; phone: 510/943–1100) bimonthly, available only to members, included in $50/annual dues. Lists about 5 or 6 positions in each issue, mostly in California.

*RiskWatch* (Public Risk and Insurance Management Association, 1117 N. 19th St., Suite 900, Arlington, VA 22209; phone: 703/528–7701) biweekly, $125/nonmember annual subscription, included in dues. Jobs listed under "Job Descriptions." Four to six job ads are in a typical issue.

## Sanitation/solid waste management

*Also see listings under "Engineering," "Public administration," and "Public works."*

### Job openings

*Employment Hotline Newsletter* (HCI Publications, 410 Archibald St, Kansas City, MO 64111; phone: 816/931–1311) weekly, $98/annual subscription, $59/six––months, $35/12 weeks. Twenty to 30 jobs in all facets of solid waste management appear in each issue. Many of these ads are the same as ads those in *Solid Waste & Power*.

*Solid Waste & Power* (HCI Publications, 410 Archibald St, Kansas City, MO 64111; phone: 816/931–1311) bimonthly, $49/annual subscription (U.S.), $60/foreign. About ten job vacancies in all aspects of solid waste management are listed under "Job Mart." Many of these ads are the same as ads those in *Employment Hotline Newsletter*.

*Biocycle* (P.O. Box 351, 18 S. Seventh St., Emmaus, PA 18049; phone: 215/967–4135) monthly, $55/annual subscription (U.S.), $75/foreign. About ten job ads in typical issue, generally focusing on recycling.

*Recycling Today* Municipal Market Edition (4012 Bridge Ave., Cleveland, OH 44113; phone: 216/961–4130) monthly, $32/annual subscription. About three vacancies for recycling coordinators, operations handlers, and directors of solid waste operations appear under "Classifieds."

*Resource Recycling* (P.O. Box 10540, Portland, OR 97210; phones: 800/227–1424, 503/227–1319) monthly, $42/annual subscription. About two recycling and solid waste management positions are listed under "Positions Available."

*Management of World Wastes* (Communication Channels, 6255 Barfield Rd., Atlanta, GA 30328; phones: 800/241–9834, 404/256–9800) monthly; $40/annual subscription (U.S.), $60/Canada. Five to ten jobs are listed under "The Job Mart."

*Waste Age* (Suite 1000, 1730 Rhode Island Ave., NW, Washington, DC 20036; phone: 202/861–0708) monthly; $45/annual subscription (U.S. and Canada), but free to professionals in the industry (U.S. and Canada only); $125/elsewhere. Jobs listed under "Classifieds."

*Solid Wastes News* (Solid Waste Association of North America, P.O. Box 7219, Silver Spring, MD 20910; phone: 301/585–2898) monthly, available only as part of membership package ($50/year membership fee for individual government employee, $10/students). Jobs listed under "Jobs." About four job ads per issue.

*Pollution Engineering* (Cahners Publishing Company, 44 Cook, St., Denver, CO 80206; phone: 303/388–4511) 13 issues/year, $24/annual subscription (U.S.), $32/Canada and Mexico, elsewhere: $72/surface mail, $92/air mail; free to qualified professionals. Among the 30 to 40 positions in the "Classified" section are a few government jobs.

*Hazardous Materials Control* (Hazardous Materials Control Research Institute, 7237A Hanover Pkwy., Greenbelt, MD 20070–3602; phone: 301/982–9500) bimonthly, $18/annual subscription (U.S.), $25/Canada, $25 elsewhere via surface mail, $50/elsewhere via air mail. Jobs listed under "Focus." Few job ads.

## Directories

*Solid Waste Management Officials Membership Directory* (Association of State Solid Waste Management Officials, 444 N. Capitol St., NW, Suite 388, Washington, DC 20001; phone: 202/624–5828) $36/nonmember. Most recently published in 1991, this directory catalogues the state government officials in this field.

*Solid Wastes Association of North American Membership Directory* (Solid Waste Association of North America, P.O. Box 7219, Silver Spring, MD 20910; phone: 301/585–2898) $500.

*Hazardous Materials Control Directory* (Hazardous Materials Control Research Institute, 7237A Hanover Pkwy., Greenbelt, MD 20070–3602; phone: 301/982–9500) $65/nonmembers, included in dues. Published each November.

*Careers in Hazardous Waste Management: A Job Hunters Guide to the Hazardous Waste Management Field* (Environmental Employment Clearinghouse, 3304 Marcus Ave., Newport Beach, CA 92663; phone: 714/675–8278) $12.95, most recent edition published January, 1992. We've generally excluded these sorts of books, but this one is different. It includes a good list of job hunting resources (periodicals and directories) and a directory of government job contacts in this specialty.

## Salary survey

*Police, Fire, and Refuse Collection, 1989* (International City Management Association, 777 N. Capitol St., NE, Washington, DC 20002; phone: 202/289–4262) $16.50 (add $4.30 shipping and handling if not prepaid). A comparative study depicting trends in salary and expenditures data from police, fire, and refuse collection and disposal services.

# Social services

*Also see listings under "Mental health," "Public administration" and "Public health." Also see the Non-Profits' Job Finder.*

## Job openings

*NASW News* (National Association of Social Workers, 7981 Eastern Ave., Silver Spring, MD 20910; phone: 301/565–0333)10 issues/year, $25/nonmember subscription, included in membership package. Jobs listed under "The Classifieds." The typical issue is filled to the brim with over 200 job ads in the arenas of social work, human services, mental health, public health, and social services.

*Social Service Jobs* (Employment Listings for Social Services, 10 Angelica Dr., Framingham, MA 01701; phone: 508/626–8644) biweekly, $39/six issues, $62/12 issues, $118/24 issues. Typical issue features 140+ positions listed by geographic region.

*Career Paths Bulletin* (P.O. Box 1142, Harrisonburg, VA 22801; phone: 703/298–2694) monthly, $48/annual subscription, $27/six-month subscription, $5/issue. Usual issue features 75 to 85 jobs in social work, mental health, developmental disabilities, rehabiliation, substance abuse, adolescent services, and related fields.

*Job Exchange* (Association for Education and Rehabilitation of the Blind, 206 N. Washington St., Suite 320, Alexandria, VA 22314; phone: 703/836–6060) monthly, available only to members: first six months free, $10/year thereafter. From 40 to 60 vacancies for administrators and practitioners (orientation and mobility specialists, teachers of persons with visual impairments, etc.) grace a typical issue.

*Occupational Therapist Weekly* (164 Rollins Ave., Suite 301, Rockville, MD 20852; phone: 301/881–2490) weekly, free to qualified professionals. About 200 positions fill the pages of this newsletter.

*The Guidepost* (American Association for Counseling and Development, 5999 Stevenson Ave., Alexandria, VA 22304; phone: 703/823–9800) 14 issues/year, $30/nonmember annual subscription, included in membership package. Jobs listed under "Classifieds—Employment." About eight to 20 job ads are published in the usual issue.

*Hospital and Community Psychiatry* (American Psychiatric Association, 1400 K St., NW, Washington, DC 20005; phone: 202/682–6228) monthly, $37/annual subscription (U.S.), $57/foreign. Jobs listed under "Classified Advertising." Typical issue runs around 75 job ads including Veterans Administration positions.

*Special Recreation Digest* (Special Recreation, Inc., 362 Koser Ave., Iowa City, IA 52246–3038; phone: 219/337–7578) quarterly, $39.95/annual subscription. From 10 to 25 activity or recreation positions such as therapists, coordinators, and administrators appear under "Recreation."

*The U.S. Journal of Drug and Alcohol Dependence* (Enterprise Center, 3201 SW 15th St., Deerfield Beach, FL 33442; phones: 800/851–9100, 305/360–9233) monthly, $49/annual subscription (U.S.); inquire for foreign rates. Jobs listed under "Classifieds." Seven to 15 job ads per issue.

*The Counselor* (National Association of Alcoholism and Drug Abuse Counselors, 3717 Columbia Pike, Arlington, VA 22204; phone: 703/920–4644) bimonthly, $36/nonmember annual subscription, included in membership package. Jobs listed under "Employment Classifieds." Typical issue features over 10 job ads, usually for upper level counselors with medical facilities; has carried openings in the federal prison system.

*Professional Report* (National Rehabilitation Counseling Association, 633 S. Washington St., Alexandria, VA 22314; phone: 703/836–7677) bimonthly, available to members only. Jobs listed under "Job Openings." Some issues have no jobs listed. Few job ads.

*AAMR News & Notes* (American Association on Mental Retardation, 1719 Kalorama Rd. NW, Washington, DC 20009; phones: 800/424–3688, 202/387–1968) six issues/year, $35/nonmember annual subscription (U.S. and Canada), $40/elsewhere, included in dues. Jobs listed under "Classifieds." Five to 20 ads appear in the typical issue.

*Mental Retardation* (American Association on Mental Retardation, 1719 Kalorama Rd. NW, Washington, DC 20009; phones: 800/424–3688, 202/387–1968) bimonthly, $70/nonmember annual subscription (U.S.), $75/elsewhere, $16/members. Jobs listed under "The Exchange." Ten to 30 ads an issue.

*TASH Newsletter* (The Association for Persons with Severe Handicaps, 11201 Greenwood Ave., North, Seattle, WA 98133; phone: 206/523-8446; note that this phone number is likely to have changed in December 1991 when TASH moved to this new address) monthly; available as part of membership package. Jobs listed under "Positions Open." About ten positions advertised in the typical issue.

*See also NELS* listed under "Law enforcement."

## Job services

*CU Career Connection* (University of Colorado, Campus Box 133, Boulder, CO 80309-0133; phone: 303/492-4127) $20/two-month fee entitles you to a "passcode" which unlocks this job hotline. You need a touchtone phone to call and request the field in which you are interested and geographic area in which you want to hear job openings. The hotline is turned off Monday through Friday, 2 to 4 p.m. for daily updating.

*Career Guidance and Placement Service* (Special Recreation, Inc., 362 Koser Ave., Iowa City, IA 52246-3038; phone: 219/337-7578) free. Submit your resume and this service will match you with appropriate activity or recreation coordinator, specialist, or therapist positions.

*The Job Bank* (Occupational Therapist Weekly, 164 Rollins Ave., Suite 301, Rockville, MD 20852; phone: 301/881-2490). This is an on-line databank that computers can access to learn about 650 jobs in occupational therapy. Contact for details.

## Directories

*Public Welfare Directory* (American Public Welfare Association, 810 First St., NE, Washington, DC 20002; phone: 202/682-0100) $70/nonmembers, $60/members, plus $5 shipping if not prepaid. Lists federal social service agencies, state and local social service agencies by state, Canadian provincial, and federal agencies. Published every August.

*National Staff Development and Training Association Directory* 810 First St., NE, Suite 500, Washington, DC 20002; phone: 202/682–0100) $70/nonmembers, $65/members. In depth directory of public welfare program and agencies by state. Published each summer.

*Directory of Adventure Alternatives in Corrections, Mental Health and Special Populations* (Association for Experiential Education, CU 249, Boulder, CO 80309; phone: 303/492–1547) $7/nonmembers, $12/members; add $3.50 shipping. This is a state–by–state listing of adventure alternative programs which use adventure programming as part of their therapeutic process.

*Experience Based Training and Development: International and Domestic Programs* (Association for Experiential Education, CU 249, Boulder, CO 80309; phone: 303/492–1547) $12.50/nonmembers, $15/members; add $3.50 shipping. Descriptions of training and development programs in the U.S. and abroad.

*National Association of Area Agencies on Aging Membership Directory* (National Association of Area Agencies on Aging, 1112 16th St., NW, Suite 100, Washington, DC 20036; phone: 202/296–8130) $30/nonmembers, included in dues. Lists state and area agencies on aging as well as providers of services to elderly persons. Published every three years.

*Senior Citizen Services* (Gale Research, Inc., 835 Penobscot Bldg., Detroit, MI 48226; phone: 800/877–4253) $90/set of four volumes: Northest, Southeast, Midwest, West; $29.95/each volume individually; 1991. Features information on 21,000 local government and private agencies and organizations that furnish services for America's older citizens including adult day care, case management, respite care, and home delivered meals.

## Salary survey

*AAMR News & Notes* (American Association on Mental Retardation, 1719 Kalorama Rd. NW, Washington, DC 20009; phones: 800/424–3688, 202/387–1968). The March/April 1991 issue contains salary survey findings.

# Trades and labor

*Also see advice in Chapter 1 on how to use this book to find trades, labor, technical, and office support positions. Also see the Index.*

## Job openings

*W.I.T.* (Step-Up for Women, 1 Prospect Ave., St. Johnbury, VT 05819; phone: 802/748-3308) quarterly, first issue free. Two or three job vacancies are advertised under "Jobs."

*Trade Trax Newsletter* (Tradeswomen, Inc., P.O. Box 40664, San Francisco, CA 94140; phone: 415/821-7334) monthly, $15/annual nonmember subscription, $20/Canada, $25/elsewhere, free to members. Four or five skilled trade jobs and apprenticeships, primarily in the San Francisco Bay Area, appear under "Employment."

## Job services

*Job-Matching Service* (Step-Up for Women, 1 Prospect Ave., St. Johnbury, VT 05819; phone: 802/748-3308) free. Job seeker submits resume and service forwards it to potential employers who are responsible for contacting the job aspirant.

# Traffic engineering and parking

*Also see the listings under "Transit management."*

## Job openings

*ITE Journal* (Institute of Transportation Engineers, Suite 410, 525 School St., SW, Washington, DC 20024-2729; phone: 202/554-8050) monthly; $50/annual subscription (U.S., Canada, and Mexico), $65/elsewhere. Jobs listed under "Positions." Usually 10 to 30 ads appear each issue.

*Traffic World* (International Thomson Transport Press, 529 14th St., NW, Washington, DC 20045; phone: 202/626-4500) weekly; $108/annual subscription; $72/six-month subscription, write for student rates. Jobs listed under "Classified."

*Roads & Bridges* (Scranton Gillette Commuications, Inc., 380 Northwest Highway, Des Plaines, IL 60016; phone: 708/298-6622) monthly, $15/annual subscription, $22.50/foreign. Jobs listed under "Classified." Seven to ten job ads in typical issue.

*Better Roads* (P.O. Box 558, Park Ridge, IL 60068; phone: 312/693-7710) monthly, $15/annual subscription (U.S. and Canada), $90/elsewhere. As many as six job with highway departments appear under "Help Wanted."

*Parking Professional* (Institutional and Municipal Parking Congress, 901 Kenmore Ave., Fredericksburg, VA 22402; phone: 703/371-7535) monthly, $48/annual subscription (U.S. and Canada), $60/elsewhere. One or two ads for parking administrators or directors appear in a typical issue.

*See also APCO—Journal of Public-Safety Communications* listed under "Public safety."

## Job services

*The Professional Register* (Institutional and Municipal Parking Congress, 901 Kenmore Ave., Fredericksburg, VA 22402; phone: 703/371-7535) At this writing, procedures and the fee schedule had not be established. Contact IMPC for details.

## Directory

*Transportation Officials and Engineers Directory* (American Road and Transportation Builders Association, 501 School St., SW, Washington, DC 20024; phone: 202/488-2722) $35/nonmembers, $30/members. This directory features a state-by-state listing of over 4,000 transportation decisionmakers and engineers at the local, state, and federal levels. 170 pages. Published each May.

# Transit management

## Job openings

*Passenger Transport* (American Public Transport Association, 1201 New York Ave., NW, Washington, DC 20005; phone: 202/898–4119) weekly, $65/annual subscription (U.S. and Canada, $77/elsewhere. "Help Wanted" features six to 15 vacancies for transit and transportation managers and planners, transportation engineers, marketing directors, and administrators.

*Mass Transit* (P.O. Box 1478, Riverton, NJ 08077; phone: 516/845–2700) 9 issues/year, $30/annual subscription (U.S. and Canada), $55/elsewhere. Jobs listed under "Classified." Four to ten job ads per issue.

*Community Transportation Reporter* (Community Transportation Association of America, Suite 900, 725 15th St., NW, Washington, DC 20005; phones: 800/527–8279, 202/628–1480) 10 issues/year, $35/annual subscription (U.S), $47/foreign, free to members. Jobs listed under "Employment—Help Wanted." About four ads for transit managers and operators per issue.

*METRO Magazine* (Bobit Publishing Co., 2512 Artesia Blvd., Redondo Beach, CA 90278; phone: 213/376–8788) 7 issues/year, $12/annual subscription (U.S.), $18/Canada, $50/elsewhere. Jobs listed under "Classified Ads." Few job ads.

*Railway Age* (Simmons–Boardman Publishing, 345 W. Hudson St., New York, NY 10014; phones: 800/228–9670, 212/620–7200) monthly, $45/annual subscription. Three to five for all aspect of railroad management and operations appear under "Classified."

## Directories

*APTA Membership Directory* (American Public Transport Association, 1201 New York Ave., NW, Washington, DC 20005; phone: 202/898–4119) available only to members. Published each January.

*Community Transportation Resource Guide* (Community Transportation Association of America, Suite 900, 725 15th St., NW, Washington, DC 20005; phones: 800/527–8279, 202/628–1480) $10. Includes transportation/transit industry. Published every January.

## Transportation planning

*Also see listings under "Planning" and "Transit management."*

### Directory

*AASHTO Reference Book* (American Association of State Highway and Transportation Officials, Suite 225, 444 N. Capitol St., Washington, DC 20001; phone: 202/624–8500) published annually; $10. Extensive listing of key personnel in the highway and/or transportation departments of each state and U.S. possession; the U.S. Department of Transportation, U.S. Coast Guard, Federal Aviation Administration, Federal Highway Administration, Federal Railroad Administration, National Highway Traffic Safety Administration, U.S. Mass Transportation Administration, Saint Lawrence Seaway Development Corporation, and Maritime Administration; and Canadian provincial transportation departments.

## Utilities management

*Also see listings under "Engineering," "Public administration," and "Public works."*

### Job openings

*Public Utilities Fortnightly* (Public Utilities Reports, Inc., Suite 200, 2111 Wilson Rd., Arlington, VA 22201; phone: 703/243–7000) biweekly; $92/annual subscription. Few job ads.

*Public Power* (American Public Power Association, 2301 M. St., NW, Washington, DC 20037; phone: 202/467–2970) bimonthly, $35/nonmember annual subscription, included in dues. Jobs listed under "Classified." Four to 12 job ads in a typical issue.

*Power* (McGraw–Hill, 11 W. 19th St., New York, NY 10011; phone: 609/426–7233) monthly, $50/annual subscription (U.S.), $55/Canada, $110/elsewhere, free to qualified executives, engineering, and supervisory personnel in electric utilities and process industries. About ten ads for electric utility supervisors, management, engineers, and instrument technicians appear under "Employment Opportunities."

*Journal of Petroleum Marketing* (Petroleum Marketers Association of America, 1120 Vermont Ave., NW, Washington, DC 20005; phone: 202//331–1198) monthly, free to qualified professionals. A few ads in utilities management appear under "Help Wanted."

*Journal of Petroleum Technology* (Society of Petroleum Engineers, P.O. Box 833836, Richardson, TX 75083–3836; phone: 214/669–3377) monthly, $30/annual nonmember subscription, $15/members. A number of government positions are among the 35 jobs for petroleum engineers, drilling engineers, and oilfield production engineers listed under "Positions Open." Also lists "Positions Wanted."

*AEE Energy Insight* (Association of Energy Engineers, 4025 Pleasant-dale Rd., Suite 420, Atlanta, GA 30340; phone: 404/447–5083) quarterly, available only to members, included in dues. Two or three ads for energy engineers appear under "AEE Referral Service."

*APGA Newsletter* (American Public Gas Association, P.O. Box 11094D, Vienna, VA 22183; phone: 703/352–3890) biweekly, available only to members, included in dues. Jobs listed under "Position Available." Few job ads; job ads not in every issue.

## Directories

*Public Power Directory* (American Public Power Association, 2301 M. St., NW, Washington, DC 20037; phone: 202/467–2970) $75/nonmember, included in membership package. Published in the January–February issue of *Public Power*.

*Publicly Owned Natural Gas System Directory* (American Public Gas Association, P.O. Box 11094D, Vienna, VA 22183; phone: 703/352–3890) $17/nonmember, free/members. Published annually.

*Annual Membership Issue* of the *Journal of Petroleum Technology* (Society of Petroleum Engineers, P.O. Box 833836, Richardson, TX 75083–3836; phone: 214/669–3377) $100/nonmembers, $25/members. This is the May issue. It's obviously less expensive to just subscribe as described above under "Job openings."

*The Geophysical Directory* (The Geophysical Directory, Inc., P.O. Box 130508, Houston, TX 77219; phone: 713/529–8789) $40/U.S. (Texas residents add 8.25 percent sales tax), $55/foreign (via air mail). Includes government agencies that utilize geophysics.

# Water/wastewater operations

*Also see listings under "Engineering," "Environment," and "Public works."*

## Job openings

*The Jobank* (Water Pollution Control Federation, 601 Wythe St., Alexandria, VA 22314; phone: 703/684–2400) bimonthly, $36/nonmember six–month subscription, $18/members. About 16 positions in pollution control and wastewater operations are in the typical issue.

*Water Environment Technology* (Water Pollution Control Federation, 601 Wythe St., Alexandria, VA 22314; phone: 703/684–2400) monthly, $144/nonmember annual subscription (U.S.), $187/nonmember elsewhere; included in membership package. Jobs listed under "Classifieds." About 10 to 15 ads in typical issue.

*Water Well Journal* (National Water Well Association, 6375 Riverside Dr., Dublin, OH 43017; phone: 614/761–3222) monthly, $12/annual subscription, free/members. About eight vacancies for drillers, hydrogeologists, and hydrologists are listed under "Opportunities."

*Water Engineering & Management* (Scranton Gillette Communications, 380 Northwest Highway, Des Plaines, IL 60016; phone: 708/298–6622) monthly, $25/annual subscription. Jobs listed under "Classified."

*Journal AWWA* (American Water Works Association, 6666 W. Quincy, Denver, CO 80235; phone: 303/794–7711) monthly, $85/nonmember annual subscription (North America), $110/elsewhere; included in annual dues ($65/U.S., $93/foreign). Jobs listed under "Classified." Fifteen to 18 job ads grace these pages each issue.

*Groundwater* (Association of Groundwater Scientists, 6375 Riverside Dr., Dublin, OH 43017; phones: 800/423-7748 (outside Ohio), 614/761-1711) bimonthly, $63/annual nonmember subscription, $20/members. Among the 40 to 50 ads for geologists, hydrogeologists, environmental engineers, and hazardous waste engineers presented under "Ground–Water Employment Opportunities" are a handful in government.

*Mainstream* (American Water Works Association, 6666 W. Quincy, Denver, CO 80235; phone: 303/794–7711) monthly, $13/nonmember annual subscription (U.S.), $18.50/foreign, included in dues (annual dues: $65/U.S., $93/foreign). Jobs listed under "Employment." About 20 job ads appear in the typical issue.

*Waterworld News* (American Water Works Association, 6666 W. Quincy, Denver, CO 80235; phone: 303/794–7711) bimonthly, free to qualified people in the profession, write for application form, subscription included in membership package. About 12 jobs for engineers, utility directors, and related positions are listed under "Classified."

## Job services

*Job Mart Program* (National Water Well Association, 6375 Riverside Dr., Dublin, OH 43017; phone: 614/761-3222) $20/12 months. Job seeker completes resume forms and a "blind ad." The blind ads are sent to employers who pay a fee to see the full resume of promising candidates. It's up to the employer to contact the job seeker. Resumes are kept on file until you find a job, or one year.

## Directory

*AWWA Membership Roster* (American Water Works Association, 6666 W. Quincy, Denver, CO 80235; phone: 303/794–7711) $26.50/members only. Most recent issue published in 1989. A new issue should be in the works by now.

# Chapter 3:

# Local sources for local and state government jobs

This chapter is divided into several sections. First come a few publications that carry government job ads for multi-state regions. These are followed by listings of national directories of local governments and officials. A second set of directories identifies state officials and agencies for each of the 50 states, and in many cases, U.S. possessions and territories as well. Several direct sources of job vacancies are also presented.

Each of the directories listed in these two sections furnishes the names, addresses, and phone numbers of department and agency heads plus the other officials they identify. These directories will help you identify the proper person or agency to contact to learn of job openings in local or state government.

The bulk of this chapter consists of a state-by-state listing of job sources for positions at the local, state, and federal levels of government. These include periodicals, job-matching services, job hotlines, and state directories of local governments and officials.

Specific information on how to find state jobs is also provided. In addition, you are guided to information on state-operated Job Service Centers which often operate computer-based job-matching services for professional and office support, trades, labor, and technical positions in local and state government. You are also directed to the appropriate Federal Job Information Center.

Information on several U.S. possessions is also included at the end of this chapter. Be sure to read the discussion at the beginning of the section entitled "Job sources: State–by–state."

## Job sources for multi–state regions

Only a few periodicals provide job information for multi–state regions in the U.S. However, for several states these are among the better sources for job announcements.

### Job openings

*Rocky Mountain Employment Newsletter* (Intermountain Publishing, 703 S. Broadway, Suite 100–B0, Denver, CO 80209; phone: 303/988–6707) 18 issues/year, $19/three–month subscription to one edition, $30/any two editions, $39/three editions. Two and one month subscriptions also available. Published in three editions: Colorado–Wyoming, Arizona–New Mexico, and Idaho–Montana. Combined, the three editions include over 400 positions, about 20 to 25 percent of them in government. The positions tend to orient toward the outdoors, with quite a few in natural resources, environmental, and wildlife.

*The Job Finder: A Checklist of Openings for Administrative and Governmental Research Employment in the West* (Western Governmental Research Association, c/o Graduate Center for Public Policy and Administration, CSU–Long Beach, 1250 Bellflower Blvd., Long Beach, CA 90840; phone 213/985–5419) monthly; $20/annual, $15/student for membership in Western Governmental Research Association which includes subscription. Typical issue features about 40 to 50 job openings in planning and public administration. Serves: 14 western states.

*Western Planner* (Western Planning Resources, Inc., c/o David Conine, City of North Bend, P.O. Box 896, North Bend, WA 98045; phone: 206/888–1211) bimonthly; $24/annual subscription; $15/annual student subscription. This has been a pretty mobile publication. Whenever *Western Planner* relocates, the the editor of *JobMart* published by the American Planning Association (1313 E. 60th St.,

Chicago, IL 60637; phone: 312/955-9100) usually knows its where-abouts. Serves: Alaska, Colorado, Idaho, Montana, Nebraska, Nevada, New Mexico, North and South Dakota, Utah, Washington, and Wyoming. About five planning and related positions are listed under ''Jobs Wanted.''

## National sources for local government jobs

### Directories

*The Municipal Yearbook* (International City Management Association, 777 N. Capitol St., NE, Washington, DC 20002; phone: 202/289-4262) $77.50 plus $4.30 shipping if not prepaid. The price is expected to rise with each new edition. Contact ICMA for the price of the new edition published each May.

Includes the following directories: officials in U.S. municipalities which features the form of government, manager/administrator, city clerk, finance officer, fire chief, police chief, and public works director; county officials in U.S. counties which lists county board chairperson, county executive or appointed administrator, clerk, chief financial officer, personnel director, and chief law enforcement officer; state municipal leagues, state agencies for community affairs; state, provincial (Canadian), and international municipal management associations; state associations of counties; provincial (Canadian) and territorial associations; provincial and territorial agencies for local affairs in Canada; directors of councils of governments recognized by ICMA; local government chief administrators in other countries; and professional, special assistance, and educational organizations serving local and state governments.

*Braddock's Federal–State–Local Government Directory* (Braddock Communications, 909 N. Washington St., Suite 310, Alexandria, VA 22314; phone: 703/549-6500) $59.95 plus $3.50 shipping. Published in the summer of odd-numbered years. Lists names, address, and phone numbers of over 10,000 elected officials and key personnel at all levels of government.

*Municipal Yellow Book* (Monitor Publishing, Co., 104 Fifth Ave., New York, NY 10011; phone: 212/627–4140) semiannual, $150/annual subscription. In over 500 pages, this directory supplies the names, addresses, and phone numbers of nearly 20,000 key elected and administrative officials of the leading cities, counties, and regional jurisdictions as well as a complete breakdown of municipal and county departments, agencies, and subdivisions.

**For Better or For Worse®**                              **by Lynn Johnston**

For Better or For Worse © 1988 Lynn Johnston Productions. Reprinted with permission of Universal Press Syndicate. All rights reserved.

*Municipal Executive Directory* (Carroll Publishing Co., 1058 Thomas Jefferson St., NW, Washington, DC 20077–0007; phone: 202/333–8620) $110/annual subscription, updated and published in full twice a year. 500+ pages. Over 65,000 entries covering all U.S. municipalities. Lists 32,000 elected, appointed, and career officials and provides information about each municipality over 15,000 in population.

*Directory of City Policy Officials* (National League of Cities, 1301 Pennsylvania Ave., NW, Washington, DC 20004; phone: 202/626–3000) $35/nonmembers, $15/members; published annually. Lists 16,500 chief elected officials, administrative officers, and members of governing bodies in the 1,750 NLC member cities plus other municipalities over 30,000 population. 115 pages.

*County Executive Directory* (Carroll Publishing Co., 1058 Thomas Jefferson St., NW, Washington, DC 20077–0007; phone: 202/333–8620) $110/annual subscription, updated and published in full twice a year. 375 pages. Over 60,000 entries covering all U.S. counties or equivalent listed by state. Provides information about each county over 25,000 in population. Covers 27,150 officials in more than 3,100 county governments. Organizational listing includes managers of government functions.

*Municipal/County Executive Directory* (Carroll Publishing Co., 1058 Thomas Jefferson St., NW, Washington, DC 20077–0007; phone: 202/333–8620) $117. Published annually, it guides you to more than 32,000 elected and appointed municipal and county officials throughout the country. Details are given about every municipality of 15,000 or more and every county of 25,000, including a locator phone number and the names and numbers of key personnel.

*State Municipal League Directory* (National League of Cities, 1301 Pennsylvania Ave., NW, Washington, DC 20004; phone: 202/626–3000) $10/nonmembers, $5/members; published annually. Lists profiles of 49 state municipal leagues, personnel policies, programs, facilities, and publications. 60 pages.

*State and Regional Associations* (Columbia Books, 1212 New York Ave., NW, Suite 300, Washington, DC 20005; phone: 202/898–0662) $40. Published annually, this volume guides you to thousands of associations at the state and regional levels including those in government. As discussed under ''Job sources: State—by—state,'' many of these localized groups offer job services. For purely practical reasons, the *Government Job Finder* does not generally report on these because there are just so many of them that they could fill a book this size on their own.

## Salary survey

*Compensation 90: An Annual Report on Local Government Executive Salaries and Fringe Benefits* (International City Management Association, 777 N. Capitol St., NE, Washington, DC 20002; phone: 202/289–4262) $180/nonmembers, $125 members (add $4.30 shipping and handling if not prepaid). Presents salary and fringe benefit information on city and county managers, councils of governments directors, assistant managers, police and fire chiefs, finance directors, parks and recreation directors, and public works directors. Includes average salaries by state, region, and jurisdiction size. Published annually.

# National sources for state government jobs

## Job openings

*Opportunities in State Government* (ACCESS: Networking in the Public Interest, 50 Beacon St., Boston, MA 02108; phone: 617/720–5627) three issues/year, $250/annual subscription. In fall, winter, and autumn, you receive listings of over 450 new job vacancies in all aspects of state government, including: aging, agriculture, arts and culture, commerce, consumer affairs, economic devvelopment, education, environment, fish and game, general services, governors' offices, health, housing, justice/law enforcement, labor, personnel/human resources, public utilities, revenue, transportation, welfare, and youth services.

*State Legislatures* (National Conference of State Legislators, 1560 Broadway, Suite 700, Denver, CO 80202; phone: 303/830–2200) monthly, $49/annual subscription (U.S.), $55/foreign. A small munchkin's handful of positions with legislatures and organizations that lobby legislators appear under "Classified Advertising."

*Internships in State Government* (Graduate Group, 86 Norwood Rd., West Hartford, CT 06117; phones: 203/232–3100, 203/236–5570) $27.50, published annually.

## Directories

*State Administrative Officials Classified by Function* (The Council of State Governments, Iron Works Pike, P.O. Box 11910, Lexington, KY 40578; phones: 800/800–1910, 606/231–1939) $30 plus $3.75 postage. Published in November of odd–numbered years. Lists names, addresses, and phone numbers of directors of state agencies in over 130 categories along with definitions of each function.

*State Yellow Book* (Monitor Publishing, Co., 104 Fifth Ave., New York, NY 10011; phone: 212/627–4140) semiannual, $150/annual subscription. Over 1,000 pages furnish detailed information on the executive and legislative branches of every states' government as well as information on the counties in each state.

*State Executive Directory* (Carroll Publishing Co., 1058 Thomas Jefferson St., NW, Washington, DC 20077-0007; phone: 202/333-8620) $135/annual subscription, updated and published in full three times a year. 500+ pages. Over 92,000 entries listing officers, committee heads, legislators, mangers of boards and authorities, and department heads.

*State Legislative Leadership, Committees and Staff* (The Council of State Governments, Iron Works Pike, P.O. Box 11910, Lexington, KY 40578-9989; phones: 800/800-1910, 606/231-1939) $30 plus $3.75 postage. Published in June of odd-numbered years. Lists names, addresses, and phone numbers of state legislative leaders, committee and chairpersons, principal legislative staff officers, and staff members, plus organizational patterns.

*State Elective Officials and the Legislatures* (The Council of State Governments, Iron Works Pike, P.O. Box 11910, Lexington, KY 40578-9989; phones: 800/800-1910, 606/231-1939) $30 plus $3.75 postage. Published in March of odd-numbered years. Lists names, addresses, and phone numbers members of state legislative bodies and elected officials with statewide jurisdiction.

*50 State Legislative Directory* (California Journal, 1714 Capitol Ave., Sacramento, CA 95814-9925; phone: 916/444-2840) In over 400 pages, this directory provides the names, district and capitol addresses for all state legislators plus all committees and frequently called phone numbers. $75 plus 6.5 percent sales tax and $2.50 shipping.

*Legislators on Diskette* (California Journal, 1714 Capitol Ave., Sacramento, CA 95814-9925; phone: 916/444-2840) For each state legislator, includes party, district, house and state, home or district address, generic capitol address. Available for every state legislator in the country ($425; version including committee assignments costs $1,500) or for individual states ($30/state plus $25 processing fee). Available in 5.25-inch MS-DOS diskettes in ASCII, comma-delimited fields, in dBase, or WordPerfect. Also available on magnetic tape.

*National Organizations of State Government Officials Directory* (The Council of State Governments, Iron Works Pike, P.O. Box 11910, Lexington, KY 40578-9989; phones: 800/800-1910, 606/231-1939) $25 plus $3.75 postage. Most recent edition: 1989. Lists more than 140 organizations associated with state government. Includes addresses, phone numbers, membership requirements, programs, publications, and organizational structures.

*BNA's Directory of State Courts, Judges, and Clerks* (Bureau of National Affairs Books Distribution Center, 300 Raritan Center Parkway, Edison, NJ 08818; phone: 201/225–1900) $50. Published in the summer of even–numbered years. Gives names, address, phone number, court number, district, and geographical area served, for over 13,000 state judges and court clerks in more than 2,100 state courts in the U.S. and possessions.

Broom Hilda reprinted by permission of Tribune Media Services.
Copyright © 1990. All rights reserved.

*List of State Departments of Community Affairs* (Council of State Community Affairs Agencies, Suite 251, 444 North Capitol St., NW, Washington, DC 20001; phone: 202/393–6435) free. Lists directors of State Departments of Community Affairs. Four pages.

*National Association of Secretaries of State Handbook* (The Council of State Governments, Iron Works Pike, P.O. Box 11910, Lexington, KY 40578–9989; phones: 800/800–1910, 606/231–1939) $30 plus $3.75 postage. Published annually. Lists services each state's secretary of state (or lieutenant governor who functions as secretary of state) furnishes.

*Interstate Conference of Employment Security Agencies State Administrators* (ICESA, 444 N. Capitol St., NW, Suite 126, Washington, DC 20001; phone: 202/628–5588) free. Published each January. Lists the name, address, phone, and fax numbers of director of the state or U.S. possession's employment security agency, such as a department of labor, employment security, or department of employment and training.

*National Association of State Alcohol and Drug Abuse Members Directory* (NASADA 444 N. Capitol St., NW, Suite 642, Washington, DC 20001; phone: 202/783–6868) free. Updated monthly.

*National Assembly of State Arts Agencies Membership Directory* (NASAA, 1010 Vermont St., NW, Suite 920, Washington, DC 20005; phone: 202/347–6352) $10, revised monthly. This is simply a list of the names, addresses, and phone numbers of state arts agencies.

*National Association of State Budget Officers Membership Directory* (NASBO, 400 N. Capitol St., NW, Suite 295, Washington, DC 20001; phone: 202/624–5382) free, available only to members. Published annually.

*National Association of State Departments of Agriculture Membership Directory* (NASDA, 1616 H St., NW, Suite 2000, Washington, DC 20006; phone: 202/296–1800) free. Published each August.

*National Association of State Units on Aging Membership Directory* (NASUA, 2033 K St., NW, Suite 304, Washington, DC 20006; phone: 202/785–0707) available only to members. Published annually.

*American Association of Motor Vehicle Administrators Membership Directory* (AAMVA, Suite 600, 4200 Wilson Blvd., Arlington, VA 22203; phone: 703/522–4200) $100/nonmembers, $50/members.

*State Government Research Directory* (Gale Research, Inc., 835 Penobscot Bldg., Detroit, MI 48226; phone: 800/233–4253) $175; last edition 1987. Provides details on 850 state research units, on subjects ranging from agriculture to women's rights. Keyword, agency, and subject indexes. 349 pages.

*Regional, State, and Local Organizations* (Gale Research, Inc., 835 Penobscot Bldg., Detroit, MI 48226; phone: 800/233–4253) $450/set, $95/each for five regional volumes; call for details. Most recent edition published in 1990. Among its 47,000 listings of non-profit organizations, are professional associations, social welfare and public affairs organizations, resource and referral centers, and more. Each volume carries about 6,000 entries in 700+ pages.

See also the listing for the *Federal/State Executive Directory* in Chapter 4.

# Job sources: State—by—state

The listings that follow provide job sources for both local and state government positions, as well as information on applicable Federal Job Information Centers for each state.

**State—Operated Job Services.** Most states offer employment services that include career counseling and a job—matching service of some type. The state—by—state listings that follow include information to enable you to locate each state's employment services, including Job Service Offices. You should write directly for more information from the state(s) of your choice.

Many of these state employment services periodically publish a listing of available job openings with locations and starting salaries. Some states offer a job hotline. Only a few states publish directories of state officials. The national directories of state officials described earlier in this chapter are usually your best source for information on specific state agencies and departments.

In addition, state—operated Job Service Offices or Centers provide information on local, state, and federal government job openings. Job Service Offices participate in the Interstate Job Bank Service which the U.S. Department of Labor's Employment and Training Administration developed. Jobs in other states are on microfiche which can be read at your local Job Service office, and in some instances, as accessible by computer including computer terminals you can use yourself. Any Job Service Office can also call the Interstate Job Bank on its toll—free number to get further information on out—of—state positions. You can learn about government job openings in other states through this job bank which should be accessible from virtually every Job Service Center that has a personal computer.

The job—matching services furnished by Job Service Offices really amount to a free employment service for government professionals and technical, labor, and clerical workers. However, habitually—employed individuals rarely take advantage of these services. Perhaps they are turned off by the generic moniker for these offices: the "unemployment office." Don't let misconceptions steer you away from a state's Job Service Offices no matter how high in the government hierarchy you wish to work. They are usually an effective source of government job openings.

**State jobs.** The state–by–state listings include specific information on locating state government positions. Some states offer easily accessible and extensive listings of state government jobs. Others pretty much let job seekers twist slowly in the wind. Some, like Illinois, are so patronage–laden that you're wasting your time if you try to get a state job without a political sponsor. Generally, a state's Job Service Offices carry listings of jobs with that state's government.

**Chapter newsletters of speciality organizations.** The newsletters produced by the state chapters of many professional organizations frequently carry job advertisements. Usually, these newsletters are available only to chapter members. Some chapters, however, allow nonmembers to subscribe or join only the chapter. Because officers of state chapters change so frequently, you should contact the national headquarters of the appropriate professional organization to obtain the address of any chapter president you wish to contact.

**Local Newspapers.** As mentioned earlier, the classified section of local newspapers is sometimes the best source of local and, occasionally, state government job ads.

Many municipal and county governments advertise job openings only in local papers because the lead time for ads is much shorter than for magazines and newsletters. Local ads also help to minimize the number of applicants. Some local governments limit their advertising to local papers in the hope of keeping the jobs in the family, so to speak. In a handful of states, local newspaper advertisements are just about the only decent source of ads for local government positions.

**Municipal League Publications.** The listings in the remainder of this chapter often include both a periodical and directory published by the state's municipal league. In such instances, the municipal league's address and phone is given only in the description of the periodical.

# Types of job sources listed

For each state, the following types of job sources are identified:

*Periodicals.* Periodicals are listed if they carry ads for local and/or state government jobs within that state. When a local newspaper is the best source for government job ads, it is identified as such.

*Job–matching services and job hotlines.* Job–matching services and job hotlines that handle local and/or state government positions are described.

*Directories.* Directories of local governments and/or officials are included to get you to the right official concerning local or state government jobs. These include names, addresses, and phone numbers. Each listing identifies the types of officials that the directory includes.

*State Jobs.* Periodicals, job banks, and job hotlines that service only state government jobs are identified under this heading. Many of these also carry announcements of local and federal government positions in the state.

*Job Service Offices.* Information is provided to enable you to find the locations of Job Service Offices (also known in some states as Employment Security Offices) throughout each state. This information is usually listed under the "State Jobs" heading for each state.

*State Agency Locator.* By calling this phone number, you can track down the phone and address of any state department, agency, or employee. When you find that the phone number of a state agency listed in the *Government Job Finder* has been changed, disconnected, or the agency has moved without leaving a forwarding address, call the state agency locator to quickly obtain the new phone number or address.

*FJIC.* The addresses and telephone numbers of the Federal Job Information Center or centers that list federal positions for that state are identified. When a state is split between several FJICs, the *Government Job Finder* tells you which parts of a state are assigned to which FJIC. If a FJIC answers its phone only during certain hours, those hours are cited. For an in-depth discussion of using FJICs, see Chapter 4.

# State job sources

## Alabama

*Alabama Municipal Journal* (Alabama League of Municipalities, 535 Adams Ave., Montgomery, AL 36104; phone: 205/263-1042) monthly; $12/annual subscription. Few job ads.

*Directory* (Alabama League of Municipalities) published annually; $20/nonmembers; first copy free to members; extra copies $20/each. Lists elected officials and city managers.

### State Jobs

Contact the State Personnel Department (64 N. Union St., Montgomery, AL 36130; phone: 205/242-3389).

To locate **Job Service Offices**, contact the Employment Services Division (Department of Industrial Relations, 649 Monroe St., Montgomery, AL 36131; director's phone: 205/242-8003).

*Alabama State Agency locator: 205/261-2500*

**FJIC:** Suite 347, Building 600, 3322 Memorial Parkway South, Huntsville, AL 35801-5311; phone: 205/544-5802.

## Alaska

*AML Newsletter* (Alaska Municipal League, Suite 200, 217 Second St., Juneau, AK 99801; phone: 907/586-1325; FAX: 907/463-5480) monthly, $20/annual subscription. Two or three jobs are listed under "Job Opportunities."

*AML Legislative Bulletin* (Alaska Municipal League, Suite 200, 217 Second St., Juneau, AK 99801; phone: 907/586-1325; FAX: 907/463-5480) weekly, available only to members. Two or three jobs are listed under "Job Opportunities."

*Alaska Municipal Officials Directory* (Alaska Municipal League, Suite 200, 217 Second St., Juneau, AK 99801; phone: 907/586-1325; FAX: 907/463-5480) $30. Published annually. 160 pages.

*Municipal Salary Survey* (Alaska Municipal League, Suite 200, 217 Second St., Juneau, AK 99801; phone: 907/586-1325; FAX: 907/463-5480) $50. Published each September.

### State jobs

The state uses a pre-qualification system for most positions. Generally, you can learn about the different job classifications, their requirements, and how to apply by contacting the Department of Administration, Division of Personnel (P.O. Box C, Juneau, AK 99811-0201; phone: 907/465-4430). Job seekers found eligible are placed on a list from which agencies hire when actual vacancies occur. When there are not enough qualified candidates on the list for a position, a vacancy announcement is issued at this office.

About 95 percent of the state government positions are available only to Alaska residents. There are, however, about 20 classifications at any one time which are open non-residents. To learn which these are, contact the Division of Personnel and ask for a copy of the *Current Out-of-State Recruitment List*." Also ask for an application form (they do accept photocopies).

When the state has difficulty filling a vacancy, it may also advertises in newspapers in the vicinity of the job's location.

Find **Job Service Offices** by contacting the Employment Security Division, (Department of Labor, P.O. Box 3-7000, Juneau, AK 99802; phone: 907/465-2712).

*Alaska State Agency locator: 907/465-4648*

**FJIC:** 222 W. 7th Ave., Suite 222, Anchorage, AK 99513; phone: 907/271-5821.

## Arizona

*Also see the listings under "Job sources for multi-state regions" at the beginning of this chapter.*

*Local Government Directory* (League of Arizona Cities and Towns, 1820 W. Washington St., Phoenix, AZ 85007; phone: 602/258-5786) published each January and July; $10. Lists all elected officials, managers, and department heads for cities and towns, counties, councils of governments, and selected state offices.

### State jobs

*Job Hotline* (State Personnel Division, Department of Administration, 1831 W. Jefferson, Phoenix, AZ 85007; phone: 602/542-5216). For a recording of state jobs that are currently open (usually for only a week), call the 24-hour hotline 602/542-4266. Updated weekly.

*Open Continuous Job Listing* (State Personnel Division, Department of Administration, 1831 W. Jefferson, Phoenix, AZ 85007; phone: 602/542-5216) monthly, free. This lists jobs for which the state is continuously recruiting. It is also available at all state Job Service Offices. The State Personnel Division will mail it to out-of-staters and to state residents who live outside Maricopa and Pima counties.

To locate **Job Service Offices**, contact the Employment and Rehabilitation Services Division (Department of Economic Security, P.O. Box 6123-010A, Phoenix, AZ 85007; director's phone: 602/542-4016).

*Arizona State Agency locator: 602/542-4900*

**FJIC:** Room 1415, 3225 N. Central Ave., Phoenix, AZ 85012; phone: 602/640-5800.

## Arkansas

*City & Town* (Arkansas Municipal League, P.O. Box 38, North Little Rock, AR 72115; phone: 501/758-1610) 10 issues/year; $15/annual subscription. Jobs listed under "Municipal Mart."

*Directory of Arkansas Municipal Officials* (Arkansas Municipal League) published annually; $10.

*Arkansas Employment Security Division Job–Matching Service* (Employment Security Division, Capitol Mall, Little Rock, AR 72201; administrator's phone: 501/682–2121; available at any of the 34 local Employment Security Division office) free. A job seeker completes the service's resume form and is then matched with jobs. The service contacts matched applicants to arrange job interviews with employers. Applications are kept active for 60 days.

### State jobs

Each state agency does its own hiring. They generally advertise in the local newspapers and at the Job Service Offices. Eventually every job applicant will go through the Employment Security Department (Room 506, ESD Building, P.O. Box 2981, Little Rock, AR 72203; phone: 501/682–2121).

For information on the location of the 34 **Job Service Offices** (known in Arkansas as local Employment Security Department offices), contact the Employment Security Department, (Room 506, ESD Building, P.O. Box 2981, Little Rock, AR 72203; phone: 501/682–2121).

*Arkansas State Agency locator: 501/682–3000*

**FJIC:** 200 NW Fifth St., 2nd Floor, Oklahoma City, OK 73102; phone: 405/231–4948; **TDD** 405/231–4614. For forms call: 405/231–5208.

## California

*Also see Jobs Available listed under "Government jobs in general" in Chapter 2.*

**Western City** (California League of Cities, 1400 K St., Sacramento, CA 95814; phone: 916/444–5790) monthly; $24/annual U.S. subscription, $32/annual foreign subscription, $15/annual student subscription (U.S.) Jobs listed under "Job Opportunities." About 50 job ads in typical issue.

Job openings are listed in the monthly membership newsletters of the following three municipal management assistance groups. Addresses are particularly subject to change, but as of this printing you can contact the following assistance group presidents for information on how to join and receive the membership newsletter:

**Municipal Management Assistants of Northern California** (c/o Jennifer Britton, Administrative Assistant, City of Sunnyvale, P.O. Box 3707, Sunnyvale, CA 94088-3707; phone: 408/730-7475).

*MMANC Newsletter* (Municipal Management Assistants of Northern California, c/o Dave Milheim, Personnel Director, City of Morgan Hill, 17555 Peak Ave., Morgan Hill, CA 95037; phone: 408/779-7273) $25/annual nonmember subscription, included in dues. About eight to 12 "Job Announcements" for all types of professional positions in municipal management are in a typical issue.

*MMANC Roster* (Municipal Management Assistants of Northern California, c/o Dave Milheim, Personnel Director, City of Morgan Hill, 17555 Peak Ave., Morgan Hill, CA 95037; phone: 408/779-7273) $10/nonmembers, free/members. Published each February.

**Municipal Management Assistants of Southern California.** We have been unable to confirm the name and address of the new president. Sorry.

**Public Management Assistants of Central California.** We have been unable to confirm the name and address of the new president. Sorry again.

*Public Interest Employment Report* (Public Interest Clearinghouse, 200 McAllister St., San Francisco, CA 94102-4978; phone: 415/565-4695) semimonthly, three-month subscription for individuals: $30/employed nonmembers, $15/unemployed nonmembers, $15/members; annual subscription: $125/schools and institutions, $60/non-profit organizations. About 90 professional and support positions described per issue are in legal services.

*Directory of Bay Area Public Interest Organizations* (Public Interest Clearinghouse) $25. Features 600 organizations working for social change in the nine-county San Francisco Bay Area. Indexed by subject and county. Most recent edition published in 1991.

*Public Interest, Private Practice: A Directory of Public Interest Law Firms in Northern California* (Public Interest Clearinghouse) $10. Lists over 200 for-profit law firms that devote a substantial portion of their legal work to the public interest.

*Public Interest Employment Service Resource Center Clipboards* (Public Interest Clearinghouse) free. Members and subscribers to the Public Interest Clearinghouse's publications can drop in between 9 a.m. and 5 p.m. Monday through Friday (open to 7 p.m. on Wednesdays) to examine the five *Job Clipboards* (attorneys, paralegals, more non–attorneys, law students, and other public interest jobs) which are updated daily with new job openings. These vacancies later appear in the next issue of the *Public Interest Employment Report* described above. Also available for examination are other job newsletters adn resource files on potential employers.

*The California Directories* (California Journal, 1714 Capitol Ave., Sacramento, CA 95814-9925; phone: 916/444-2840) *Vol. 1: State Government* provides names, district and capitol addresses, phone, and staff of the legislature; description of state departments and top staff. 144 pages. $50 plus $6.5 percent sales tax and $2.50 shipping. *Vol. 3: Local Government* gives address, phone, top elected and appointed officials for every California city and county. $50 plus $6.5 percent sales tax and $2.50 shipping. Get both directories for $85 plus 6.5 percent tax and $2.50 shipping.

*California City Hall Address Book* (California League of Cities, 1400 K St., Sacramento, CA 95814; phone: 916/444–8960) $20.

*California Roster* [Stock No. 7540-930-0301-4; $8.75; published irregularly, most recent edition: 1990; lists city, county, state, and federal officials in California] and *The California Planner's 1991 Book of Lists* [Stock No. 7540-931-1005-0; $9; published each January; includes directories of city and county planing agencies, councils of government, and local agency formation commissions; usually sold out before September] (Department of General Services, 4675 Watt Ave., P.O. Box 1015, North Highland, CA 95660; phone: 916/973-3700) Add $1.50 per copy to ship via UPS. Prepayment required; no telephone orders. Prices include sales tax. Make check payable to "State of California," and include stock number of each book ordered.

## State jobs

*Capitol Weekly* (1930 9th St., Suite 200, Sacramento, CA 95814; phone: 916/444-7665) weekly, $59/annual subscription plus $4.57 sales tax for California residents, $39/six–month subscription plus $3.02 sales tax for California residents. This is the closest thing to a central listing of jobs vacancies with the State of California. Hundreds of vacancies are listed under "State Jobs." Each issue also includes about 50 exams for state positions listed under "The Exam Section."

Although there is no official central listing of state jobs in California, many are listed at the state's 135 **Job Service Centers.** An exam is required to obtain a job with the State of California. Contact the State Personnel Board (801 Capitol Mall, Sacramento, CA 94244; phone: 916/322-2530, **TDD:** 916/323-7490) for a copy of the pamphlet *How to Get a Job with the State of California* and a copy of the three-page list of Testing Offices. All open job examinations are announced on the 24-hour job hotlines operated by the State Personnel Board and are update at 5 p.m. every Friday.

## State Job Hotlines

*24-hour, seven days-a-week recordings except for the information staff*

| Type of Job | Sacramento | San Francisco | Los Angeles |
|---|---|---|---|
| Information staff | 916/322-2530 | | |
| Legal, professional, technical | 916/323-3471 | 415/557-9357 | 213/620-4199 |
| | | | *619/292-7334 |
| Law enforcement and social services | 916/323-3472 | 415/557-9358 | 213/620-4175 |
| Health and related | 916/323-3473 | 415/557-9359 | 213/620-4192 |
| | | | *619/236-9239 |
| Trades and labor | 916/323-3474 | 415/557-9350 | 213/620-4210 |
| Office services | 916/323-3475 | 415/557-0310 | 213/620-4210 |
| | | | *619/695-8891 |
| Promotions only (general) | 916/323-3470 | — | 213/620-4172 |
| Promotions only (career executive assignments) | 916/323-3291 | — | — |
| TDD hotline | 916/323-7490 | — | — |
| * Indicates the number of the Los Angeles office to call from the San Diego area toll-free | | | |

*California Journal Roster and Government Guide* (California Journal Press, 1714 Capitol Ave., Sacramento, CA 95814–9925; phone: 916/444–2840) $2.25 plus 7.25 percent sales tax for California residents plus $2.50 shipping. Published annually. Lists state agencies and boards, legislators, and legislative committees. Most recently published in 1991.

This is also available on 5.25 inch MS-DOS compatible computer disks in ASCII comma delimited format, dBase, or Word-Perfect. $49 plus 7.25 percent sales tax for California residents plus $2.50 shipping. Monthly updates available for $5.

To locate **Job Service Offices**, contact the Employment Development Department (P.O. Box 944216, Sacramento, CA 94244–2160; phone: 916/445–8008).

*California State Agency locator: 916/322–9900*

**FJIC: Los Angeles area:** 9650 Flair Dr., Suite 100A, El Monte, CA 91731, phone: 818/575–6510; **Sacramento area:** North entrance, 4695 Watt Ave., North Highlands, CA, 916/551–1464, send mail to: 1029 J St., Sacramento, 95814; **San Diego area:** Federal Building, Room 4-S-9, 880 Front St., San Diego, CA 92188, phone: 619/557–6165; **San Francisco area:** Room 235, 211 Main St., San Francisco, phone: 415/744–5627, send mail to: P.O. Box 7405, San Francisco, CA 94120.

## Colorado

*Also see the listings under ''Job sources for multi-state regions'' at the beginning of this chapter.*

*Colorado Job Finder* (Colorado Municipal League, Suite 2100, 1660 Lincoln, Denver, CO 80264; phone: 303/831–6411) biweekly; $30 annual/subscription, $16/six-month subscription, plus sales tax for Colorado residents. Typical issue features about 25 to 30 ads.

*Directory of Municipal and County Officials* (Colorado Municipal League) $35/nonmembers, $25/Colorado state agencies, $17.50/members and associate members, plus sales tax for Colorado residents, and 10 percent for shipping and handling. Published annually in September. Lists elected officials and major department heads plus Councils of Governments, Regional Planning Commissions, selected state and federal offices, selected state associations.

*Salaries and Fringe Benefits: Executive Compensation* (Colorado Municipal League) $30/nonmembers, $15/members, plus sales tax for Colorado residents and 10 percent for shipping and handling. Published annually in July. Covers 25 types of municipal executive and administrative positions.

*Salaries and Fringe Benefits: Benchmark Employee Compensation Report* (Colorado Municipal League) $50/nonmembers, $25/members, plus sales tax for Colorado residents, and 10 percent for shipping and handling. Published annually in April. Covers 46 jobs classifications.

*Salaries and Fringe Benefits in Colorado Cities and Towns under 3,000 Population* (Colorado Municipal League) $30/nonmembers, $15/members, plus sales tax for Colorado residents, and 10 percent for shipping and handling. Published annually in August.

## Local job hotlines in Colorado

### Municipalities

Arvada (24 hour): 303/431–3012

Aurora (24 hour): 303/695–7222

Boulder (24 hour): 303/441–3434

Brighton: 303/659–4050, extension 294

Commerce City (24 hour): 303/289–3618

Englewood: 303/762–2304

Fort Collins (24 hour): 303/221–6586

Golden (24 hour): 303/279–3331, ext. 223

Lakewood: 303/987–7777

Littleton (24 hour): 303/795–3858

Loveland: 303/667–6130, extension 374 (8 a.m.—5 p.m.), 303/667–0145 (recording: 5 p.m.—8 a.m.)

Northglenn (24 hour): 303/450–8789

Thornton (24 hour): 303/538–7240

Westminster (24 hour): 303/650–0115

Wheat Ridge (24 hour): 303/234–5927

## Counties

Adams County: 303/659-2120, extension 175 (8 a.m.—4:45 p.m.)

Arapahoe County (24 hour): 303/795-4480

Douglas County: 303/668-6260 (Monday—Friday, 8 a.m.—4:30 p.m.)

Eagle County (24 hour): 303/328-8891

Jefferson County (24 hour): 303/277-8686

Larimer County (24 hour): 303/498-7379

Weld County: 303/352-1993

### State jobs

*Department of Personnel Job Bulletin* (Department of Personnel, Room 110, 1313 Sherman, Denver, CO 80203) biweekly. Write for details.

### Colorado state job hotlines

Department of Personnel

Professional/administrative jobs: 303/866-4225

Clerical and skilled jobs: 303/866-4230

To locate **Job Service Offices**, contact the Department of Labor and Employment (600 Grant St., Denver, CO 8020-3528; phone: 303/837-3801).

*Colorado State Agency locator: 303/866-5000*

**FJIC:** 12345 W. Alameda Parkway, Lakewood, CO; 303/969-7050; send mail to: P.O. Box 25167, Lakewood, CO 80225; for forms and local supplements, call 303/969-7055.

## Connecticut

*Connecticut Town and City* (Connecticut Conference of Municipalities, 900 Chapel St., New Haven, CT 06510; phone: 203/772-2168) six issues/year, free to job seekers (be sure to mention your job seeking status when requesting a subscription; note, though, that a subscription fee will be established in 1989 or 1990). Jobs listed under "Classified." Four to seven job ads appear in the usual issue.

*Connecticut Municipal Directory* (Connecticut Conference of Municipalities) $85/nonmembers, $50/members. Published annually. Lists demographic information about each city, elected officials and major department heads, Regional Planning Agencies, Regional Councils of Government, and organizations of Connecticut municipal officials.

## State jobs

All state job vacancies are listed at the state's Job Service Offices and at the office of the State Recruitment and Testing Center (1 Hartford Square West, Suite 101A, Hartford, CT 06106; phone: 203/566-2501). Active examinations for state jobs are announced each Sunday in the display and classified advertising sections of the following Connecticut newspapers: *Bridgeport Post, Danbury New-Times, Hartford Courant, Meriden Record-Journal, New Haven Register, New London Day, Norwalk Hour* [Monday edition], *Norwich Bulletin, Register Citizen* (Torrington) [Monday edition], *Stamford Advocate, Waterbury American,* and *Willimantic Chronicle* [Monday edition].

For an explanation of the hiring process, ask the State Recruitment and Testing Center to send you a copy of the brochure "Working for the State of Connecticut" which explains the difference between competitive and non-competitive positions. The best way to find out about the non-competitive positions which do not require a merit system examination, is to call the individual agency and ask.

To locate the state **Job Service Offices** in Ansonia, Bridgeport, Bristol, Danbury, Danielson, Enfield, Hamden, Hartford, Manchester, Meriden, Middleton, New Britain, New London, Norwalk, Norwich, Stamford, Torrington, Waterbury, and Willimantic, see the state government section (the blue pages) of the local white pages telephone directory or contact the Connecticut Department of Labor (200 Foly Brook Blvd., Wethersfield, CT 06109; phone: 203/566-8818) for a list of Job Service Offices.

*Connecticut State Agency locator: 203/566-2211*

**FJIC:** Room 613, 450 Main St., Hartford, CT 06103; phone: 203/240-3263.

## TANK M<sup>c</sup>NAMARA®

## Delaware

*League Directory* (Delaware League of Local Governments, P.O. Box 484, Dover, DE 19901; phone: 302/678–0991) published annually with monthly updates; $25/nonmembers; $15/associate members, commercial, and governmental; free/members. Lists elected officials for each municipality.

### State jobs

*Weekly Recruitment Listings* (State Personnel Office, Townsend Bldg., Dover, DE 19903; phone: 302/739–5458 and Carvel State Office Bldg., 820 N. French St., Wilmington, DE 19801; phone: 302/571–3289) weekly, free. Call or write to get on mailing list. Issued each Monday, this list consists of jobs that are being filled at the time and for which you can apply right away.

*Continuous Job Listings* (State Personnel Office, Townsend Bldg., Dover, DE 19903; phone: 302/739–5458 and Carvel State Office Bldg., 820 N. French St., Wilmington, DE 19801; phone: 302/571–3289) monthly, available for viewing at either of these personnel offices. This is a listing of state jobs for which applications are taken continuously. When a position opens, hiring is done from the list of people who have applied instead of announcing the job opening and taking new applications. These jobs do not appear in the *Weekly Recruitment Listings*.

You can obtain actual job announcements from Applicant Services in either personnel office. Also, be sure to ask for a copy of the brochure *Steps to State Employment*.

To locate **Job Service Offices**, contact the Division of Employment and Training (Delaware Dept. of Labor, P.O. Box 9499, Newark, DE 19714-9499; phone: 302/368-6825).

*Delaware State Agency locator: 302/739-4000*

**FJIC:** Room 168, 600 Arch St., Philadelphia, PA 19106; phone: 215/597-7440.

## District of Columbia

*Also see nationwide job sources enumerated in Chapter 2 and federal job sources noted in Chapter 4.*

*1992 Internships* (Petersons Guides, PO Box 2123, Princeton, NJ 08543-2123; phone: 800/338-3282) $27.95. Updated annually, this 300+ page this book describes more than 200 internship opportunities in and around the District of Columbia, mostly with the federal government.

*Internships in Congress* (Graduate Group, 86 Norwood Rd., West Hartford, CT 06117; phones: 203/232-3100, 203/236-5570) $27.50, published annually.

*Internships + Job Opportunities in New York City and Washington, DC* (Graduate Group, 86 Norwood Rd., West Hartford, CT 06117; phones: 203/232-3100, 203/236-5570) $27.50, published annually.

*Washington 91* (Columbia Books, 1212 New York Ave., NW, Suite 300, Washington, DC 20005; phone: 202/898-0662) $60, published annually. Nearly 600 pages of addresses, phone numbers, and information including one chapter on local government in the District and surrounding counties and towens with populations over 5,000, and regional authorities. Also includes chapters on the media, business, national associations, labor unions, law firms, medicine and health, foundations and philanthropy, science and policy research, education, religion, cultural institutions, clubs, and community affairs.

*The Capitol Source: The Who's Who, What, Where in Washington* (National Journal, Inc., 1730 M St., NW, Washington, DC 20036; phones: 800/424-2921, 202/862-0644) $30. Published in April and November, this directory includes names, addresses, and phone numbers for the District of Columbia. Also included are corporations, interest groups, think tanks, labor unions, real estate, financial institutions, trade and professional organizations, law firms, political consultants, advertising and public relations firms, private clubs, and the media. All entries are also available on computer diskette. Call 202/857-1469 for information.

## District Government Jobs

*The Job Opportunities Bulletin* (District of Columbia Office of Personnel, Suite 301, 613 G St., NW, Washington, DC 20001; phone: 202/727-6099) biweekly, one free copy is available to nonresidents who are also eligible write once for job descriptions; posted on bulletin boards at all District personnel offices and city agencies; obtain actual detailed vacancy announcements at personnel offices, see the next paragraph for details. Lists titles, closing dates, and job announcement numbers of job openings for all District government offices and independent agencies. Each issue tells you how to obtain full individual position vacancy announcements (including a **TDD** phone number) and gives advice on how to apply (the District currently uses the same SF-171 form the federal government requires, but is developing its own, more manageable application form), how to obtain a detailed vacancy announcement, and how rankings are determined. Note that D.C. residency is required within six months of starting the job. The typical issue lists about 300 positions. Relatively few entry level positions.

The District operates four Servicing Personnel Offices where this bulletin is available and full job descriptions can be obtained. They are open on weekdays from 8:15 a.m. to 4:45 p.m. For information on jobs with the departments of Human Services and Recreation, call 202/727-0803 (801 N. Capitol St., NE); with the departments of Consumer and Regulatory Affairs, Public Works, Administrative Services, and the D.C. Energy Office, call 202/939-8700 (2000 14th St., NW); for information on vacancies with the police and fire departments and the Department of Corrections and Board of Parole, call 202/727-4272 (300 Indiana Ave., NW);

and for the remaining District agencies, call 202/525-1050 (Room 326, 1133 North Capital St., NE).

*District of Columbia Agency Locator: 202/727-1000*

**FJIC:** Room 1416, 1900 E St., NW, Washington, DC 20415; phone: 202/606-2700; includes federal jobs for D.C. metropolitan area.

## Florida

*Quality Cities '89* (Florida League of Cities, P.O. Box 1757, 201 W. Park Ave., Tallahassee, FL 32302-1757; phone: 904/222-9684) 11 issues/year; $20/annual nonmember subscription, $6/members, $15/government agencies. Jobs listed under "Report from City Hall."

*Officials of Florida Municipalities* (Florida League of Cities) $50/nonmembers; free/members, published each May. Lists all local officials.

*County Reporter* (Florida Association of Counties, P.O. Box 549, Tallahasse, FL 32302; phone: 904/224-3148) monthly; $25/annual subscription. Jobs listed under "JobLine."

*Membership Directory* (Florida Association of Counties) $35. Published in odd-numbered years. Lists county elected officials and major department heads.

*Directory of Planning Officials* (Florida Department of Community Affairs, Division of Resource Planning and Management, Bureau of Local Planning, 2740 Centerview Dr., Tallahassee, FL 32399-3000) write for price; published annually. Lists state, regional, and local planning officials.

### State jobs

*Job Hotline* (Florida Department of Administration, 435 Carlton Building, Tallahassee, FL 32399-1550; phone: 904/487-1749). Call 800/848-8477 (from within Florida only) or 904/487-2851 to hear a recording of available state positions of all types. But before you call, obtain the free *Employment Information Packet* which contains application instructions and job classifications and classification codes so you can use the job hotline. You need a touch-tone phone to call the hotline because you'll have to punch in the classification code to indicate each job for which you want vacancy information as well as to indicate the county in which you wish to work, and whether you are interested in career service (technical, labor, clerical) or management (professional).

*Resource Listing* (Florida Department of Administration, 435 Carlton Building, Tallahassee, FL 32399-1550; phone: 904/487-1749). This periodic bulletin contains a description of every available position with the State of Florida. It is not available to individuals by mail. However, it is available for your perusal at all Job Service Offices, the Department of Administration, and the personnel office of all state agencies.

To locate **Job Service Offices**, contact the Department of Labor and Employment Security (2012 Capital Cr., SE, Tallahassee, FL 32399-2154; phone: 904/488-4398).

*Florida State Agency locator: 904/488-1234*

**FJIC:** Suite 125, 3444 McCrory Pl., Orlando, FL 32803; phone: 407/648-6148.

# Georgia

*Georgia's Cities* (Georgia Municipal Association, 201 Pryor St, SW, Atlanta, GA 30303; phone: 404/688-0472) monthly; $30/annual subscription. Jobs listed under "City Exchange." Few job ads.

*Directory* (Georgia Municipal Association) published annually; $40/nonmembers; free/members.

## State, local, and federal jobs

*Job Information Service* (Georgia Department of Labor, 148 International Blvd., NE, Atlanta, GA 30303) Local, state, and federal government job openings maintained on computerized statewide database. Job opening information can be viewed at any of the department's 35 field offices throughout the state. The largest office is in Atlanta (2811 Lakewood Ave., SW, Atlanta, GA 30315; phone: 404/669-3300). Contact the department for a list of all field offices or check the local phone book. Jobs are also listed in the *State Merit System Public Annoucement.* Contact the Georgia Department of Labor for further information.

*Georgia State Agency locator: 404/656-2000*

**FJIC:** Room 940A, 75 Spring St., SW, Atlanta, GA 30303; phone: 404/331-4315.

## Hawaii

*The Honolulu Advertiser/Star–Bulletin* (605 Kapiolani Blvd., Honolulu, HI 96813; phone: 808/935–3916) published weekly on Sunday. Write for subscription prices. Government jobs usually listed under "300 – General Help Wanted." Local and state jobs ads.

Contact each county directly for the list of available government jobs it maintains:

*County of Hawaii:* Department of Civil Service (101 Aupuni St., Suite 133, Hilo, HI 96720; phone: 808/961–8361)

*County of Kauai:* Department of Personnel Services (4280 Rice St., Lihue, HI 96766; phone: 808/245–4791)

*City and County of Honolulu:* Department of Civil Service (550 S. King St., Honolulu, HI 96813; phone: 808/523–4301; **24–hour Job Hotline:** 808/523–4303) Job listings updated weekly and posted at this address and at Satellite City Halls. *Job applicants must be legal residents of Hawaii at the time they apply for a government job with this city or county.*

*County of Maui:* Department of Personnel Services (County Building, 200 S. High St., Wailuku, Maui, HI 96793; phone: 808/243–7850).

*Directory of State, County, and Federal Officials* (Legislative Reference Bureau, State Capitol, Honolulu, HI 96813; phone: 808/548–6237) Write for price of the most recent edition.

### State jobs

*For all but a few positions, the State of Hawaii requires prior residency to even apply for a state job.*

*Professional Recruiting Office* (3345 Queen St., Suite 410, Honolulu, HI 96813; phone: 808/587–0904). These positions are generally exempt from the prior residency requirements, so mainlanders can apply for them. They are generally in health or education and only about 15 are available at any one time.

*Non–exempt positions.* (Hawaii Department of Personnel Services, Recruitment and Examination Division, 830 Pnchbowl St,. Honolulu, HI 96813; phone: 808/548–4031). At any one time, 300 to 400 of these state jobs are open, but remember, you must be a resident of Hawaii even to merely apply. Job descriptions are available at this office and also at the state's Job Service Offices.

The state does expect to implement a new hiring systtem in 1992 or 1993 that will enable you to complete just one application form and use it for all state jobs you seek instead of having to fill out separate form for different types of jobs.

For information on **Job Service Offices,** contact the Department of Labor and Industrial Relations, 830 Punchbowl St., Honolulu, HI 96813; phone: 808/548-3150).

*Hawaii State Agency locator: 808/548-2211*

**FJIC:** Room 5316, 300 Ala Moana Blvd., Honolulu, HI 96850; phone: 808/541-2791; call 808/541-2784 for federal jobs overseas.

## Idaho

*Also see the listings under "Job sources for multi-state regions" at the beginning of this chapter and listings under "Montana."*

*Idaho Cities* (Association of Idaho Cities, 3314 Grace St., Boise, ID 83703; phone: 208/344-8594) monthly; $5/annual subscription. Jobs listed under "Employment." Job ad are rare.

*Directory of Idaho Government Officials* (Association of Idaho Cities) published annually, $20. Lists city, county, and state elected officials and department heads as well as highway district officials, area-wide planning organizations and state legislators.

### State jobs

*Idaho Personnel Commission* (700 W. State St., Boise, ID 83720; phone: 208/334-2263). Contact for information and procedures. Job announcements for state, as well as local government positions are available at Job Service Offices throughout the state. Call the **Job hotline** recording for current listings: 208/334-2568.

For the addresses and phones of **Job Service Offices,** contact the Department of Employment, 317 Main St., Boise, ID 83735; phone: 208/334-6110).

*Idaho State Agency locator: 208/334-2411*

**FJIC:** 915 Second Ave, Seattle, WA 98174; phone: 206/553-4365.

## Illinois

*Illinois Municipal Review* (Illinois Municipal League, 500 E. Capitol, Springfield, IL 62701; phone: 217/525-1220) monthly; $5/annual subscription. Jobs listed under "Municipal Exchange Service." About 15 ads per issue.

*Illinois Municipal Directory* (Illinois Municipal League) $25. Published near the end of odd-numbered years. Lists elected officials and department heads.

### State jobs

*Roster of State Government Officials* (Illinois Issues, Building K, Room 80, Sangamon State University, Springfield, IL 62794-9243; phone: 217/786-6084 $3.95 plus $2 shipping; make checks payable to "Bursar, Sangamon State University." Published in April. Contains the names, addresses, and phone numbers of the state's constitutional officers, legislators, agency directors, board and commission members, etc.

The hiring situation  in Illinois state government continues to be less than promising. With over 100,000 applications on file, the state hires only about 5,000 employees a year, generally to replace retiring workers. Despite the U.S. Supreme Court's decision in *Ruttan v. Illinois Republican Party* that party affiliation could not be a factor in hiring, promoting, or transferring most state employees, patronage's  grip on state jobs is stronger than ever under the current Republican governor. Combine that with severe budget difficulties, and finding a job with the State of Illinois, outside of law enforcement, can be a nightmare.

**To Apply:** For any state position, obtain a state job application from the Bureau of Personnel (Department of Central Management Services, 500 Stratton Bldg., Springfield, IL 62706; phone: 217/782-7110). Complete the application and return it to the bureau. Some jobs, like clerical positions, also require a written test. Individuals for different job categories are ranked according to application, and where applicable, test scores. All state agencies and departments are supposed to hire from the ranked lists.

**To Identify State Job Openings:** There is no easily accessible single source of state job openings. To find available positions, contact the personnel division of each agency or department for which you wish to work. You can get their phone numbers from the State Agency Locator, any of the directories of state agencies enumerated at the beginning of this chapter, or the Springfield, Illinois, telephone directory.

**Employee Information System Computer.** Many, but not all, state departments and agencies voluntarily list job openings on this user-friendly computer which operates via artificial intelligence (no, this is not a reference to Dan Quayle—I don't know why we bother to keep making jokes about Dan Quayle since he's so good at it himself). You can easily print out lists of available state jobs by type of position, location, and department. These computers are located in the State of Illinois Center in Chicago (100 W. Randolph) and in Springfield, the state capitol, at the Stratton Office Building (basement), Willard Ice Building, Transportation Building, Harris Public Aid Building, and Centennial Building.

**Illinois Department of Employment Security Offices** (Office Manager, Employment Security Consolidated Office South, 1300 S. 9th St., Springfield, IL 62705; phone: 217/524-7838 and 401 S. State St., Chicago, IL 60605; 312/793-8138). Sixty-three of these **Job Service Offices** across the state offer computer-based job searches that include some state, local and federal government jobs. For a list of Job Service Offices, contact one of these offices or see the state government section of your local white pages telephone directory.

*Illinois State Agency locator: 217/782-2000*

**FJIC:** Room 530, 175 W. Jackson, Chicago, IL 60604; phone: 312/353-6192 (only on weekdays from 9 a.m. to noon) Self-service only. *Madison and St. Clair Counties, East St. Louis area:* Room 400, 815 Olive St., St. Louis, MO 63101; 314/539-2285.

## Indiana

*ACTionlines* (Indiana Association of Cities and Towns, ISTA Center, 150 W. Market St., Indianapolis, IN 46204-2882; phone: 317/237-6200) monthly; $45/annual subscription. Very few job ads.

*Roster of Indiana City and Town Officials* (Indiana Association of Cities and Towns) $25/nonmembers, one copy included in membership package. Published in U.S. Presidential election years. Updated once during the four-year period; small fee to be established for nonmember purchases of the update. Lists elected officials and major department heads.

*Informal Job Registry* The Executive Director of the Indiana Association of Cities and Towns (ISTA Center, 150 W. Market St., Indianapolis, IN 46204-2882; phone: 317/237-6200) maintains a very informal job registry. Send your resume to him and he will keep it on file. Upon request, he sends the resumes of qualified individuals to municipalities to fill positions.

*IACT Salaries, Wages & Benefits Surveys* (Indiana Association of Cities and Towns) Complete survey costs $25. Most recent survey published in 1991.

## State jobs

*Indiana Department of Employment and Training Service (IDETS)* (Room 331, 10 N. Senate Ave., Indianapolis, IN 46204; phone: 317/232-3270) has personnel who specialize in matching applicants with government jobs through the statewide automated **Job Service** Matching System. This service is available only by an in-person visit to a IDETS office. Write for a list of offices or consult the state government section in local telephone directories. All these services are free.

For information on specific positions and residency requirements, contact the Indiana Department of Employmennt and Training Services, (10 N. Senate Ave., Indianapolis, IN 46204; phone: 317/232-3270).

*Indiana State Agency Locator: 317/232-3140*

**FJIC:** 575 N. Pennsylvania Ave., Indianapolis, IN 46204; phone: 317/226-7161; *for information on federal jobs in Clark, Dearborn, and Floyd counties:* Room 506, 200 W. Second St., Dayton, OH 45402; phone: 513/225-2720.

# Iowa

*Iowa Municipalities* and *Iowa Interlink* (League of Iowa Municipalities, Suite 209, 100 Court Ave., Des Moines, IA 50309; phone: 515/244-7282) both bimonthly; $18/annual subscription for both for Iowa residents; $20/outside Iowa for both. Jobs listed under "Classifieds."

*Directory* (League of Iowa Municipalities) published in every even-numbered year; $25/nonmembers; free/member municipalities. Lists elected officials, department heads, and local government offices.

## Local and state jobs

For information on available local and state government jobs contact the Department of Employment Services (Capitol Complex, Des Moines, IA 50319; phone: 515/281-5387) or the Department of Personnel (Capitol Complex, Des Moines, IA 50319; phone: 515/281-3087).

## State jobs

*Job Class Opening Announcement* (Department of Personnel, Grimes State Office Building, E. 14th and Grand, Des Moines, IA 50319-0150; phone: 515/281-3087, **TDD**: 515/281-7825) weekly, available for inspection at the department's Job Information Center. Local and federal jobs are also listed at the center. Contact this department for a copy of the brochure *Working for the State of Iowa: Getting on Board.*

*JOBLINE* Recording that lists state job openings: 800/247-6002 from within Iowa, except Des Moines; from out of state and Des Moines, call 515/281-5820.

*Iowa State Agency Locator: 515/281-5011*

**FJIC:** Room 134, 601 E. 12th St., Kansas City, MO 64106; phone: 816/426-7757; m*for information on federal jobs in Scott County:* Room 530, 175 W. Jackson, Chicago, IL 60604; phone: 312/353-6192 (only on weekdays 9 a.m. until noon) self-service only; *for information on federal jobs in Pottawattamie County:* Room 101, 120 S. Market St., Wichita, KS 67202; phone: 316/269-6794.

## Kansas

*Kansas Government Journal* (League of Kansas Municipalities, 112 SW 7th, Topeka, KS 66603; phone: 913/354–9565) monthly; $18/annual subscription. Jobs listed under "Want Ads."

### State jobs

Contact the Department of Recruitment and Employment Information, Division of Personnel Services, Room 951–South, Landon State Office Building, 900 SW Jackson St., Topeka, KS 66612–1251; phones: 913/296–5390, **TDD**: 913/296–4798)

*Jobline* (Kansas Department of Administration, Personnel Services, Room 129–S, State Office Building, Topeka, KS 66612; phone: 913/296–4278). Call 913/296–2208 for a recording that lists state vacancies. Updated every Friday at 4 p.m., this 24–hour service gives you the name and phone of the person to contact about a vacancy. It also tells you which openings are limited to current state employees.

To find **Job Service Offices**, contact the Department of Human Resources (401 SW Topeka Blvd., Topeka, KS 66603; phone: 913/296–7474) for a copy of the "DHR Office Directory" which lists 36 Department of Human Resources offices that offer job services.

*Kansas State Agency Locator: 913/296–0111*

**FJIC**: Room 101, 120 S. Market St., Wichita, KS 67202; phone: 316/269–6764. *Residents of Johnson, Leavenworth, and Wyandotte counties:* Federal Building, Room 134, 601 E. 12th St., Kansas City, MO 64106; phone: 816/426–5702.

## Kentucky

*The Kentucky City* (Kentucky Municipal League, 2201 Regency Rd., Suite 100, Lexington, KY 40503; phone: 606/277–2886) monthly; $11/annual subscription. Jobs listed under "Career Opportunities." Few job ads.

*Directory* (Kentucky Municipal League) published every two years, $21/nonmembers, $10/members.

## State jobs

Contact the Department of Personnel (Room 373, Capitol Annex, Frankfort, KY 40601; phone: 502/564-4460).

To locate **Job Service Offices**, contact Examination and Recruitment (Department for Employment Services, 275 E. Main St., Frankfort, KY 40621; phone: 502/564-5331).

*Kentucky State Agency Locator: 502/564-2500*

**FJIC:** Room 506, 200 W. Second St., Dayton, OH 45402; phone: 513/225-2720; *for information on federal jobs in Henderson County:* 575 N. Pennsylvania Ave., Indianapolis, IN 46204; phone: 317/269-7161.

## Louisiana

*Louisiana Municipal Review* (Louisiana Municipal Association, 700 N. 19th St., P.O. Box 4327, Baton Rouge, LA 70821; phone: 504/344-5001) monthly; $12.84/annual subscription. Few job ads.

*LAM News* (Louisiana Municipal Association) monthly, available only to members, free upon request. Occassionally sports a job announcement or two.

*Directory of Louisiana Municipal Officials* (Louisiana Municipal Association) $26. Published in January of odd-numbered years. Lists elected officials and major department heads.

## State jobs

*Information Hotline* (State Department of Civil Service, Information and Recruiting Office, 5825 Florida Blvd., Baton Rouge, LA 70806; phone: 504/925-1911). If you call this number between 2:30 p.m. and 4:45 p.m., Monday through Firday, you'll get a live person. Call between 8 a.m. and 2:30 p.m. and you'll get a recording that will tell you the following: You need to complete a job application form for each state job that interests you. You can obtain these forms at this Information and Recruiting Office or any Louisiana Job Service Office. The Job Service Offices have the titles and descriptions of state jobs. You must submit a separate application for each job, but you may submit photocopies. Within four weeks of applying, you'll be notified if your application was accepted and you will be told when any civil service exam, if required, will be held. You'll get your grade about four weeks after taking the test. Passing candidates are then placed on a list from which each agency selects people to interview when a job opens.

For information on the location of **Job Service Offices**, contact the Department of Employment and Training (P.O. Box 94094, Baton Rouge, LA 70804–9094; phone: 504/342–3111).

*Louisiana State Agency Locator: 504/342–6600*

**FJIC:** Suite 608, 1515 Poydras, New Orleans, LA 70112; phone: 504/589–2764.

## Maine

*Maine Sunday Telegram* and *Portland Press Herald* (390 Congress, Portland, ME 04101; phone: 207/780–9000) are the state's best sources of job ads for government positions.

*Maine Townsman* (Maine Municipal Association, Local Government Center, 37 Community Drive, Augusta, ME 04330; phone: 207/623–8428) monthly; $13/annual subscription. Jobs listed under "Classifieds." Few job ads.

*Municipal Directory* (Maine Municipal Association) $25/nonmembers, $15/members. Published annually.

### State jobs

Contact the Bureau of Human Resources, Department of Administration (State House Station #4, Augusta, ME 04333; phone: 207/289–3854/4419).

To locate **Job Service Offices**, contact the Bureau of Employment Security (Department of Labor, State House Station #54, Augusta, ME 04333; director's phone: 207/289–3431).

*Maine State Agency Locator: 207/289–1110*

**FJIC:** Room 104, 80 Daniel St., Portsmouth, NH 03801–3879; phone: 603/431–7115.

## Maryland

*Maryland Municipal League Information Bulletin* (Maryland Municipal League, 1212 West St., Annapolis, MD 21401; phone: 301/268–5514) biweekly, $50/annual nonmember subscription, $25/members. Four or five positions in all aspects of local government appear under "Jobs and Equipment."

*Municipal Maryland* (Maryland Municipal League, 1212 West St., Annapolis, MD 21401; phone: 301/268–5514) 10 issues/year; $188.50/annual subscription. Jobs listed under "Market Place." Few job ads.

*Maryland Municipal League Personnel Exchange Program* (Maryland Municipal League, 1212 West St., Annapolis, MD 21401; phone: 301/268–5514) $5/six months. Job seeker submits copy of resume which is kept on file for six months. When this program matches a job seeker's resume with an available local government job, it sends a copy of the job announcement to the job hunter who is then responsible for contacting the potential employer.

*Directory of Maryland Municipal Officials* (Maryland Municipal League, 1212 West St., Annapolis, MD 21401; phone: 301/268–5514)) $17/nonmembers, $8.50/members. Published annually. Lists city and town officials.

*Washington 91* (Columbia Books, 1212 New York Ave., NW, Suite 300, Washington, DC 20005; phone: 202/898–0662) $60, published annually. Nearly 600 pages of addresses, phone numbers, and information including one chapter on local government in the District and surrounding counties and towens with populations over 5,000, and regional authorities. Also includes chapters on the media, business, national associations, labor unions, law firms, medicine and health, foundations and philanthropy, science and policy research, education, religion, cultural institutions, clubs, and community affairs.

### State jobs

Contact the Department of Personnel (Room 609, 301 W. Preston St., Baltimore, MD 21201; phone: 301/225–4715).

To pinpoint **Job Service Offices**, contact the Job Training and Placement Administration (Department of Economic and Employee Development, Room 700, 1100 N. Eutaw St., Baltimore, MD 21201; director's phone: 301/333–5070).

*Job–Matching Service* (Job Training and Placement Administration, Department of Economic and Employment Development, 1100 1100 N. Eutaw St., Baltimore, MD 21201; director's phone: 301/333–7574) free. Matches your skills to job vacancies in the government, private, and non–profit sectors.

*Maryland State Agency Locator: 301/974–2000*

**FJIC:** 101 W. Lombard St., Baltimore, MD 21201; phone: 301/962–3822.

## Massachusetts

*The Beacon* (Massachusetts Municipal Association, 60 Temple Place, Boston, MA 02111; phones: 800/882–1498, 617/426–7272) 11 issues/year, $36/nonmember annual subscription, included in dues. Jobs listed under "Employment Opportunities." Typical issue carries 10 to 20 job ads.

*Municipal Directory* (Massachusetts Municipal Association) published annually; $25/nonmembers, $12/members, published annually in early winter. Lists all elected local officials and department heads, planning agencies, statewide municipal associations.

Mother Goose and Grim reprinted by permission of MCM L&M and Grimmy, Inc. © 1991. All rights reserved.

### State jobs

Notices for civil service exams for all job openings are posted by all local municipal clerks. Within the Department of Personnel Administration's Examination Administration Group (1 Ashburton Place, Room 205, Boston, MA 02108), the Public Information Unit (Room 201; general phone: 617/727–8370) provides information on job exam entrance requirements (800/392–6178, **TDD** 617/727–8370) and a recording of upcoming civil service exams (617/727–9244). The exam for each job area is given every other year. Write or call to receive an exam schedule from the Public Information Unit. The schedule released in November lists exams given during January through June of the coming year. The schedule published in February lists exams given in July through December.

To locate **Job Service Offices**, contact the Department of Employment and Training (19 Stainford St., Boston, MA 02108; phone: 617/727-6529).

*Massachusetts State Agency Locator: 617/727-2121*

**FJIC:** 10 Causeway St., Boston, MA 02222-1031; phone: 617/565-5900.

## Michigan

*Michigan Municipal Review* (Michigan Municipal League, 1675 Green Rd., P.O. Box 1487, Ann Arbor, MI 48106; phone: 313/662-3246) 10 issues/year, $15/annual subscription. Jobs listed under "Municipal Want Ads." About 20 ads per issue.

*Directory of Michigan Municipal Officials* (Michigan Municipal League) published each January and July, $28/nonmembers, free/members. Lists elected officials and department heads.

*Resume Referral Service* (Michigan Municipal League, 1675 Green Rd., P.O. Box 1487, Ann Arbor, MI 48106; phone: 313/662-3246). Contact for information on this service which is actually operated by the Michigan City Management Association.

*Planning & Zoning News* (Planning and Zoning Center, Inc., 302 S. Waverly Rd., Lansing, MI 48917; phone: 514/886-0555) monthly, $130/annual subscription. Jobs listed under "Jobs Available." Few job ads.

### State jobs

Each state agency does its own hiring. To learn of current vacancies, you must contact the individual agency's placement office. For a list of state agencies, see the various directory of state agencies near the beginning of this chapter.

To learn the requirements for state jobs, contact the Recruitment Office (Michigan Department of Civil Service, 400 S. Pine St., Lansing, MI 48933; phone: 517/373-3030). This office can tell you the qualifications for each job and whether a civil service exam is required. Civil service exam dates are posted here, at the service's other two offices, and at the state's Job Service Offices. Educational institutions are eligible to be sent notices of civil service exams.

To find **Job Service Offices**, contact the Employment Security Commission (7310 Woodward Ave., Detroit, MI 48202; phone: 313/876-5022).

*Michigan State Agency Locator: 517/373-1837*

**FJIC:** Room 565, 477 Michigan Ave., Detroit, MI 48226; phone: 313/226-6950.

## Minnesota

*Cities Bulletin* (League of Minnesota Cities, 183 University Ave., East, St. Paul, MN 55101; phone: 612/227-5600) weekly during legislative session, semimonthly during rest of the year, $50/annual nonmember subscription, $35/members. Lists five or more local government jobs, primarily professional.

*Minnesota Cities* (League of Minnesota Cities, 183 University Ave., East, St. Paul, MN 55101; phone: 612/227-5600) monthly; $18/annual subscription. Jobs listed under ''Municipal Ads.'' About eight ads per issue.

*Directory for Minnesota Municipal Officials* (League of Minnesota Cities) published each January, $20 plus sales tax for Minnesota residents, plus $1/postage.

### State jobs

*Minnesota Career Opportunities* (Department of Employee Relations, 658 Cedar St., St. Paul, MN 55155; phone: 612/296-6700) biweekly, first issue free, $30/annual subscription, $24/six-month subscription; send subscription requests and a check payable to the State of Minnesota to: Minnesota Book Store, 117 University Ave, St. Paul, MN 55155; phones: 800/657-9747, 612/297-3000. Copies are available at all state Job Service Offices. Includes information on filling out job applications, examination procedures, and training classes. Fifteen to 30 job vacancies are described in each issue.

*Job Hotline* (Minnesota Department of Employee Relations, 658 Cedar St., St. Paul, MN 55155; phone: 612/296-6700). Call 612/296-2616 for a 24-hour recording of available state government jobs. Updated every two weeks. For assistance from a real person, call 612/296-2616 between 9 a.m. and 4 p.m. Monday through Friday.

For information on the location of **Job Service Offices,** contact Jobs, Opportunity and Insurance (Department of Jobs and Training, 390 N. Robert St., St. Paul, MN 55101; director's phone: 612/296-3625).

*Minnesota State Agency Locator: 612/296-6013*

**FJIC:** Federal Bldg., Room 501, Ft. Snelling, Twin Cities, MN 55111; phone: 612/725-3430.

## Mississippi

*Mississippi Municipalities* (Mississippi Municipal Association, 455 N. Lamar Jackson, MS 39202; phone: 601/353-5854) monthly; $10/annual subscription. Jobs listed under "MMA Employment Service."

*Mississippi Municipal Directory* (Mississippi Municipal Association) published every four years; most recent edition is 1989. $50. Lists all municipal elected officials and department heads.

### State jobs

Job openings are announced through a computer network connected to the State Employment Service (Job Service) offices. Job descriptions can be viewed at these offices. County positions are sometimes also listed on this system. These state job vacancies are also available for review at the State Personnel Board (301 N. Lamar St., Jackson, MS 39201; phone: 601/359-1406). Although the State Personnel Board does not mail out job notices, you can find out what Mississippi state jobs are available through the Interstate Job Bank in which your local Job Service Office almost certainly participates.

For a list of **Job Service Offices,** contact the Mississippi State Employment Service (1520 W. Capitol St., Jackson, MS 39215-1699) for a copy of the Directory of Employment Service Offices.

*Mississippi State Agency Locator: 601/359-1000*

**FJIC:** Suite 341, Building 600, 3322 Memorial Parkway South, Huntsville, AL 35801-5311; phone: 205/544-5802.

## Missouri

*Missouri Municipal Review* (Missouri Municipal League, 1913 William St., Jefferson City, MO 65109; phone: 314/635-9134) monthly; $15/annual subscription. Jobs listed under "Municipal Hunting Ground." About 10 job ads per issue.

*Missouri Municipal Officials Directory* (Missouri Municipal League) published annually; $30/nonmembers ($27 if prepaid), free/members. Lists municipal elected officials and department heads.

### State jobs

*Job Opportunity Announcements* Division of Personnel, Office of Administration (P.O. Box 388, Jefferson City, MO 65102; phone: 314/751-4162) are sent periodically to Job Service offices throughout the state. These announcements describe the positions available on the merit system.

To locate **Job Service Offices**, contact the Division of Employment Security (Labor and Industrial Relations Department, 421 E. Dunklin, Box 59, Jefferson City, MO 65104; director's phone: 314/751-3215).

*Missouri State Agency Locator: 314/751-2000*

**FJIC:** Room 400, 815 Olive St., St. Louis, MO 63101; phone: 314/539-2285; Room 134, 601 E. 12th St., Kansas City, MO 64106; phone: 816/426-5702.

## Montana

*Also see the listings under "Job sources for multi-state regions" at the beginning of this chapter.*

*Montana League of Cities and Towns Newsletter* (Montana League of Cities and Towns, Suite 201, 208 N. Montana Ave., P.O. Box 1704, Helena, MT 59624; phone: 406/442-8768) 3-4 issues/annually; free. Ads are rare, but when they do appear they cover Montana, Idaho, and Oregon.

*Directory of Montana Municipal Officials* (Montana League of Cities and Towns) published in even-numbered years; $12.50. Lists elected officials and department heads of incorporated municipalities.

*Montana Planners Directory* (Montana Department of Commerce, Local Government Assistance Division, Cogswell Bldg., Helena, MT 59620; phone: 406/444-3757) $3.75, except free to Montana local government planners. Last published in 1989. The State Library (1515 E. Sixth Ave., Helena, MT 59620; phone: 406/444-3004) has copies available for inter-library loan. Lists all planners in the state and planning agencies, Councils of Governments, and related federal departments.

### State and local jobs

Most state agencies use the Job Service for recruitment.

*Directory of Job Service Offices* (Job Service Division, Department of Labor and Industry, P.O. Box 1728, Helena, MT 59624; phone: 406/444-4100) Lists detailed information on the state's 24 Job Service Offices. Competition for government jobs is intense. For information on available local and state government positions, inquire at the Job Service Office in the area in which you wish to live.

*Montana State Agency Locator: 406/444-2511*

**FJIC:** P.O. Box 25167, 12345 W. Alameda Parkway, Lakewood, CO 80225; 303/969-7050; for forms and local supplements, call 303/969-7055.

## Nebraska

*Nebraska Municipal Review* (League of Nebraska Municipalities, 1335 L St., Lincoln, NE 68508; phone: 402/476-2829) monthly; $10/annual subscription. Jobs listed under "Classifieds."

*Nebraska Directory of Municipal Officials* (League of Nebraska Municipalities) published annually; $13

### State jobs

*State Job Listings* (Department of Personnel (301 Centennial Mall S., P.O. Box 94905, Lincoln, NE 68509-4905; phone: 402/471-2075) free. Complete the application form and attach your resume and recommendation letters. Check the job listings each week and call or write to activate your file when you find jobs that interest you.

*Job Hotline* (Department of Personnel (301 Centennial Mall S., P.O. Box 94905, Lincoln, NE 68509-4905; phone: 402/471-2075). Call 402/471-2200 for the latest vacancies in state government.

To locate **Job Service Offices**, contact the Job Service Division (Department of Labor, 550 S. 16th St., Lincoln, NE 68509; phone: 402/471–9828).

*Nebraska State Agency Locator: 402/471–2311*

**FJIC:** Room 101, 120 S. Market St., Wichita, KS 67202; phone: 316/269–6774.

# Nevada

*Information Exchange* (Nevada League of Cities, Box 2307, Carson City, NV 89701; phone: 702/882–2121) monthly, subscription, free to public officials in Nevada. Job ads appear occasionally.

*Nevada League of Cities Directory* (Nevada League of Cities) published annually; $7.50/nonmembers; free/members.

*Nevada Association of Counties Directory* (Nevada Association of Counties, Suite 205, 308 N. Curry St., Carson City, NV 89703; phone: 702/883–7863) $20. Published annually in February. Lists elected county officials and department heads, state and federal officials.

## State jobs

*Job Recording Line* (Department of Personnel, 209 E. Musser St., Carson City, NV 89710; phone: 702/687–4050) Call 702/687–4160 for a 24–hour recording of available jobs (titles, department, location). To receive a full job description and application form, contact the Department of Personnel.

*Job Announcements* (Department of Personnel, 209 E. Musser St., Carson City, NV 89710; phone: 702/687–4050) weekly. Distributed only to state agencies, including Job Service Offices, and universities. Copies cannot be mailed to individuals, but you can see it at state agencies. Lists state government positions.

To obtain a list of **Job Service Centers**, contact the Employment Security Department (500 E. Third St., Carson City, NV 89710; phone: 702/687–4630).

*Nevada State Agency Locator: 702/885–5000*

**FJIC:** North entrance, 4695 Watt Ave., North Highlands, CA, 916/551–1464, send mail to: 1029 J St., Sacramento, 95814; Room 100, 1029 J St., Sacramento, CA 95814.

## New Hampshire

Local government job openings are advertised in local newspapers and the *New Hampshire Sunday News* (35 Amherst St,. Manchester, NH 03101; phone: 603/668–4321), *Maine Sunday Telegram* (390 Congress, Portland, ME 04101; phone: 207/775–5811), and *Boston Globe* (135 Morrissey Blvd., Boston, MA 02107; phone: 617/929–2000).

*New Hampshire Town and City* (New Hampshire Municipal Association, 25 Triangle Park Dr., P.O. Box 617, Concord, NH 03302; phone: 603/224–7447) 10 issues/year; $10/annual subscription. Jobs listed under "Municipal Want Ads." Few job ads.

*Directory of New Hampshire Municipal Officials* (New Hampshire Municipal Association, P.O. Box 617, Concord, NH 03302; phone: 603/224–7447) $25. Published every July. Lists elected officials and major department heads.

*County Directory of New Hampshire* (New Hampshire Association of Counties, 16 Centre St., Concord, NH 03301; phone: 603/224–9222) $5. Published in March of odd–numbered years. Lists elected and appointed officials.

### State jobs

*Opportunities in New Hampshire State Government* (Division of Personnel, State House Annex, Room 1, School Street, Concord, NH 03301; phone: 603/271–3261) Write for details on how to receive this job vacancy notice and to receive the published list of state job vacancies.

To locate **Job Service Offices**, contact the Bureau of Employment Services (Department of Employment Security, 32 S. Main St., Concord, NH 03301; phone: 603/224–3311).

*New Hampshire State Agency Locator: 603/271–1110*

**FJIC:** Room 104, 80 Daniel St., Portsmouth, NH 03801–3879; phone: 603/431–7115.

## New Jersey

*New Jersey Municipalities* (New Jersey State League of Municipalities, 407 W. State St., Trenton, NJ 08618; phone: 609/695-3481) 9 issues/year; $9/nonmember annual subscription, $6/members, $10/foreign. Jobs listed under "Municipal Job Line." About 25 job ads per issue.

*Municipal Directory* (New Jersey State League of Municipalities) $20/nonmembers, $12/municipal members. Published each February. Lists elected officials and major department heads.

*Revised Statutes, Administrative Rules and Regulations, Roster* (New Jersey Board of Professional Planners, 124 Halsey St., P.O. Box 45016, Newark, NJ 07101; phone: 201/648-2465) Contact the board for the current price, if any.

### State jobs

*Job Opportunities in State Government* (Department of Personnel, 44 S. Clinton Plaza, Trenton, NJ 08625, Attention: Artis Hamilton; phone: 609/292-7467) mailed on the first of each month; no subscription fee is charged; you must, however, send actual postage stamps (four ounces per issue); do *not* send cash or a check. They'd really appreciate if you could send a self-addressed, stamped 9 inch by 12 inch envelope for each issue you want. Each issue includes instructions on applying for state jobs and a state job application you can photocopy to submit. A typical issue features at least 40 to 50 job announcements for state government positions.

*Job Service Offices* (Division of Employment Services, Department of Labor, John Fitch Plaza, Trenton, NJ 08625; phone: 609/292-2400) Request a list of the 23 full-service offices and 16 satellite offices. Many state, local, and federal jobs can be found in their computers.

*New Jersey State Agency Locator: 609/292-2121*

**FJIC:** 970 Broad St., Newark, NJ 07102; phone: 201/645-3673 (from Camden, call 215/597-7440).

## New Mexico

*Also see the listings under "Job sources for multi-state regions" at the beginning of this chapter.*

*Albuquerque Journal* (7777 Jefferson, NE, Albuquerque, NM 87109; phone: 505/823-4400) The Sunday edition is the best source of ads for local government positions in three-fourths of the state. For the southern and southeast portions of the state, see the Sunday *El Paso Times* (401 Mills St., El Paso, TX 79901; phone: 915/546-6260). For jobs in the extreme southern section, beginning with Clovis and going south, the Sunday editions of the local newspapers from nearby Texas are the best sources in which to find ads for local government job openings.

*The Municipal Reporter* (New Mexico Municipal League, 1229 Paseo de Peralta, Santa Fe, NM 87501; phone: 505/982-5573) monthly, $20/annual subscription. Jobs listed under "Positions Available." When there are ads, there will be two or three.

*Directory of New Mexico Municipal Officials* (New Mexico Municipal League) $28. Published each May. Lists municipal elected officials and department heads, Councils of Government, and relevant state officials and agencies.

*Directory of New Mexico County Officials* (New Mexico Association of Counties, 1215 Paeo de Peralta, Santa Fe, NM 87501; phone: 505/983-2101) $25. Published in January of odd-numbered years. Lists elected county officials, managers, attorneys, and extension agents.

### State jobs

Contact the State Personnel Office (810 W. San Mateo, Santa Fe, NM 87503; phone: 505/827-8190).

To locate **Job Service Offices**, contact the Department of Labor (P.O. Box 1928, Albuquerque, NM 87103; phone: 505/841-8609).

*New Mexico State Agency Locator: 505/827-4011*

**FJIC:** Federal Building, Room 101, 421 Gold Ave., SW, Albuquerque, NM 87102; phone: 505/766-2906.

## New York

*The Chief–Civil Service Leader* (150 Nassau St., New York, NY 10038; phone: 212/962-2690) weekly; $20/annual subscription. Includes ads and anouncements of civil service exams for hundreds of professional, trades, labor, technical, and clerical jobs both the state government and for New York City.

*The New State Municipal Bulletin* (New York Conference of Mayors, 119 Washington Ave., Albany, NY 12210; phone: 518/463–1185) bimonthly, $25/nonmember annual subscription. Job ads printed at the rear. Few job ads.

*Directory for City and Village Officials* (New York Conference of Mayors) $50, $20/state agencies. Published each January. Lists elected officials and major department heads of cities and villages. The state's 932 towns, which range in population from 40 to over 700,000 are not included. The nationwide directories of local officials described at the beginning of this chapter include New York towns.

*NYSAC News* (New York State Association of Counties, 150 State St., Albany, NY 12207; phone: 518/465–1473) $24/annual nonmember subscription, included in dues. A handful of jobs in county government of all types appear under "Municipal Want Ads."

*NWSAC County Directory* (New York State Association of Counties) $20/nonmembers, included in dues; published each March.

*Regional and County Planning Directors* (New York Department of State, Office of Local Government Services, 162 Washington Ave., Albany, NY 12231; phone: 518/473–3355) free. Revised frequently. One–page list of county and regional planning directors with addresses and phone numbers.

*Directory, New York Metropolitan Chapter American Planning Association* (c/o Peter Hart, Buckhurst Fish Hutton Katz Inc., 72 Fifth Ave., New York, NY 10011; phone: 212/620–0050; if no longer at that address, obtain the new address from APA's Director of Chapter Services [1776 Massachusetts Ave., NW, Washington, DC 20036; phone: 202/872–0611]). Contact Mr. Hart for price, if any. Published in even–numbered years. Lists public planning agencies in New York City and surrounding region, consulting firms, and the 800 + members of APA's New York Metropolitan Chapter.

*Internships + Job Opportunities in New York City and Washington, DC* (Graduate Group, 86 Norwood Rd., West Hartford, CT 06117; phones: 203/232–3100, 203/236–5570) $27.50, published annually.

## Town jobs

Many of the state's 932 "towns" advertise positions in national specialty publications and local newspapers. However, half of these towns have populations of 5,000 or less. Local officials make oral vacancy announcements at town board meetings. Newspaper coverage and word of mouth seem to suffice for filling these jobs.

Those jobs covered by civil service require civil service examinations. Use the government section of the local telephone directory to locate a civil service office (often only at the county level) to contact for information on which local jobs are subject to civil service and how to apply.

## State jobs

*Guide to Career Opportunities in New York State Government* (New York State Department of Labor, Publications Unit, Room

401, State Office Campus Building #12, Albany, NY 12240; phone: 518/457–3801) $50, free/first annual update, $25/subsequent annual updates; most recent edition, 1991. This extremely detailed, but lively, book is the authoritative guide to 178 civil service occupations in 26 state agencies, occupations which either offer a large number of employment opportunities or for which the state has historically had difficulty finding qualified applicants. It specifies detailed job duties, salary schedule, qualifications, testing requirements, job and office locations, state agency functions, and the job environment, promotion opportunities and career ladders, total positions and annual hiring by job title, and an outline of the civil service law. Comes in a two–volume loose–leaf binder. This guide is expected to be available also on computer disk. Contact for details.

Contact the New York State Department of Civil Services (State Office Campus Building #1, Albany, NY 12239; phone: 518/457–3701).

*The New York State Directory* (Cambridge Information Group, 7200 Wisconsin Ave., Bethesda, MD 20814; phones: 800/843–7751, 301/961–6750) $112. Published annually in the summer. Over 440 pages. Lists executive and legislative state offices in 25 major policy areas; senior officials in all counties; senior government officials in Albany, Binghamton, Buffalo, New York City, Rochester, Syracuse, and Yonkers; public school administrators; judges; chambers of commerce; statewide and county political party chairpersons; registered lobbyists and political action committees.

To find **Job Service Offices**, called Community Service Centers in New York, contact the Department of Labor (Room 590, State Campus Building #12, Albany, NY 12240; phone: 518/457–7030).

*New York State Agency Locator: 518/474–2121*

**FJIC: New York City area:** Jacob Javits Federal Building, Room 120 (second floor), 26 Federal Plaza, New York, NY 10278, phone: 212/264–0422/0423; **Syracuse area:** James Hanley Federal Building, 100 S. Clinton St., Syracuse, NY 13260; phone: 315/423–5660.

## North Carolina

*Southern City* (North Carolina League of Municipalities, 215 N. Dawson St., Raleigh, NC 27601; phone: 919/834–1311) monthly; $6/annual subscription. Jobs listed under "Career Opportunities."

*Directory of North Carolina Municipal Officials* (North Carolina League of Municipalities) $30 plus sales tax for North Carolina residents. Published each March. Lists only municipal elected officials and department heads.

*County Lines* (North Carolina Association of County Commissioners, 215 N. Dawson, P.O. Box 1488, Raleigh, NC 27602; phone: 919/832–2893) biweekly; $20/annual subscription, $10/six–month subscription. Jobs listed under "Classifieds." About ten to 15 job ads per issue.

*Directory of North Carolina County Officials* (North Carolina Association of County Commissioners) $22 plus sales tax for North Carolina residents. Published in odd–numbered years. Lists elected officials and department heads.

## State jobs

State hiring is decentralized. To learn about job vacancies, go to a state Job Service Office. Obtain an application form there and send it to the agency to which you are applying. For a list of agencies, see the various directories of state agencies at the beginning of this chapter.

To locate *Job Service Offices,* contact the Employment Security Commission (P.O. Box 25903, Raleigh, NC 27611; phone: 919/733-7546).

*North Carolina State Agency Locator: 919/733-1110*

**FJIC:** 4505 Falls of the Neuse Rd., P.O. Box 25069, Raleigh, NC 27611-5069; phone: 919/856-4361.

## North Dakota

*North Dakota League of Cities Bulletin* (North Dakota League of Cities, 1731 N. 13th St., Box 2235, Bismarck, ND 58502; phone: 701/223-3518) 10 issues/annual; $10/annual subscription. Very few job ads. Jobs listed under "Jobs Available."

*Directory of North Dakota Officials* (North Dakota League of Cities) $12/nonmembers, free/members. Published in even-numbered years. Lists elected city officials and selected department heads.

## State jobs

*Job Service North Dakota* (1000 E. Divide Ave., P.O. Box 1537, Bismarck, ND 58502; phone: 701/224-2825) State and many other government jobs announcements can be viewed at any local Job Service Office. Write for a list of local offices.

*North Dakota State Agency Locator: 701/224-2000*

**FJIC:** Federal Bldg., Room 501, Ft. Snelling, Twin Cities, MN 55111; phone: 612/725-3430.

## Ohio

*Cities & Villages* (Ohio Municipal League, Suite 510, 175 S. Third St., Columbus, OH 43215; phone: 614/221-4349) monthly; $10/annual subscription. Five to ten jobs are listed under "Classified Ads."

*County Information and Data Service* (County Commissioners Association of Ohio, Suite 500, 175 S. Third St., Columbus, OH 43215; phone: 614/221-5627) $150/annual nonmember subscription, included in dues. Only one or two job ads make it into the "Classifieds."

## State jobs

Each state agency does its own hiring. There is no civil service exam. To get a list of the personnel offices of state agencies, contact the Division of Personnel, Department of Administrative Services (28th Floor, 30 E. Broad St., Columbus, OH 43266; phone: 614/466-3455). Also see the various directories that include state agencies near the beginning of this chapter to identify state government agencies in Ohio.

The state operates a **Job Information Center** (30 E. Broad St., B1 Level, Columbus, OH 43266-0405; phone: 614/466-4026).

To obtain a list of the state's 76 **Job Service Offices**, contact the Public Information Office (Bureau of Employment Services, 145 S. Front St., P.O. Box 1618, Columbus, OH 43216; phone: 614/466-3859.

*Ohio State Agency Locator: 614/466-2000*

**FJIC:** Room 506, 200 W. Second St., Dayton, OH 45402; phone: 513/225-2720. *Residents of the counties north of and including Van Wert, Auglaize, Hardin, Marion, Crawford, Richland, Ashland, Wayne, Stark, Carroll, and Columbiana:* Room 565, 477 Michigan Ave., Detroit, MI 48226; phone: 313/226-6950.

## Oklahoma

*Oklahoma Cities & Towns* (Oklahoma Municipal League, 201 N.E. 23rd St., Oklahoma City, OK 73105; phone: 405/528-7515) biweekly; $10/annual subscription for nonmembers, $8/annual subscription for member cities and towns. A pretty extensive listing of government jobs vacancies appears under "Employment Opportunities."

*Directory of Oklahoma City and Town Officials* (Oklahoma Municipal League) published annually; $20.

## State jobs

Contact the Office of Personnel Management (B–22 Jim Thorpe Bldg., 2101 N. Lincoln Blvd., Oklahoma City, OK 73105; phone: 405/521–2177).

To pinpoint **Job Service Offices**, contact Employment Security Commission (320 Will Rogers Memorial Dr., Oklahoma City, OK 73105; phone: 405/557–7105).

*Oklahoma State Agency Locator: 405/521–2011*

**FJIC:** 200 NW Fifth St., 2nd Floor, Oklahoma City, OK 73102; phone: 405/231–4948; **TDD** 405/231–4614. For forms call: 405/231–5208.

## Oregon

*Newsletter* (League of Oregon Cities, P.O. Box 928, Salem, OR 97308; phone: 503/588–6550) monthly; $48/annual subscription. Jobs listed under "Career Opportunities."

## State and local jobs

*Job Hotline* (Executive Department, Attention: Announcement Clerk, 155 Cottage St., NE, Salem, OR 97310; phone: 503/378–3006). Updated daily, this 24–hour hotline gives detailed information on currently available state jobs and how to apply for them. Out-of-state job seekers can request up to three recruitment announcements of specific jobs at a time. You must send a self-addressed, stamped #10 business envelope with your request. These job vacancies are also listed on the computers at the state's Job Service Offices where you can print out as many as you like. You can also request a free copy of the brochure, *Job Hunter's Guide to Oregon State Service* which takes you through the hiring process.

*Announcement Bulletin* (Executive Department, Attention: Announcement Clerk, 155 Cottage St., NE, Salem, OR 97310; phone: 503/378–3006) weekly, $5/month. This bulletin, affectionately known by staff as the "OC Bulletin," lists all the jobs on the "Job Hotline" but with less detail. Out-of-state job seekers can request up to three recruitment announcements of specific jobs at a time. You must send a self-addressed, stamped #10 business envelope with your request. You can also request a free copy of the brochure, *Job Hunter's Guide to Oregon State Service* which takes you through the hiring process.

*Local Office Directory* (Employment Division, Department of Human Resources, 875 Union St., NE, Salem, OR 97301; phones: 503/378–3211, 800/237–3710 within Oregon only). Contact these folks for this list of 33 local **Job Service** offices from which listings of local and state government jobs are available.

*Oregon State Agency Locator: 503/378–3131*

**FJIC:** Room 376, 1220 SW Third St., Portland, OR 97204; phone: 503/221–3141.

## Pennsylvania

*Pennsylvanian* (Local Pennsylvanian, Room 207, 2941 N. Front St., Harrisburg, PA 17110; phone: 717/236–9526) monthly; $17/annual subscription. Six to ten jobs are listed under "Classifieds."

*Pennsylvania State Association of Township Supervisors Magazine* (PSATS, 3001 Gettysburg Rd., Camp Hill, PA 17011; phone: 717/763–0930) monthly, $22/annual subscription. Few job ads.

*Pennsylvania League of Cities Directory* (Pennsylvania League of Cities, 2608 N. Third St., Harrisburg, Pa 17110; phone: 717/236–9469) $50/nonmember, $20/member. Published each March. Lists elected officials and major department heads.

*Directory of City Officials* (Distribution Services Unit, P.O. Box 2028, Harrisburg, PA 17105; phone: 717/787–6746) $2; when ordering, give publication number 137. Published each May by the Pennsylvania Department of Transportation, Local Government Services (717/787–2183). Lists elected officials and major department heads.

*Directory of County Commissioners* (Distribution Services Unit, P.O. Box 2028, Harrisburg, PA 17105; phone: 717/787–6746) $2; when ordering, give publication number 136. Published each May by the Pennsylvania Department of Transportation, Local Government Services (717/787–2183). Lists elected officials and major department heads.

*Directory of Borough Officials* (Distribution Services Unit, P.O. Box 2028, Harrisburg, PA 17105; phone: 717/787-6746) $7; when ordering, give publication number 138. Published each May by the Pennsylvania Department of Transportation, Local Government Services (717/787-2183). Lists elected officials and major department heads.

*Pennsylvania Municipal Yearbook* (Pennsylvania State Association of Boroughs, 2941 Front St., Harrisburg, PA 17110; phone: 717/236-9526) $100/nonmember, $30/member. Published each summer. Lists many top elected and administrative officials for each of the state's 970 boroughs.

*State Association of Township Commissioners Directory* (Pennsylvania League of Cities, 2608 N. Third St., Harrisburg, Pa 17110; phone: 717/236-9469) $50/nonmember, $20/member. Published each March. Lists elected officials and major department heads for townships and member boroughs.

*Directory of First Class Township Officials* (Distribution Services Unit, P.O. Box 2028, Harrisburg, PA 17105; phone: 717/787-6746) $2; when ordering, give publication number 139. Published each May by the Pennsylvania Department of Transportation, Local Government Services (717/787-2183). Lists elected officials and major department heads.

*Directory of Second Class Township Officials* (Distribution Services Unit, P.O. Box 2028, Harrisburg, PA 17105; phone: 717/787-6746) $11; when ordering, give publication number 140. Published each May by the Pennsylvania Department of Transportation, Local Government Services (717/787-2183). Lists elected officials and major department heads.

## State jobs

**Civil service positions**: To determine your eligibility, contact the Pennsylvania Civil Service Commission (P.O. Box 569, Harrisburg, PA 17108-0569; phone: 703/783-3058) or Job Service Offices. Obtain locations of **Job Service Offices** from the Office of Employment Security (Department of Labor and Industry, Room 1115, Seventh and Forster Streets, Harrisburg, PA 17121; pyhone: 717/787-3354).

**Positions exempt from civil service**: For trades, labor, technical, and office support positions with all state agencies, submit your resume to the Division of State Employment (Room 110, Finance Building, Harrisburg, PA 17120; phone: 717/787–5703). Resumes are kept on file for one year. State agency personnel officials examine the resumes and contact qualified applicants for an interview when a vacancy occurs.

*Pennsylvania State Agency Locator: 717/787–2121*

**FJIC: Harrisburg area:** Room 168, Federal Bldg., P.O. Box 761, Harrisburg, PA 17108, phone: 717/782–4494; **Philadelphia area:** Room 1416, William Green Jr. Federal Building, 600 Arch St., Philadelphia, PA 19106, phone: 215/597–7440; **Pittsburgh:** Room 119, 1000 Liberty Ave., Pittsburgh, PA 15222; phone: 412/644–2755.

## Rhode Island

There is no central source for local government job openings in Rhode Island. See the classified advertising sections of the Sunday editions of local Rhode Island newspapers for local government job ads.

Also contact the personnel offices of the cities in which you might be interested in working. The Rhode Island League of Cities and Towns (Suite 502, 1 State St., Providence, RI 02903; phone: 401/272–3434) is willing, on an informal basis, to help job seekers from out-of-state find job openings. The league will, upon request, informally check to see if there are any local government positions available.

*Directory of State and Local Government Officials* (Rhode Island Dept. of Administration, Office of Community Affairs, 1 Capitol Hill, Providence, RI 02908; phone: 401/277–2854) $3. Published each March. Lists all state department heads and divisions chiefs as well as municipal elected officials and department heads.

### State jobs

Contact the Department of Administration, Office of Personnel (1 Capitol Hill, Providence, RI 02908; phone: 401/277–2160).

Find the ten **Job Service Offices,** by contacting the Department of Employment and Training (101 Friendship St., Providence, RI 02903; phone: 401/277–3722) or see your telephone directory. Job Service staff will match job seekers with positions and refer them to potential employers.

*Rhode Island State Agency Locator: 401/277–2000 (8 a.m. to 4 p.m. only)*

**FJIC:** Room 310, John O. Pastore Federal Bldg., Kennedy Plaza, Providence, RI 02903; phone: 401/528–5251.

## South Carolina

*Uptown* (Municipal Association of South Carolina, 1529 Washington St., Columbia, SC 29211; phones: 800/658–3633, 803/799–9574) monthly, $10/annual nonmembersubscription, in dues. Two or three jobs in municipal government appear under "Job Market."

*South Carolina Municipal Officials Directory* (Municipal Association of South Carolina, 1529 Washington St., Columbia, SC 29211; phones: 800/658–3633, 803/799–9574) published annually; $15/nonmembers, free/members. Lists municipal elected officials and department heads.

### State jobs

*Career Lines* (State Recruitment Unit, Department of Human Resources Management, 2221 Devine, Columbia, SC 29205; phone: 803/734–9080). For a 24-hour recording of professional positions with the State of South Carolina, call 803/734–9333; for clerical, technical, and skilled labor positions, call 803/734–9334.

While many state jobs are listed on the *Career Lines,* many others are posted on the bulletin board at the State Recruitment Unit. All should be available at Job Service Offices. Each state agency does its own hiring. See the directories of state agencies at the beginning of this chapter.

To locate **Job Service Offices,** contact the Employment Security Commission (1550 Gadsden St., Columbia, SC 29202; phone: 803/737–2400).

*South Carolina State Agency Locator: 803/734–1000*

**FJIC:** 310 New Bern Ave., P.O. Box 25069, Raleigh, NC 27611; phone: 919/856–4361.

## South Dakota

*South Dakota Municipalities* (South Dakota Municipal League, 214 E. Capitol, Pierre, SD 57501; phone: 605/224-8654) monthly; $20/annual subscription. Jobs listed under "Classified Ads." Few job ads.

*Directory of South Dakota Municipal Officials* (South Dakota Municipal League) $15. Published each July. Lists elected officials and major department heads.

*SDACC County Comment* (South Dakota Association of County Commissioners, 207 E. Capitol, Pierre, SD 57501; phone: 605/224-4554) monthly, $10/nonmember annual subscription, included in membership package. Few job ads.

*South Dakota Directory of County Officials* (South Dakota Association of County Commissioners) $10/nonmembers, included in membership package. Pubished in January of odd-numbered years. Lists elected county officials and some department heads.

*South Dakota Directory of Local Development Corporations* (Governor's Office of Economic Development, Capitol Lake Plaza, Pierre, SD 57501; phone: 605/773-5032) free. Published each autumn. Lists local development corporations, planning districts, etc.

### State, local, and federal jobs

*South Dakota Job Order Index* (Labor Market Information Center, P.O. Box 4730, Aberdeen, SD 57402-4730; phone: 605/622-2314, from within South Dakota only call 800/592-1881) weekly; free. Lists local, state, and federal government, as well as private sector, jobs by geographic area. Includes list of local Job Service Offices.

*State Job Hotline* (South Dakota Bureau of Personnel  For a 24-hours a day recording of open state government jobs (including agency, title, salary, qualifications, closing date), call 605/773-3326.

*South Dakota State Agency Locator: 605/773-3011*

**FJIC:** Federal Bldg., Ft. Snelling, Twin Cities, MN 55111; phone: 612/725-3430.

## Tennessee

*Tennessee Town and City* (Tennessee Municipal League, 226 Capitol Blvd., Nashville, TN 37219; phone: 615/255-6416) 23 issues/year; $10/nonmember annual subscription, $6/members. Jobs listed under "Classified Ads." Few job ads. Local newspapers are the best source of job ads.

*Directory of Tennessee Municipal Officials* (University of Tennessee, Municipal Technical Advisory Service, 600 Henley, Knoxville, TN 37996-4105; phone: 615/974-0411) $50 (bound version), $100 (looseleaf, updated monthly), free to Tennessee municipal government officials. Bound version published each January. Lists municipal elected officials and department heads plus state and regional government agencies.

*Directory of Tennessee County Officials* (University of Tennessee, County Technical Assistance Service, Suite 400, 226 Capitol Boulevard Bldg., Nashville, TN 37219-1804; phone: 615/242-0358) $25 plus postage, first copy free to Tennessee county government officials. Published every October. Lists elected county officials and department heads.

### State jobs

Contact individual state agencies directly to learn of job vacancies. For a list of state agency phone numbers and addresses, contact the Tennessee Department of Personnel, 505 Deadericck St., Nashville, TN 37243-0635; phone: 615/741-7973).

To obtain a list of **Job Service Offices**, contact the Department of Employment Security (500 James Robertson Parkway, 12th Floor, Nashville, TN 37245-0900; phone: 615/741-7973).

*Tennessee State Agency Locator: 615/741-3011*

**FJIC:** 200 Jefferson Ave., Suite 1312, Memphis, TN 38103-2335; phone: 901/544-3956.

## Texas

*TML Texas Town & City* (Texas Municipal League, 211 E. 7th, Austin, TX 78701-3283; phone: 512/478-6601) monthly; $15/annual subscription. Jobs listed under "Classifieds." With about 40 job ads per issue, this is one of the most comprehensive sources for local government employment.

*Prospects* (Texas Municipal League) monthly, $25/nonmember annual subscription, included in membership package. This job announcement newsletter describes 15 to 20 municipal and county goverment positions each issue.

*Directory of Texas City Officials* (Texas Municipal League) $50/nonmembers, $30/members. Published each August. Lists elected city officials and major department heads, Regional Planning Agencies, Councils of Government, etc.

### State jobs

Each state agency hires its own staff. See the various directories that include state agencies near the beginning of this chapter to identify state government agencies in Texas. Many state job openings, however, are listed on the Texas Employment Commission's statewide, computer-assisted job matching system. Request a list of the more than 100 local Texas Employment Commission (**Job Service Offices**) offices throughout the state from the TEC State Office (101 E. 15th St., Austin, TX 78778-0001; phone: 512/463-2222) or see the state government section of the local telephone directory.

*Texas State Agency Locator: 512/463-4630*

**FJIC: Dallas area:** Room 6B10, 1100 Commerce St., Dallas, TX 75242; phone: 214/767-8035; **Houston, and San Antonio areas:** phone recording only: 713/226-2375; 8610 Broadway, Room 305, San Antonio, TX 78217, phones: 512/229-6611/6600; **Corpus Christi area:** 512/884-8113, use San Antonio office.

## Utah

*Directory of Local Government Officials* (Utah League of Cities and Towns, 50 South 600 East, Salt Lake City, UT 84102; phone: 801/328-1601) $20.

### Local and state jobs

Jobs listings are available by in-person application from the Utah **Job Service**, 720 South 200 East, Salt Lake City, UT 84111 (phone: 801/536-7000 or 5735 S. Readwood Rd., Salt Lake City, UT 84107; phone: 801/269-4700).

## State jobs

*State of Utah Job Opportunities* (Room 2229, State Office Building, Salt Lake City, UT 84114; phone: 801/538-3025) weekly, $20/six-month subscription.

To locate **Job Service Offices**, contact the Utah Department of Employment Security (174 Social Hall Ave., Salt Lake City, UT 84147; phone: 801/533-2202).

*Utah State Agency Locator: 801/538-3000*

**FJIC:** 12345 W. Alameda Parkway, Lakewood, CO; 303/969-7053; send mail to: P.O. Box 25167, Lakewood, CO 80225; for forms and local supplements, call 303/969-7055.

## Vermont

*Vermont Job Service* (Vermont Department of Employment and Training, P.O. Box 648, Barre, VT 05641; phone: 802/229-1757) free. Provides job matching services including municipal and state government positions. Resumes are kept on file up to three years.

*VLCT Newsletter* (Vermont League of Cities and Towns, 12 1/2 Main St., Montpelier, VT 05602; phone: 802/229-9111) monthly, $80/nonmember annual subscription, included in membership package. Jobs listed under "Classified." Few job ads, primarily for planners and community development. City manager ads are very rare.

*List of Mayors and Managers* (Vermont League of Cities and Towns, 12 1/2 Main St., Montpelier, VT 05602; phone: 802/229-9111) available as mailing labels. Contact for prices.

## State jobs

*Open Competitive Recruitment Announcements* (Vermont Department of Personnel, 110 State St., Montpelier, VT 05602; phone 802/828-3483) monthly, free. Lists open state job positions, location, and starting salary.

*24 Hour JOBLINE* (Vermont Department of Personnel). Call 802/828-3484 for frequently updated tape recording of state job openings.

To locate **Job Service Offices**, contact the Department of Employment and Training (P.O. Box 488, Montpelier, VT 05602; phone: 802/229-0311).

*Vermont State Agency Locator: 802/828–1110*

**FJIC:** Room 104, 80 Daniel St., Portsmouth, NH 03801–3879; phone: 603/431–7115.

## Virginia

*Virginia Town and City* (Virginia Municipal League, 13 E. Franklin St., P.O. Box 12164, Richmond, VA 23241; phone: 804/649–8471) monthly; $8/annual subscription for nonmembers, $4 for members. Jobs listed under "Market Place."

*Virginia Municipal League Letter* (Virginia Municipal League, 13 E. Franklin St., P.O. Box 12164, Richmond, VA 23241; phone: 804/649–8471) ) biweekly, $25/annual subscription. Jobs listed under "Available Positions."

*Virginia Review* (County Publications, Inc., P.O. Box 860, Chester, VA 23831; phone: 804/748–6351) 10 issues/year, $14/annual subscription. A small number of government positions, if any, are advertised in here.

*Virginia Review Directory of State and Local Government Officials* (County Publications, Inc., P.O. Box 860, Chester, VA 23831; phone: 804/748–6351) $26.07 plus sales tax for Virginia residents, published each spring. 280 pages. One of the most thorough state and local government directories in the country.

*Virginia Municipal League Directory* (Virginia Municipal League, 13 E. Franklin St., P.O. Box 12164, Richmond, VA 23241; phone: 804/649–8471) ) published in odd–numbered years; $20.90. Lists elected officials and department heads for all municipalities and counties, planning district commissions, regional planning agencies, some state and federal offices, and statewide government professional organizations.

*Washington 91* (Columbia Books, 1212 New York Ave., NW, Suite 300, Washington, DC 20005; phone: 202/898–0662) $60, published annually. Nearly 600 pages of addresses, phone numbers, and information including one chapter on local government in the District and surrounding counties and towens with populations over 5,000, and regional authorities. Also includes chapters on the media, business, national associations, labor unions, law firms, medicine and health, foundations and philanthropy, science and policy research, education, religion, cultural institutions, clubs, and community affairs.

*Directory of Local Planning in Virginia* (Dept. of Housing and Community Development, Office of Local Development Programs, 205 N. Fourth St., Richmond, VA 23219; 804/786–4966) free. Published in even–numbered years. Lists all county, city and town planning directors, zoning and subdivision administrators, and planning district commission executive directors as well as the status of various planning activities.

### State jobs

Locate a local State Employment Service Office (Job Service) through a local telephone directory's state government section or obtain a list of the 42 local **Job Service Offices** from the Virginia Employment Commission (703 E. Main St., Richmond, VA 23219; phone: 804/786–3001). Announcements of local, state, and federal job openings are available for examination.

Virginia is one of the first states to use ALEX, the *A*utomated *L*abor *EX*change computer service that enables job seekers to look up job vacancies in Virginia, and nationwide, themselves. If a job is listed with some state Job Service office anywhere in the country, it will be accessible through ALEX. ALEX terminals are being set up at Job Service Offices and in shopping malls, libraries, and schools.

*Virginia State Agency Locator: 804/786–0000 (that's not a typographical error, honest)*

**FJIC:** Federal Building, Room 220, 200 Granby St., Norfolk, VA 23510–1886; phone: 804/441–3355.

## Washington

*AWC Job–Net* (Association of Washington Cities, 1076 S. Franklin St., Olympia, WA 98501; phone: 206/753–4137) monthly, $15/annual subscription. Lists managerial, administrative, and professional government job openings.

*Officials of Washington Cities* (Association of Washington Cities and Municipal Research and Services Center of Washington, 10517 NE 38th Pl, Kirkland, WA 98033–7926; phone: 206/827–4334) $11.50/nonmembers, free/members of Association of Washington Cities. Published in even–numbered years. Lists elected city and county officials and major department heads.

*Directory of County Officials in Washington State* (Washington State Association of Counties, 206 10th Ave., SE, Olympia, WA 98501; phone: 206/753–1886) $5. Published every January. Lists county elected officials and major department heads, members of state boards and committees, and members of the following Washington state associations: County Administrative, County Engineers, Local Public Health Officials, County Human Services, County/Park Recreation Boards and Departments, County and Regional Planning Directors.

HAGAR the HORRIBLE is reprinted with special permission
of King Features Syndicate, Inc. Copyright 1991

*The Directory of Planning and Community Development Agencies* (Washington State Department of Community Development, Local Government Assistance Division, Ninth and Columbia Building, M/S GH–51, Olympia, WA 98504–4151; phone: 206/753–4978) free. 139 pages. Lists all city, county, and regional planning agencies; major state departments and agencies; federal agencies; housing authorities and state housing contacts; community action agencies; economic development organizations; social service agencies; government–related professional associations and organizations; hearing examiners; boundary review boards; Indian tribes; university and college planning departments; county extension offices.

## State jobs

*Washington State Department of Personnel* (521 Capitol Way, South, P.O. Box 1789, Olympia, WA 98507–1789; phone: 206/753–5368) mails job announcements on a weekly basis with semi-monthly summaries on the first and third Wednesday each month. To receive this list, send a stamped, self-addressed #10 envelope for each issue you wish to receive. This list, as well as announcements of jobs at other levels of government are posted at each of the state's 33 Job Service Centers.

*Joblines* (P.O. Box 1789, Olympia, WA 98507–1789; phone: 206/753–5368). Call any of these numbers for a recorded announcement of new state job openings available each week: 206/586–0545 (Olympia), 206/464–7378 (Seattle), and 509/456–2889 (Spokane).

To locate **Job Service Offices**, contact the Division of Employment Services (Employment Security Department, 212 Maple Park, Olympia, WA 98504; phone: 206/438–4804).

*Washington State Agency Locator: 206/753–5000*

**FJIC:** 915 Second Ave, Seattle, WA 98174; phone: 206/553–4365.

## West Virginia

*West Virginia Municipal League Directory* (West Virginia Municipal League, 1620 Kanawha Blvd., East, Suite 1B, Charleston, WV 25311; phone: 304/342–5564) $25. Updated regularly. Lists elected municipal officials, city managers, clerk/recorders.

## State jobs

Contact Personnel, Civil Service System (B–456, 1900 Washington St., E, Charleston, WV 25305; phone: 304/348–3950).

To locate **Job Service Offices**, contact the Bureau of Employment Programs (112 California Ave., Charleston, WV 25305; phone: 304/348–2660).

*West Virginia State Agency Locator: 304/348–3456*

**FJIC:** Room 506, 200 W. Second St., Dayton, OH 45402; phone: 513/225–2720; for information on West Virginia, call 513/225–2866.

# Wisconsin

*The Municipality* (League of Wisconsin Municipalities, 122 W. Washington Ave., Madison, WI 53703-2757; phone: 608/267-2380) monthly, $12/annual subscription. Very extensive listing of jobs under "Municipal Want Ads."

*Wisconsin State Current Employment Opportunities Bulletin* (State Division of Merit Recruitment, Department of Employment Relations, 137 E. Wilson St., P.O. Box 7855, Madison, WI 5307-7855; phone: 608/266-1731; TDD/VOICE: 608/266-1731) biweekly; $18/annual subscription, $9/six-month subscription. To subscribe, send check and order to State Document Sales, 202 S. Thornton, P.O. Box 7840, Madison, WI 53707. Each issue is posted at state Job Service offices, colleges, and all state offices. Includes state and some local positions.

*Wisconsin Counties* (Wisconsin Counties Association, 802 W. Broadway, Suite 308, Madison, WI 53713; phone: 608/266-6480) monthly, $19.50/annual subscription. One or two positions appear under "County Classified."

*League of Wisconsin Municipalities Directory* (League of Wisconsin Municipalities, 122 W. Washington Ave., Madison, WI 53703-2757; phone: 608/267-2380) $25/nonmembers, $12/members. Published annually. Lists elected officials and department heads.

## State jobs

*Wisconsin State Continuous Recruitment Bulletin* (Job Information Receptionist, State Division of Merit Recruitment and Selection, 137 E. Wilson St., P.O. Box 7855, Madison, WI 53707-7855; phone: 608/266-1731) annually; free. Lists state job classifications for which there is a continual need or for which applicants are in very short supply (health care, data processing, power plant operators, labor/service, typists). Each edition is posted at state Job Service offices, colleges, and all state offices.

To locate **Job Service Offices**, contact the Job Service Division (Department of Industry, Labor, and Human Relations, P.O. Box 7903, Madison, WI 53707; director's phone: 608/266-8561).

*Wisconsin State Agency Locator: 608/266-2211*

**FJIC:** Federal Bldg., Room 501, Ft. Snelling, Twin Cities, MN 55111; phone: 612/725-3430; *for federal job information in Dane, Grant, Green, Iowa, Jefferson, Kenosha, Milwaukee, Racine, Rock, Walworth, Waukesha counties:* Room 530, 175 W. Jackson, Chicago, IL 60604; phone: 312/353-6189.

## Wyoming

*Also see the listings under "Job sources for multi-state regions" at the beginning of this chapter.*

*The WAM News* (Wyoming Association of Municipalities, P.O. Box 3110, Cheyenne, WY 82803-3110; phone: 307/632-0398) monthly; $5/annual subscription. Jobs listed under "Job Opportunities." Few jobs ads.

*Official Municipal Roster* (Association of Municipalities) $10/non-members, free to members, published each February.

### State, local, and federal jobs

*Job Service of Wyoming* (Department of Employment, P.O. Box 2760, Casper, WY 82602; phone: 307/235-3200) Local, state and federal government job openings kept at 16 Job Service Centers throughout the state. No publication available. Write or call for the addresses of local Job Service Centers.

*Wyoming State Agency Locator: 307/777-7220*

**FJIC:** P.O. Box 25167, 12345 W. Alameda Parkway, Lakewood, CO 80225; 303/969-7054; for forms and local supplements, call 303/969-7055.

## U.S. possessions and territories

## American Samoa

Contact *Department of Manpower Resources* (Pago Pago, AS 96799; phone: 684/633-4485).

American Samoa government main switchboard: 684/633-4116

## Guam

Guam government main switchboard: 671/472-8931.

## Northern Mariana Islands

Contact *Personnel Management Office* (Civil Service Commission, Personnel Management Office, Office of the Governor, P.O. Box 150, Saipan, CHRB MP 96950; phones: 670/234-6958, 670/234-7327, 670/234-8036).

## Puerto Rico

Contact the *Bureau of Employment Security* (Labor and Human Resources Department, 505 Munoz Rivera Ave., Hato Rey, PR 00918; phone: 809/753-9550) for information on state jobs as well as locations of Job Service Offices.

**FJIC:** U.S. Federal Bldg., Room 340, 150 Carlos Chardon Ave., Hato Rey, PR 00918-1710; phone: 809/766-5242.

Puerto Rico main government switchboard: 809/721-6040

## Virgin Islands

### Territorial government jobs

Virgin Islands main government switchboard: 809/774-0880

To locate **Job Service Offices**, contact the Department of Labor (2131 Hospital St., Christenstead, St. Croix, VI 00820-0094; phone: 809/773-1994).

**FJIC:** U.S. Federal Bldg., Room 340, 150 Carlos Chardon Ave., Hato Rey, PR 00918-1710; phone: 809/766-5242.

# Chapter 4

# Finding federal government jobs

Even during the current Reagan–Bush era, federal agencies still hire thousands of trained government professionals and technical, trades, and labor, and office support staff every month, albeit in smaller numbers than in the pre–Reagan years. Federal jobs offer good pay, excellent benefits, and a high level of job security. In addition, federal employees generally enjoy greater prestige than many state and local officials, as well as a greater opportunity to travel.

## Federal government hiring process

### Office of Personnel Management

A federal government position can fall under one of two different hiring procedures. Most federal positions are Competitive Service jobs which are filled through the Office of Personnel Management (OPM), manager of the Civil Service System. The OPM acts as the recruiting agency for these positions and establishes job qualifications, distributes job announcements, and manages hiring procedures.

While each agency has its own personnel office, the Office of Personnel Management (OPM), an independent executive agency, stands at the apex of the federal personnel system. Until the mid–1980s, OPM played a central role in directly recruiting and screening applicants for many types of positions and for certain agencies. This agency was responsible for testing applicants, examining SF–171s, giving ratings, and maintaining registers of qualified applicants. When agencies had a personnel need, OPM would forward lists of qualified candidates to the agency for consideration. The agency, in turn, interviewed candidates and made the final selection decisions. Overall, the process was a mixture of centralized and decentralized hiring functions. Applicants understood that one had to first stop at OPM to get information on job vacancies, take any required tests, submit their SF–171 for evaluation, receive a rating, and wait on the register to be called for an interview. Such hiring procedures were very time consuming. Consequently, the employment process in the federal government rightfully deserved a reputation for being centralized, complicated, and lengthy. If you wanted to quickly find a job, the federal government was the last place to stop. Finding a federal job required a major investment of time and patience while this centralized bureaucracy tried to cope with thousands of applications that eventually had to be acted upon at the lowest level in the bureaucracy—the operating units.

However, the role of OPM in the hiring process has undergone major needed changes during the past five years. Unfortunately, few job applicants—including many federal employees—know about these changes. As a result, many people approach the federal hiring process as if it still operates according to the procedures of the 1960s, 1970s, and early 1980s. For example, they first approach OPM in search of a "rating" and then wonder how they can get on a "register"— the two most frequently asked questions that are inappropriate for today's new hiring procedures. In fact, if you want to demonstrate your ignorance of the federal hiring process, just ask these questions at your local Federal Job Information Center (FJIC). Indeed, personnel at the FJICs have learned to be very patient in answering what appears to be many of the same old questions over and over again. Applicants even go so far as to argue with OPM personnel about these procedures. After all, their friend the expert, who just happens to work in the federal government, told them this is what they had to do to get a federal job! Well, so much for advice from well–meaning friends.

Key personnel functions, such as issuing vacancy announcements, rating applicants, and training, has been increasingly decentralized to individual agencies since the mid–1980s. Today, OPM plays a more supportive role in helping agencies meet their personnel needs. While OPM is still the

government's central personnel agency, it delegates hiring authority to other agencies and maintains oversight responsibilities at the same time. The degree to which it delegates this authority will depend on the capabilities of individual agencies to conduct their own hiring. In general, however, OPM is responsible for issuing government-wide personnel regulations; providing support services to agencies; managing some application, testing, and screening processes; disseminating job vacancy information; providing limited training services; assisting agencies in meeting their personnel needs; and extending benefits to employees and government retirees. This agency still remains important to the federal government hiring process, but it is not as a central personnel office that conducts hiring for individual agencies—a common misunderstanding of job applicants who continue to pester OPM with inappropriate questions when they should be addressing these questions to individual agencies.

Many federal agencies, however, hire their employees through their own personnel departments. These are called "exempted" or "excepted" service positions and their employees are not subject to the OPM's application procedures or job qualifications. Job candidates apply directly to these agencies rather than through the OPM.

## Competitive service

The federal government does not have a single, unified personnel system. Its over 3 million employees are classified into different services and positions. The federal civil service, for example, classifies positions into competitive or exempted services. The majority of federal government positions (80 percent) are in the *competitive service.* These positions fall under the civil service regulations, codified in the Civil Service Reform Act of 1978, which are administered by the Office of Personnel Management. Such positions are made public through Job Vacancy Announcements and must adhere to the "merit principles" of openness, fairness, and nondiscrimination. These positions come under Presidential authority, are subject to periodic reductions-in-force regulations and hiring freezes, and follow internal seniority rules.

## Exempted or excepted service

At the same time, Congress, the judiciary, and several agency positions are exempted from these regulations. These positions lie outside the authority of OPM and are subject to individual agency personnel regulations. Individuals in these positions do not accumulate civil service seniority which would apply to other positions in the competitive service. Executive agencies in the *exempted or excepted services* include:

- Central Intelligence Agency
- Defense Intelligence Agency
- Executive Protective Service (Secret Service—Uniformed Branch)
- Federal Bureau of Investigation
- Federal Reserve System, Board of Governors
- General Accounting Office
- U.S. Agency for International Development
- National Science Foundation (only scientific, engineering, and a few high-level managerial positions are exempted)
- National Security Agency
- Nuclear Regulatory Commission
- Postal Rate Commission
- U.S. Postal Service
- U.S. Department of State (skilled specialists and experienced secretaries only; all others take the foreign service exam)
- Tennessee Valley Authority
- U.S. Mission to the United Nations
- Judicial branch of the federal government (except the Administrative Office of the U.S. Customs Court)
- Legislative branch of the federal government (except the Government Printing Office)

These agencies have their own set of personnel procedures for hiring and managing personnel. For information on their particular application procedures, contact these agencies directly. The directories listed in this chapter will help you find the right person to contact. Also the personnel office numbers and job hotlines of many of these agencies are listed later in this chapter.

## Exempted or excepted postions

The federal government also excludes certain positions (rather than whole agencies) from civil service regulations. These positions are not subject to OPM standards. Such positions are excepted because they are difficult to fill through normal recruitment channels. These positions include:

- Teachers in Department of Defense overseas schools
- Attorneys, doctors, dentists, and nurses with the Department of Veterans Affairs
- Scientists and engineers with the National Science Foundation

- Chaplains in Departments of Veterans Affairs and Justice
- Drug enforcement agents
- Professional and Administrative Careers (PAC)—GS–5 through GS–7. About one–third of the federal government's professional jobs fall into this PAC classification. When inquiring about a professional position, be sure to ask if it is a PAC or Excepted job.

A significant proportion of the jobs at the following agencies are PAC jobs: Department of Agriculture (11 percent), Air Force (19 percent), Army (24 percent), Department of Commerce (19 percent), General Services Administration (6 percent), Department of Health and Human Services (13 percent), Department of the Interior (20 percent), International Communication Agency (74 percent), Navy (12 percent), Department of State (85 percent), Department of Transportation (4 percent), Treasury Department (8 percent), and Veteran's Administration (31 percent).

The federal government operates a number of special hiring programs for persons with disabilities, veterans, women, and Hispanics, as well as a high school and college student program and a summer employment program. Information on these programs is available from each Federal Job Information Center and from any personnel office of the Office of Personnel Management. Descriptions and contact information on them is also presented in the *Federal Personnel Office Directory* which is described later in this chapter.

## Classifications and compensation

The total federal workforce is divided into two major classification systems. White–collar professional, administrative, scientific, clerical, and technical employees are paid according to the *General Schedule (GS)*, which is graded from GS–1 to GS–18 and uniformly applied throughout the federal government.

These salary rates encompass most white–collar positions in the competitive service. Under the 1990 Federal Employees Pay Comparability Act, the President can issue special raises of up to eight percent to federal employees who live in cities with a particularly high cost of living. The act seeks to bring federal salaries in line with those of local industries on an area–by–area basis. As of this writing, higher salary rates have been approved for clerical workers in Washington, San Francisco, New York, and Boston as well as for some engineering positions.

Trade, labor, and other blue–collar workers—70 percent of whom are employed by the Departments of Army, Navy, and Air Force—are paid on the *Federal Wage System (WG)*. Grades range from WG–1 to WG–15 and the pay in each grade varies for each of 137 geographical areas. Altogether over 600,000 employees are classified as WG.

Other pay systems operate for the Senior Executive Service—management and executive positions at the GS–16 to GS–18 levels—the U.S. Postal Service, and a few other positions.

The following table gives the GS federal salary rates by grade and step for 1991.

## General schedule of federal salary rates by grade, 1991

| Grade Levels | One | Two | Three | Four | Five | Six | Seven | Eight | Nine | Ten |
|---|---|---|---|---|---|---|---|---|---|---|
| GS-1 | 11,015 | 11,383 | 11,749 | 12,114 | 12,482 | 12,697 | 13,058 | 13,422 | 13,439 | 13,776 |
| GS-2 | 12,385 | 12,679 | 13,090 | 13,439 | 13,590 | 13,990 | 14,390 | 14,790 | 15,190 | 15,590 |
| GS-3 | 13,515 | 13,966 | 14,417 | 14,868 | 15,319 | 15,770 | 16,221 | 16,672 | 17,123 | 17,574 |
| GS-4 | 15,171 | 15,677 | 16,183 | 16,689 | 17,195 | 17,701 | 18,207 | 18,713 | 19,219 | 19,725 |
| GS-5 | 16,973 | 17,539 | 18,105 | 18,671 | 19,237 | 19,803 | 20,369 | 20,935 | 21,501 | 22,067 |
| GS-6 | 18,919 | 19,550 | 20,181 | 20,812 | 21,443 | 22,074 | 22,705 | 23,336 | 23,967 | 24,598 |
| GS-7 | 21,023 | 21,724 | 22,425 | 23,126 | 23,827 | 24,528 | 25,229 | 25,930 | 26,631 | 27,332 |
| GS-8 | 23,284 | 24,060 | 24,836 | 25,612 | 26,388 | 27,164 | 27,940 | 28,716 | 29,492 | 30,268 |
| GS-9 | 25,717 | 26,574 | 27,431 | 28,288 | 29,145 | 30,002 | 30,859 | 31,716 | 32,573 | 33,430 |
| GS-10 | 28,322 | 29,266 | 30,210 | 31,154 | 32,098 | 33,042 | 33,986 | 34,930 | 35,874 | 36,818 |
| GS-11 | 31,116 | 32,153 | 33,190 | 34,227 | 35,264 | 36,301 | 37,338 | 38,375 | 39,412 | 40,449 |
| GS-12 | 37,294 | 38,537 | 39,780 | 41,023 | 42,266 | 43,509 | 44,752 | 45,995 | 47,238 | 48,481 |
| GS-13 | 44,348 | 45,826 | 47,304 | 48,782 | 50,260 | 51,738 | 53,216 | 54,694 | 56,172 | 57,650 |
| GS-14 | 52,406 | 54,153 | 55,900 | 57,647 | 59,394 | 61,141 | 62,888 | 64,635 | 66,382 | 68,129 |
| GS-15 | 61,643 | 63,698 | 65,753 | 67,808 | 69,863 | 71,918 | 73,973 | 76,028 | 78,083 | 80,138 |
| GS-16 | 72,298 | 74,708 | 77,118 | 79,528 | 81,396 | 82,697 | 85,060 | 87,424 | 89,424 | 89,784 |
| GS-17 | 83,032 | 85,800 | 88,568 | 91,336 | 94,104 | | | | | |
| GS-18 | 97,317 | | | | | | | | | |

## Job types and alternatives

The federal government hires individuals in five categories of jobs. These consist of:

↪ *Professional occupations:* These require knowledge of science or specialized education and training at a level equal to a bachelor's degree or higher. Examples include engineers, accountants, biologists, and chemists. Engineers (105,000) and nurses (40,000) are the largest professional groups with the Federal government.

↬ *Administrative occupations:* These require increasingly responsible experience or a general college level education. Examples include personnel specialists and administrative officers.

↬ *Technical occupations:* These are associated with a professional or administrative field, but they are nonroutine in nature. Examples include computer technician and electronic technician.

↬ *Clerical occupations:* These involve work which supports office, business, or fiscal operations. Examples include clerk–typist, mail and file clerk.

↬ *Other occupations:* All other occupations not classified as professional, administrative, technical, or clerical. Includes many blue–collar and trade occupations, such as painters, carpenters, and laborers.

↬

The federal government has as many different types of positions as the private sector. A complete list of positions would take up the remainder of this book. There are other books discussed at the end of this chapter that go into detail about each of the federal classifications. Here, we'll identify the major classifications.

The Office of Personnel Management, using a numerical code, classifies all General Schedule positions into 22 occupational groups and families. These include:

## Classification of GS positions

GS–0000    Miscellaneous Occupational Group

GS–0100    Social Science, Psychology, and Welfare Group

GS–0200    Personnel Management and Industrial Relations Group

GS–0300    General Administrative, Clerical, and Office Services Group

GS–0400    Biological Sciences Group

GS–0500    Accounting and Budget Group

GS–0600    Medical, Hospital, Dental, and Public Health Group

GS–0700    Veterinary Medical Science Group

GS–0800    Engineering and Architecture Group

GS–0900    Legal and Kindred Group

GS–1000    Information and Arts Group

GS–1100    Business and Industry Group

GS–1200    Copyright, Patent, and Trademark Group

GS–1300    Physical Sciences Group

GS–1400    Library and Archives Group

GS–1500    Mathematics and Statistics Group

GS–1600    Equipment, Facilities, and Services Group

GS–1700    Education Group

GS–1800    Investigation Group

GS–1900    Quality Assurance, Inspection, and Grading Group

GS–2000    Supply Group

GS–2100    Transportation Group

Each classification is further subdivided into additional classifications. For example, here are the 23 categories of the Investigation Group of occupations (GS–1800):

GS–1801    General Inspection, Investigation, and Compliance

GS–1802    Compliance Inspection and Support

GS–1810    General Investigating

GS–1811    Criminal Investigating

GS–1812    Game Law Enforcement

GS–1815    Air Safety Investigating

GS–1816    Immigration Inspection

GS–1822    Mine Safety and Health

GS–1825    Aviation Safety

GS–1831    Securities Compliance Examining

GS–1850    Agricultural Commodity Warehouse Examining

## SYLVIA                                    by Nicole Hollander

GS–1854     Alcohol, Tobacco, and Firearms Inspection

GS–1862     Consumer Safety Inspection

GS–1863     Food Inspection

GS–1864     Public Health Quarantine Inspection

GS–1884     Customs Patrol Officer

GS–1889     Import Specialist

GS–1890     Customs Inspection

GS–1894     Customs Entry and Liquidating

GS–1895     Customs Warehouse Officer

GS–1896     Border Patrol Agent

GS–1897     Customs Aid

GS–1898     Admeasurement

Wage System occupations are also classified into groups and families. These consist of 36 WG categories as follows.

## Classification of WG positions

WG–2500     Wire Communications Equipment Installation and Maintenance Family

WG–2600     Electronic Equipment Installation and Maintenance Family

| | |
|---|---|
| WG–2800 | Electrical Installation and Maintenance Family |
| WG–3100 | Fabric and Leather Work Family |
| WG–3300 | Instrument Work Family |
| WG–3400 | Machine Tool Work Family |
| WG–3500 | General Services and Support Work Family |
| WG–3600 | Structural and Finishing Work Family |
| WG–3700 | Metal Processing Family |
| WG–3800 | Metal Work Family |
| WG–3900 | Motion Picture, Radio, Television, and Sound Equipment Operation Family |
| WG–4000 | Lens and Crystal Work Family |
| WG–4100 | Painting and Paperhanging Family |
| WG–4200 | Plumbing and Pipefitting Family |
| WG–4300 | Pliable Materials Work Family |
| WG–4400 | Printing Family |
| WG–4600 | Woodwork Family |
| WG–4700 | General Maintenance Operations Work Family |
| WG–4800 | General Equipment Maintenance Family |
| WG–5000 | Plant and Animal Work Family |
| WG–5200 | Miscellaneous Occupations Family |
| WG–5300 | Industrial Equipment Maintenance Family |
| WG–5400 | Industrial Equipment Operation Family |
| WG–5700 | Transportation/Mobile Equipment Maintenance Family |
| WG–6500 | Ammunition, Explosives, and Toxic Materials Work Family |
| WG–6600 | Armament Work Family |
| WG–6900 | Warehousing and Stock Handling Family |
| WG–7000 | Packing and Processing Family |
| WG–7300 | Laundry, Dry Cleaning, and Pressing Family |
| WG–7400 | Food Preparation and Serving Family |
| WG–7600 | Personal Services Family |

WG–8200    Fluid Systems Maintenance Family

WG–8600    Engine Overhaul Family

WG–9000    Film Processing Family

The white–collar GS positions that employ the largest number of individuals include the following:

- Accountants and auditors (GS–510)
- Administrative assistants and officers (GS–341)
- Air traffic control specialists (GS–2152)
- Budget analysts or officers (GS–560)
- Civil rights analysts (GS–160)
- Computer specialists (GS–334)
- Contract representatives (GS–962)
- Contract and procurement specialists (GS–1102)
- Criminal investigators (GS–1810 and GS–1811)
- Economists (GS–110)
- Engineers (GS–800 series)
- Equipment specialists (GS–1670)
- Financial institution examiners (GS–570)
- Foresters (GS–460)
- Internal revenue officers (GS–1169)
- Lawyers (GS–905)
- Loan specialists (GS–1165)
- Management analysts (GS–343)
- Nurses (GS–610)
- Personnel management specialists (GS–201)
- Physicians (GS–602)
- Physicists (GS–1310)
- Production controllers (GS–1152)
- Program analysts (GS–345)
- Quality assurance specialists (GS–1910)
- Social insurance representatives and administrators (GS–105)
- Social insurance claims examiners (GS–993)
- Supply management specialists (GS–2003) and inventory management specialists (GS–2010)

- Teachers (GS–1710)
- Training instructors (GS–1712)

The blue–collar occupations, both under the GS and WG systems, which employ the largest number of individuals include the following.

- Accounting technicians (GS–525)
- Aircraft mechanics (WG–8852)
- Claims clerks (GS–998)
- Clerks (GS–300 and GS–500 series)
- Clerk–typists (GS–322)
- Computer operators (GS–332)
- Data transcribers (GS–356)
- Electricians (WG–2805)
- Electronics mechanics (WG–2604)
- Engineering aids and technicians (GS–802)
- Financial administration workers (GS–503)
- Firefighters and other fire protection workers (GS–081)
- Food service workers (GS–7408)
- Forestry technicians and smoke jumpers (GS–462)
- Heavy mobile equipment mechanics (WG–5803)
- Janitors or porters (GS–3566)
- Laborers (WG–3502)
- Machinists (WG–3414)
- Mail and file clerks (GS–305)
- Maintenance mechanics (WG–4749)
- Medical technicians (GS–600)
- Nursing assistants (GS–621)
- Personnel clerks and assistants (GS–203)
- Pipefitters (WG–4205)
- Reporting stenographers, shorthand reporters, clerk stenographers (GS–312)
- Secretaries (GS–318)
- Sheet metal mechanics (WG–3806)
- Supply clerks and technicians (GS–2005)

- Tax accountants and examiners (GS–592)

If you are interested in detailed information on each of these occupational groups, including the minimum qualifications as well as the typical duties and responsibilities for each position, you should examine copies of the federal government's standard personnel reference books: *Handbook X–118: Qualification Standards for Positions Under the General Schedule,* and *Position–Classification Standards.* Both books are available through the Federal Job Information Centers (FJICs) identified in Chapter 3, federal personnel offices, and federal agency libraries. Any serious federal job seeker should review these documents before completing a SF–171. These documents give the details, including the proper language for communicating qualifications, of positions that agency personnel must adhere to when evaluating SF–171s.

For example, the "KSAPs" (job elements consisting of knowledge, skills, abilities, and personal characteristics) you include on your SF–171 in reference to a specific vacancy announcement are critical in the evaluation process. Since the language of KSAPs is found in the *Handbook X–118,* you should consult this book before presenting your qualifications on the SF–171 in reference to the KSAPs. Consequently, the closer you can bring your SF–171 in line with the requirements of positions and the language of evaluators, the better should be your position in the federal hiring process.

The Department of Labor's *The Dictionary of Occupational Titles* and *The Occupational Outlook Handbook* (Superintendent of Documents, U.S. Government Printing Office, Washington, DC 20402–9325; phone: 202/783–3238; $17/paperback, stock number 029–001–03022–3) and publications and handouts issued by the Office of Personnel Management and personnel offices of individual agencies also include information on these positions.

## Applications and special occupational categories

Because the federal hiring process is in transition, you should contact OPM, a Federal Job Information Center, or the agency for details concerning whether or not tests are required for a particular position and to whom you should send your application—directly to OPM or to the agency.

The application process will differ for different categories of positions, and especially for recent college graduates seeking entry-level positions with the federal government. Five categories of positions have special application procedures.

## Administrative Careers With America (ACWA)

The Administrative Careers With America program covers nearly 100 different entry-level administrative and professional occupations which are filled through one of two applications methods—a written examination or an application based on scholastic achievement as reflected by an applicant's grade point average. This program is especially appropriate for recent college graduates and other qualified entry-level job seekers. Positions in this category start at the GS-5 and GS-7 levels. Individuals can apply for jobs under this program within nine months of graduation, or upon completion of qualifying academic courses or three years' work experience.

Written examinations under the ACWA program are given in six different occupational groups:
- Group I: Health, Safety, and Environmental
- Group II: Writing and Public Information
- Group III: Business, Finance, and Management
- Group IV: Personnel, Administration, and Computers
- Group V: Benefits Review, Tax, and Legal
- Group VI: Law Enforcement and Investigation

The largest number of job opportunities are in Groups III, IV, V, and VI.

Individuals can also apply for entry-level administrative or professional positions based on their scholastic record rather than take an exam. The scholastic record must demonstrate a GPA of 3.5 or higher on a 4.0 scale, or the individual must have graduated in the upper 10 percent of their class.

The Administrative Careers With America program also includes 16 entry-level positions which do not require a written test. However, they do require special college course work. These positions include:

Archeology                    Geography

| | |
|---|---|
| Archival work | History |
| Community planning | International relations |
| Economics | Manpower research/analysis |
| Educational programming | Museum management |
| Foreign affairs | Psychology |
| General anthropology | Social science |
| General education/training | Sociology |

Applications for these non-test positions can be submitted to a local OPM Area Office only after the Area Office announces vacancies which are limited in number. Applications are then reviewed and rated based upon an evaluation of education and work experience or meeting GPA/scholastic requirements.

For information on entry-level opportunities available under the Administrative Careers With America program, contact one of OPM's Area Offices, a Federal Job Information Center listed in Chapter 3, or call the Career American College Hotline at 900/990-9200 (40¢ per minute charged).

## Senior Executive Service

About 8,000 federal employees are part of this high-level service. While they do face the risk of transfer to a position far from home, they can earn outstanding salaries if their work is superior. These officials focus on broader responsiblities like long-range planning, general oversight, agency-wide issues, and more contact with high-level officials in the private sector.

Agencies fill SES postiions in accord with guidelines issued by the Office of Personnel Management. An agency would nominate a candidate for SES whose qualifications are then certified by a review board. To be certified for SES, you must meet at least one of three criteria:

☞ Demonstrated executive experience;

☞ Participated succesfully in a developmental program approved by the Office of Personnel Management; or

☞ Posess special or unique qualities that suggest success as an executive.

To learn more about SES, contact the personnel office for an agency for which you wish to work or the Office of Personnel Management. Ask to see a copy of *A Guide to Executive Qualifications* published by the Office of Personnel Management.

## Specialized occupations

Entry into certain specialized occupations at the GS–5 and GS–7 levels only requires completion of certain college–level courses and a written application. These occupations include:

- Accountant/Auditor
- Biologist
- Engineer
- Forester
- Mathematical Science
- Physical Science

For application information relevant to these specialized occupations, call the Career America College Hotline (1–900/990–9200).

## Public safety occupations

Requirements for entry–level (GS–5 and GS–7) public safety occupations include a bachelor's degree or equivalent experience as well as a written test. Occupations included in this category are:

- Air Traffic Controller (employed with the Federal Aviation Administration)
- Deputy U.S. Marshal (employed with the U.S. Marshals Service, Department of Justice)
- Treasury Enforcement Agent (employed with the Internal Revenue Service, Customs Service, and the Bureau of Alcohol, Tobacco, and Firearms in the Department of Treasury)
- U.S. Park Police Officer (employed with the National Capital Region, National Park Service, Department of the Interior)

## Technical occupations

Positions in this category provide support and technical assistance to professionals. Entry requirements include practical knowledge of specialized subjects and two years of technical experience, or a combination of two years of work experience and education above high school, or a two–year degree. A written test may be required. Most of these jobs start at the GS–4 grade level. For information on these positions, contact one of OPM's Area Offices or a Federal Job Information Center listed in Chapter 3, or the agency itself.

## Clerical and administrative support positions

Representing the largest group of government employees, most clerical and administrative support positions start at the GS–2 grade level. They usually require a high school diploma. Given the increased demand for these employees, the hiring process has been streamlined to the point where some individuals can be hired within 48 hours of taking a qualifying test and submitting their application for these positions. For information on positions in this category, contact one of OPM's Area Offices or a Federal Job Information Center listed in Chapter 3.

### Job search strategies

Successful federal job applicants know how to cut through this somewhat confusing and frustrating hiring process. What separates them from unsuccessful candidates is their:

- ✌ Knowledge of the details of individual agencies, personnel procedures, and job vacancies. This knowledge enables them to quickly cut through what may appear to others to be a confusing and frustrating process.
- ✌ Skill in developing and marketing a good application (SF–171 and other documents) that clearly communicates their experience, qualifications, and strengths to agencies and hiring officials.
- ✌ Patience, persistence, and drive in seeing the process through to the end.

✌ Knowing where to find the job vacancies—a skill the remainder of this chapter will help you develop.

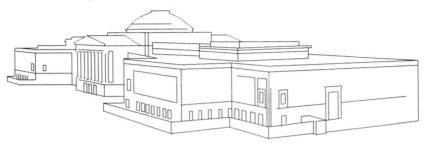

You should begin your job search with a thorough understanding of both the formal and informal hiring processes in the federal government. While you can get a job by only following the formal system of responding to vacancy announcements, taking tests, and completing application forms, your odds will improve considerably if you also pursue jobs in the informal system of prospecting, networking, informational interviews, and referrals—as well as finding job vacancies with the tools described in this chapter. The last portion of this chapter describes a number of books that will help you with even more with the federal hiring process.

## Sources of federal jobs

There are several ways to find available federal professional and non-professional positions. The first two, consulting periodicals and directly contacting a federal agency's personnel office, are the most productive and are discussed in detail later in this chapter. The others are treated immediately below in their entirety.

❑ **Periodicals.** There are a number of periodicals that carry listings of federal government job openings. These may include both Competitive Service Jobs and Excepted Service and PAC positions.

❑ **Federal Agency's Personnel Office.** Contacting a federal agency's personnel office directly or using its job hotline to learn of job openings is the most sure–fire way to learn of all current openings with a department including Excepted and PAC positions.

❑ **Newspaper Advertisements.** The advertisements for federal jobs that appear in local newspapers are generally for professional positions in the geographic area the paper serves. They usually appear in the business section. National newspapers like *The New York Times* (229 W. 43rd St., New York, NY 10036; phone: 212/556–1234), *Washington Post* (1150 15th St. NW, Washington, DC 20071; phone: 202/334–6000), *The Wall Street Journal* (420 Lexington Ave., New York, NY 10170; phone: 212/808–6700), and *U.S.A. Today* (1000 Wilson Blvd., Arlington, VA 22209; phone: 703/276–5200) are often good sources of federal job ads.

❑ **College Career Planning and Placement Offices.** If you are in college, check with your school's placement office to see if it posts vacancy notices from any federal agencies and if federal recruiters interview on campus. Other campus offices worth checking for specialized information on federal jobs include: Minority, Veteran, and Handicapped Affairs; Cooperative Education, Internship, and Student Employment offices; the Financial Aid Office; and the Counseling Center.

The OPM's regional offices distribute to colleges and universities a publication called *Career America News* which furnishes information about new federal hiring procedures and "hot" career opportunities in the federal government.

❑ **Office of Personnel Management.** The OPM's central office is aware of virtually all openings at the different federal agencies. In addition, local OPM offices should have listings of all available federal positions. You can locate offices of the OPM in the federal government section of local telephone directories or in some of the federal government directories identified later in this chapter.

❏ **Federal Job Information Centers (FJIC).** These centers function as the regional and subregional offices of the U.S. Office of Personnel Management. They post the current weekly Federal Job Opportunity List which includes both Competitive Service positions and Excepted jobs. Contact the nearest center to see job titles of available federal jobs in your area and to obtain full job announcements and required application forms.

Unfortunately, many FJICs are "self–service" centers where you'll never see nor speak to a government employee, living or dead. Announcements of federal job openings are posted on the wall. Applicants complete an address label and note the job number for which they'd like to apply. Slip the label through the mail slot and you'll receive a job application and full job description by mail within a few days. Although every FJIC has a telephone number, some answer it only during limited hours. The addresses and telephone numbers for FJICs are provided in the state–by–state listings in Chapter 3.

The FJIC in Washington, DC has a self–service telephone system (202/606–2700) you can call anytime to learn the status of your application or test results (code 550), order forms or announcements (code: 280), learn about part–time and job sharing positions (code: 410), and much more. Code 000 will allegedly get you a live "information specialist" to answer your questions on weekdays between 8 a.m. and 4 p.m. Washington time. Patricia Wood's book, *The 171 Reference Book,* discussed at the end of this chapter, includes a directory for the 30+ different information sources on this phone line.

❏ **State Job Service Offices.** Serious job seekers should visit state–operated Job Service Centers which are supposed to carry all the job listings available at the nearest FJIC plus state and often local government jobs—and you'll usually get to talk to a live employee behind the counter. Job Service Centers are discussed in Chapter 3 and identified in the state–by–state listings.

The remainder of this chapter describes the privately–published periodicals that list available federal positions and a privately–operated service that tells you which federal jobs you are qualified for. It also guides you to the personnel offices of federal departments to learn of job openings, and presents a detailed review of several books that help you weave your way through the complex and often confusing federal job application process.

## Sources of federal government vacancies

The federal government does not publish any lists of all available federal jobs. However, several private concerns publish magazines and newspapers which are the most timely inter-agency collections of federal openings for professional and technical, trades, labor, and support staff.

Remember that many of the periodicals and job services presented in Chapter 2 also include federal positions, primarily professional. See this book's index for listings under "Federal jobs." The Job Service Offices and Federal Job Information Centers noted in the state–by–state listings in Chapter 3 also carry federal government jobs. However, their lists of federal vacancies are rarely as complete as those offered by the publications described below or as the information you will receive directly from a federal agency's personnel office.

## Job openings

*Federal Jobs Digest* (Breakthrough Publications, P.O. Box 594, Millwood, NY 10546; phones: 800/824–5000, 914/762–5111) bi-weekly, $29/three–month subscription, $54/six–month subscription, $110/annual subscription (U.S.), $129/Canada, $160/elsewhere. Copies are available for inspection at the many public libraries and community colleges that subscribe. You'll actually find as many as 30,000 open federal positions listed in here by hiring agency under these general headings: National Office of Personnel Management (OPM) Announcements, Regional OPM Announce-ments, Overseas Job Vacancies, Veterans Administration Jobs, Federal Job Vacancies Nationwide, Senior Executive Service, and schedules for U.S. Postal Exams. Also listed are the addresses for the personnel offices of all Veterans Administration Hospitals. For each of the 20,000 + federal jobs located in the nation's capital and throughout the nation that are listed in each issue, *Federal Jobs Digest* gives the job title, grade, closing date, job announcement number, and application address. A number of more detailed

**TRAVELS WITH FARLEY**

Reprinted by permission of Phil Frank. Copyright © 1978.

display ads also appear in each issue. Includes Wage Grade (WG) and General Schedule (GS) jobs.

*Federal Career Opportunities* (Federal Research Service, 243 Church St., NW, Vienna, VA 22180; phone: 703/281–0200) biweekly, $38/three-month subscription, $75/six–month subscription, $160/annual subscription. Each issue provides information on about 4,000 federal job vacancies from GS–5 to Senior Executive levels.

*Federal Times* (6883 Commercial Dr., Springfield, VA 22159; phone: 703/750–8920) weekly; $48/annual subscription, $24/six–month subscription. Typical issue lists very brief descriptions of several hundred federal positions including the military. Jobs listed under "Jobs." Lists vacancies at GS–7 and above.

*Federal Research Report* (Business Publishers, Inc., 951 Pershing Dr., Silver Spring, MD 20910; phone: 301/587–6700) weekly, $160.50/annual subscription. All eight pages of this newsletter feature information on federal grants and contracts for research and development.

*Spotlight* (College Placement Council, 62 Highland Ave., Bethlehem, PA 18042; phones: 800/544–5272, 215/868–1421) 21 issues/year, $65/annual nonmember subscription, included in membership package. Under "Jobwire" there are usually five to ten positions including positions for personnel directors and career counselors in the federal government.

*VA Practitioner* (Cahners Publishing Company, 44 Cook St., Denver, CO 80206–5191; phone: 303/388–4511) 14 issues/year, $40/annual subscription (U.S.), $80/Canada and Mexico, $80/elsewhere (surface mail), $140/air mail. From five to ten ads for physician and nurse positions at Veterans Administration hospitals appear under "Classifieds."

*Business and Industry Bulletin* (Career Development and Placement Services, Campus Box 14, Emporia State University, Emporia, KS 66801; phone: 316/343–5407) weekly, $56.57/annual subscription, $31.43/six–month subscription. This three–page newsletter includes federal government positions.

*Science Education News* (Directorate for Education and Human Resources, American Association for the Advancement of Science, 1333 H St., NW, Washington, DC 20005; phone: 202/326–6620) 10 issues/year, free. Under "Opportunities," this newsletter frequently reports about federal agencies that need teachers and researchers.

*1992 Summer Employment Directory of the United States* (Petersons Guides, PO Box 2123, Princeton, NJ 08543–2123; phone: 800/338–3282) $14.95. Published annually in the autumn. Its 200+ pages list over 75,000 summer job openings at resorts, camps, amusement parks, national parks, and government, particularly federal positions with regional offices of the Department of Labor, and in the nation's capital with the Environmental Protection Agency.

*New Internships in the Federal Government* (Graduate Group, 86 Norwood Rd., West Hartford, CT 06117; phones: 203/232–3100, 203/236–5570) $27.50, published annually. This directory included internships and some permanent job openings.

*Internships in Congress* (Graduate Group, 86 Norwood Rd., West Hartford, CT 06117; phones: 203/232–3100, 203/236–5570) $27.50, published annually.

Also see several of the periodicals that focus on federal positions which are listed under "Legal services and court administration" in Chapter 2. Also look under "Federal jobs" in the Index of this book.

## Job services

*Federal Job Matching Service* (Breakthrough Publications, P.O. Box 594, Millwood, NY 10546; phones: 800/824–5000, 914/762–5111) $30 fee, $25 fee for subscribers to *Federal Jobs Digest* (submit address label with your order); fee refunded if applicant found unqualified for any federal job. Service matches candidate's education and experience to federal job requirements and gives the candidate a list of the federal job titles (with official job description and list of qualifications) and grade levels that offer the best chance of getting a federal job. First obtain the very thorough "Federal Job Questionnaire" from this service. Return the completed form with your check to Breakthrough Publications. Include any of the following additional items which you feel may be pertinent to evaluating your background: resume, school transcript (if you received a degree within the last five years), professional licenses or certificates, and/or job narrative or history. Do *not* send any original material since this supplementary material will not be returned to you. Expect a response within three weeks. Note: This service identifies jobs for which, in its judgment, you are qualified. You must still consult the various sources of federal job listings to determine if there are any open positions.

*kiNexus* (Information Kinetics, Inc., Suite 560, 640 N. LaSalle St., Chicago, IL 60610; phones: 800/828–0422, 312/642–7560) $24.95/annual fee, free if you are a student at one of the 1,500+ universities that subscribe to this service—check with your school's placement office. This is an online resume database service for college students and graduates with up to five years work experience. You complete their resume form and kiNexus puts your information into the computer. Federal government agencies that subscribe to kiNexus, such as the Internal Revenue Service, can ask kiNexus to conduct searches to identify candidates for specific positions or can conduct their own searches since the database is online. The potential employer is responsible for contacting job candidates for an interview. As of this writing, over 250,000 college students and recent graduates have their resumes in this system.

# Contacting federal personnel offices

One of the most productive sources of job openings is the main personnel office, in the District of Columbia, of the agencies for which you wish to work. Not only do they have the most up–to–date job openings, but they can also give you the appropriate application forms, full job announcements, and additional information about the department and job itself.

To help you contact these personnel offices, the *Government Job Finder* includes a list of telephone numbers for the main personnel office of over 200 federal agencies. If an agency has more than one personnel office, the list includes the phone number for the director of personnel. Her staff will direct you to the proper personnel office.

Some agencies also maintain regional or district personnel offices around the country. To locate them, call the main personnel office in Washington, D.C. for a list or for the location of the one nearest you. Alternatively, you can find these numbers in many of the directories of federal departments and agencies described later in this chapter and in the blue pages of the local telephone directory of the city in which the office is located.

A number of agencies operate 24–hour job hotlines with tape recorded messages that list the latest job vacancies as well as eligibility status and instructions for submitting an application. In the following list, these job hotlines are indicated by a black dot (•), or "bullet" as the printing industry calls it. Nearly all the phone numbers in this list are for the central personnel office of the federal agency. In a few cases, the central switchboard number is given because no separate personnel office number was available.

**Phone numbers for central personnel offices
of selected federal government agencies**

**The area code is 202 unless otherwise noted**
• *indicates job hotline phone number*

## Agency                                    Telephone Number

ACTION                                                      634–9263
                                                         • 634–1000
                                                     TDD: 634–9256
Administrative Office of U.S. Courts                 • 301/443–2262
Agency for Toxic Substances and Disease Registry      404/639–3615
Agriculture, Department of                                 447–5626
                                                         • 447–5300
Agricultural Research Service                          301/344–1124
Animal and Plant Health Inspection Service                447–2511
Army Corps of Engineers                                   272–0720
Bureau of Alcohol, Tobacco, and Firearms                  566–7321
Bureau of Engraving and Printing                          447–9840
Bureau of Indian Affairs                                  343–5547
Bureau of Land Management                                 343–3193
Bureau of Mines                                           634–1004
Bureau of Public Debt                                     447–9798
                                                         • 447–1407
Bureau of Prisons                                         724–3072
Bureau of Reclamation                                     208–4662
Bureau of the Census                                  317/358–3323
                                                     • 301/763–5537
Center for Disease Control                            404–639–3615
Central Intelligence Agency                           703/351–2141
                                                     • 703/351–2028
Commerce, Department of                                 • 377–5138
Commission on Civil Rights                                376–8364
Commodity Futures Trading Commission                      254–3275
Consumer Product Safety Commission                    301/492–6500
Courts, Administrative Office of U.S.                      633–6116

|                                                                        | 633–6061 |
|------------------------------------------------------------------------|----------|
| Defense, Department of                                                 |          |
|   Air Force                                                   | 800/847–0108 |
|   Army (jobs in District of Columbia area)                   | 325–2130 |
|   Navy                                                       | 545–6700 |
| Defense Communications Agency                                          | 692–2783 |
|                                                                        | • 703/746–1724 |
| Defense Contract Audit Agency                                          | 274–6785 |
| Defense Logistics Agency                                               | 800/458–7903 |
| Drug Enforcement Administration                                        | 307–4000 |
| Education, Department of (jobs in District of Columbia area)           | 732–5559 |
| Employment and Training Administration                                 | 535–8744 |
| Energy, Department of                                                  | 586–8563 |
|                                                                        | • 586–4333 |
| Environmental Protection Agency                                        | 382–3305 |
|                                                                        | • 755–5055 |
| Equal Employment Opportunity Commission                               | 663–4306 |
|                                                                        | TDD: 663–7025 |
| Export–Import Bank of the U.S.                                         | 566–8834 |
| Farm Credit Bureau                                                     | 800/556–8870 |
| Farmers Home Administration                                            | 382–1056 |
| Federal Aviation Administration                                        | 276–8007 |
| Federal Bureau of Investigation                                        | 324–3000 |
| Federal Communications Commission                                      | 632–7106 |
|                                                                        | TDD: 632–6999 |
| Federal Deposit Insurance Corporation                                  | 898–8890 |
| Federal Election Commission                                            | 800/424–9530 |
| Federal Emergency Management Agency                                    | 646–4040 |
|                                                                        | • 646–4041 |
| Federal Housing Finance Board                                          | 408–2576 |
| Federal Labor Relations Authority                                      | 382–0751 |
| Federal Maritime Commission                                           | 523–5733 |
| Federal Mediation and Conciliation Service                            | 653–5290 |
| Federal Regulatory Commission                                         | • 357–8791 |
| Federal Reserve System                                                | 800/448–4894 |
|                                                                        | • 452–3038 |
| Financial Management Service                                           | 287–0834 |
| Food and Drug Administration                                          | 301/443–1970 |
|                                                                        | • 301/443–1969 |

| | |
|---|---|
| Food and Nutrition Service | 703/756–3276 |
| Foreign Agricultural Service | 387–1587 |
| Forest Service | 703/235–2730 |
| General Accounting Office | 275–6092 |
|   (GS 13 & above) | • 275–6361 |
|   (GS 2–12) | • 275–6017 |
| General Services Administration | 566–1814 |
| | **TDD:** 708–5300 |
| Government Printing Office | 275–1137 |
| Health and Human Services, Department of | 245–6560 |
| Health, Office of Asst. Secretary | • 443–1986 |

Mother Goose and Grim reprinted by permission of MGM L&M
and Grimmy, Inc. Copyright 1989. All rights reserved.

| | |
|---|---|
| Health Care Financing Administration | 301/966–5505 |
| Housing and Urban Development, Department of | 708–0408 |
| Human Development Services, Office of | 245–6216 |
| Immigration and Naturalization Service | 786–3704 |
| | • 514–4301 |
| Indian Health Service | 301/443–6520 |
| Interior, Department of | 787–1414 |
| Internal Revenue Service | 566–3617 |
| | • 535–5384 |
| International Trade Administration | 377–3071 |
|   (jobs in U.S.) | |
|   (international positions) | 377–3133 |
| International Trade Commission | 252–1651 |
| Interstate Commerce Commission | 275–7288 |
| Justice, Department of | 633–4615 |
| Labor, Department of | 523–6666 |
| | • 523–6646 |

| | |
|---|---|
| Library of Congress | 707–5620 |
| | TDD: 523–6769 |
| | • 707–5295 |
| Marine Corps | • 697–7474 |
| Merit Systems Protection Board | 653–5916 |
| | TDD: 653–8896 |
| Minerals Management Service | 208–3983 |
| | • 703/787–1402 |
| National Aeronautics and Space Administration | 453–8478 |
| National Archives and Records Administration | 800/634–4898 |
| National Capital Planning Commission | 724–0206 |
| National Capitol Park Service | • 619–7111 |
| National Credit Union Administration | 682–9720 |
| National Endowment for the Arts | 682–5405 |
| National Endowment for the Humanities | 786–0415 |
| National Gallery of Art | • 842–6282 |
| National Institute of Health | 301/496–2404 |
| | • 301/496–9541 |
| National Labor Relations Board | 254–9044 |
| | TDD: 634–1669 |
| National Oceanic and Atmospheric Administration | 301/443–8834 |
| National Park Service | 343–4648 |
| National Science Foundation | 357–9681 |
| | TDD: 357–7492 |
| | • 357–7735 |
| | • 800/628–1487 |
| National Security Agency | 800/255–8415 |
| National Transportation Safety Board | 382–6717 |
| National Weather Service (Southern Region) | • 303–497–3950 |
| Naval Submarine Base (King Bay, GA) | • 800/544–1707 |
| Naval Undersea Warfare Engineering Station | • 206–396–2443 |
| Nuclear Regulatory Commission | 301/492–4661 |
| Occupational Safety and Health Administration | 523–8013 |
| Office of the Comptroller of the Currency | 447–1800 |
| Office of Inspector General | 366–2677 |
| Office of Management and Budget (OMB) | 395–3765 |
| Office of Personnel Management (OPM) | 632–2424 |
| | TDD: 606–2118 |
| OPM Job Information Center | • 653–8468 |
| Overseas Private Investment Corporation | 457–7200 |

| | |
|---|---|
| Office of U.S. Trade Representative | 395–3230 |
| Panama Canal Commission | 634–6441 |
| Patent and Trademark Office | 703/557–3631 |
| | • 703/538–3360 |
| Peace Corps | |
| (Professional staff) | 800/424–8580, ext 255 |
| | 254–5170 |
| | • 800/424–8580, ext 214 |
| (Overseas volunteer) | 800/424–8580, ext 93 |
| Pension Benefit Guaranty Corporation | 778–8800 |
| Postal Rate Commission | 789–6800 |
| Postal Service | 268–3646 |
| President, Executive Office of the | 456–1414 |
| Public Health Service (Civil Service positions) | 301/443–1986 |
| Railroad Retirement Board | 312–751–4580 |
| Securities and Exchange Commission | 272–2519 |
| Selective Service System | 724–0435 |
| Small Business Administration | 800/368–5855 |
| | • 287–3102 |
| Smithsonian Institution | |
| (Federal openings) | 357–1450 |
| (Non–federal openings) | 357–1452 |
| Social Security Administration | 301/965–4506 |
| Soil Conservation Service | 447–2631 |
| State, Department of | TDD: 647–7256 |
| (foreign service officers) | 647–4000 |
| (foreign service specialist) | 703/875–7247 |
| | • 703/875–7109 |
| (Civil Service) | 647–7152 |
| | • 647–7284 |
| Tennessee Valley Authority | 615/632–3341 |
| Training and Doctrine Command (TRADOC) | • 804/727–3336 |
| Transportation, Department of | 366–9394 |
| Treasury, Department of | 566–5411 |
| | • 447–1407 |
| Treasury, U.S. Mint | • 415–744–9364 |
| U.S. Arms Control and Disarmament Agency | 647–8677 |
| U.S. Coast Guard | 267–1706 |
| U.S. Customs Service | 634–5025 |
| U.S. Fish and Wildlife | 343–6104 |
| U.S. Geological Survey | 703/648–6131 |

|  |  |
|---|---|
|  | • 703/648–7676 |
|  | TDD: 703/6487788 |
| U.S. House of Representatives | 226–6731 |
| U.S. Information Agency | 485–2618 |
|  | • 619–4539 |
| U.S. International Development | 663–1449 |
| Cooperation Agency |  |
| U.S. Marshals Service |  |
| (administrative positions) | 307–9600 |
| (Deputy U.S. Marshal) | 307–9400 |
| U.S. Mint | 634–2133 |
| U.S. Savings Bond Division | 634–5368 |
| U.S. Secret Service | 535–5800 |
| U.S. Senate | 224–9167 |
| Veterans Administration | 800/368–5629 |
| Veterans' Affaurs | 233–3771 |
|  | TDD: 233–3225 |
| Veterans Affairs Data Processing Center (Texas) | • 512–482–7441 |
| (Department of Medicine and Surgery) | 233–2300 |
| (Department of Veteran's Benefits) | 233–5210 |
| Voice of America | 485–8117 |
|  | • 619–0909 |

## Directories of federal agencies

An extensive array of federal agency directories will also help you locate the personnel offices of any federal department and, in most cases, give you very valuable background information before you apply for a specific federal job. They are well–worth consulting. Public libraries tend to have at least one of these directories on the reference shelves.

The single best source for addresses and phone numbers of federal personnel offices continues to be the *Federal Personnel Office Directory* (Federal Reports, Inc., Suite 408, 1010 Vermont Ave., NW, Washington, DC 20005; phone: 202/393–3311; 1990–1991 edition: $20/individuals, $27.50/institutions, plus $2 postage) which provides information on over 1,500 U.S. government hiring offices throughout the country and overseas, as well as a detailed description of the federal employment system and cross–references by state and agency. It also includes full information, including agency coordinator lists, about special federal recruit-ment programs for persons with disabilities, women, minorities, veterans, and summer employment. Information on application procedures is also included.

An essential source when you don't know exactly what federal job you want to seek, is *The Almanac of American Government Jobs and Careers* by Ronald and Caryl Krannich ($14.95, 1991; available from Planning/Communications; see the catalog in the back of this book). In its 392 pages, this book gives detailed information about virtually every federal department, commission, and agency in all three branches, including occupational titles, college majors, and the address and phone of the personnel office official to contact.

Other sources of value include:

*Federal Yellow Book* (Monitor Publishing, Co., 104 Fifth Ave., New York, NY 10011; phone: 212/627–4140) quarterly, $175/annual subscription. Thanks to its frequency of publication, this is the most up–to–date of all the directories of federal departments and agencies. It's 800 pages give you details on over 35,000 top decision makers in the White House, Executive Office of the President, and all federal departments and agencies, including regional offices.

*Washington Information Directory* (Congres-sional Quarterly, Inc., 1414 22nd St., NW, Washington, DC 20037; phones: 800/673–2730, 202/887–8500) published each June, $69.95. 1084 pages. Divides the federal gov-ernment into 17 broad subject catego-ries and furnishes detailed information on each federal department and agency. Also provides details on regional federal information sources, non–governmental organizations in the Washington area, and Con-gressional committees and subcommittees.

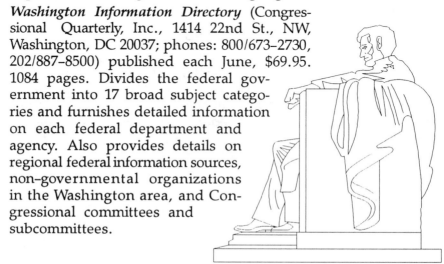

*Federal Staff Directory* (Staff Directories, Ltd., P.O. Box 62, Mt. Vernon, VA 22121; phone: 703/739-0900) $59 per volume. Published every January (volume 1, hardcover) and August (volume 2, paperback) which updates volume one. Lists 30,000 key decision makers and staff for all federal departments and agencies, including the White House. Includes personnel departments. Also contains biographies of 2,400 key federal executives and senior staff. Keyword index.

*Congressional Staff Directory* (Staff Directories, Ltd., P.O. Box 62, Mt. Vernon, VA 22121; phone: 703/739-0900) $59 per volume. Published every April (volume 1, hardcover) and September (volume 2, paperback) which updates volume one. Complete listing of members of Congressional committees, subcommittees, and staffs and the 20,000 people who make Congress work. Includes biographies of 3,200 key staff. Keyword index.

*Congressional Staff Directory on DISK* (Staff Directories, Ltd., P.O. Box 62, Mt. Vernon, VA 22121; phone: 703/739-0900) $250, released in May. An effective tool to track a Congressman, her staff, and home district, this database and program include a zip code locator, print labels feature, user file for customized data, and the ability to export data in ASCII format for use with most word processors. Includes all 16,000 names and addresses as they appear in the *Congressional Staff Directory*.

*Congressional Yellow Book* (Monitor Publishing, Co., 104 Fifth Ave., New York, NY 10011; phone: 212/627-4140) quarterly, $175/annual subscription. Over 700 pages in each edition give you detailed information on Congressional staff positions, committees and subcommittees, top staff in Congressional support agencies like the Congressional Budget Office, General Accounting Office, and Library of Congress.

*Washington 91* (Columbia Books, 1212 New York Ave., NW, Suite 300, Washington, DC 20005; phone: 202/898-0662) $60, published annually. Nearly 600 pages of addresses, phone numbers, and information including chapters on the federal government, international affairs, national issues, and community affairs. Also includes chapters on the media, business, national associations, labor unions, law firms, medicine and health, foundations and philanthropy, science and policy research, education, religion, cultural institutions, clubs, and community affairs.

*The Capitol Source: The Who's Who, What, Where in Washington* (National Journal, Inc., 1730 M St., NW, Washington, DC 20036; phones: 800/424–2921, 202/862–0644) $30. Published in April and November, this directory includes names, addresses, and phone numbers for the District of Columbia. Also included are corporations, interest groups, think tanks, labor unions, real estate, financial institutions, trade and professional organizations, law firms, political consultants, advertising and public relations firms, private clubs, and the media. All entries are also available on computer diskette. Call 202/857–1469 for information.

*Federal Executive Directory* (Carroll Publishing Co., 1058 Thomas Jefferson St., NW, Washington, DC 20077–0007; phone: 202/333–8620) updated and published in full six times a year, $155/annual subscription. 535 pages. Contains more than 86,000 entries in both the executive and legislative branches, including Cabinet depart-  ments, federal administrative agencies, Congressional committee members and staff, areas of responsibility for legal and administrative assistants. Features alphabetical, organizational for congress and executive branches, and keyword indexes.

*Federal Executive Directory Annual* (Carroll Publishing Co., 1058 Thomas Jefferson St., NW, Washington, DC 20077–0007; phone: 202/333–8620) published annually, $117. This is essentially an annual edition of the *Federal Executive Directory* discussed immediately above.

*Federal Regional Executive Directory* (Carroll Publishing Co., 1058 Thomas Jefferson St., NW, Washington, DC 20077–0007; phone: 202/333–8620) updated and published in full twice a year, $110/annual subscription. 390 pages. Over 65,000 entries of non–Washington based executive managers in Cabinet departments, Congress, the courts, and administrative agencies. Includes alphabetical, organizational, geographical (city within state), and keyword indexes.

*Federal Organization Service/Civil* (Carroll Publishing Co., 1058 Thomas Jefferson St., NW, Washington, DC 20077-0007; phone: 202/333-8620) updated every six weeks, $450/annual subscription. Delineates the complex infrastructure of the civil branch of the federal government, with nearly 140 fold-out charts identifying who's who in over 1,600 departments and offices. The direct-dial phone numbers for more than 10,000 federal employees are given.

*Federal Statistical Specialists: The Official Directory of Names and Numbers* (Oryx Press, 4041 N. Central, Phoenix, AZ 85012-3997; phone: 800/279-6799) $37.50, 160 pages, November 1991. Lists federal employees' addresses, phone, and fax numbers by department, agency, or organization.

*Federal Fast Finder* (Washington Researchers Publishing, 2612 P St., NW, Washington, DC 20007; phone: 202/333-3533) $30, published each May. This is a key word telephone directory to over 1,500 federal government departments, agencies, and electronic bulletin boards operated by the federal government.

*Directory of Military Bases in the U.S.* (Oryx Press, 4041 N. Central, Phoenix, AZ 85012-3997; phone: 800/279-6799) $95, 1990, 208 pages. Details on over 700 bases in all branches of the military including both FTS and Autovon main telephone numbers.

*Federal Managers' Association Membership Directory* (FMA, 1000 16th St., NW, Suite 701, Washington, DC 20036; phone: 202/778-1500) available only to members, $50/annual dues. Published each month, this directory guides you to managers and supervisors who work for the federal government.

*International Military Club Executive Association Membership Directory* (IMCEA, 1438 Duke St., Alexandria, VA 22314; phone: 703/548-0093) $200, published each May.

*Federal Organization Service/Military* (Carroll Publishing Co., 1058 Thomas Jefferson St., NW, Washington, DC 20077-0007; phone: 202/333-8620) updated every six weeks, $625/annual subscription plus $30 shipping. Provides direct-dial phone numbers for 11,500 key individuals in 1,500 military departments and offices.

*Defense Organization Service/RDT&E* (Carroll Publishing Co., 1058 Thomas Jefferson St., NW, Washington, DC 20077–0007; phone: 202/333–8620) updated every 60 days, $800/annual subscription plus $30 shipping. This directory gets you to the Army, Navy, Air Force, and defense industry officials responsible for over 300 line item programs in research, development, test, and evaluation.

*The Capitol Source: The Who's Who, What, Where in Washington* (National Journal, Inc., 1730 M St., NW, Washington, DC 20036; phones: 800/424–2921, 202/862–0644) $30. Published in April and November, this directory includes names, addresses, and phone numbers for all branches of the federal government. All entries are also available on computer diskette. Call 202/857–1469 for information.

*Judicial Staff Directory* (Staff Directories, Ltd., P.O. Box 62, Mt. Vernon, VA 22121; phone: 703/739–0900) $59, published every November. Complete listing of staff and judges in all of the federal courts. Keyword index.

*Encyclopedia of Governmental Advisory Organizations* (Gale Research, Inc., 835 Penobscot Bldg., Detroit, MI 48226; phones: 800/877–4253, 313/961–2242) $485, 1991. 1,500 pages. Over 6,000 entries describing the activities and personnel of groups and committees that advise the President and federal departments and bureaus.

*New Governmental Advisory Organizations Supplement* (Gale Research, Inc., 835 Penobscot Bldg., Detroit, MI 48226; phones: 800/877–4253, 313/961–2242) $335, June 1992. Updates the *Encyclopedia of Governmental Advisory Organizations*.

*Federal Regulatory Directory* (Congressional Quarterly, Inc., 1414 22nd St., NW, Washington, DC 20037; phones: 800/673–2730, 202/887–8500) $80, most recent edition 1990. 986 pages. Provides details on more than 100 federal regulatory agencies including each agency's functions, the laws they enforce, and the names, addresses, and phone numbers of key personnel in Washington and regional offices.

*Government Research Directory* (Gale Research, Inc., 835 Penobscot Bldg., Detroit, MI 48226; phones: 800/877–4253, 313/961–2242) $390, 1991. 1,200 pages. Describes over 3,700 research facilities and programs of the United States government. Includes government agencies and bureaus that are research organizations and user-oriented facilities supported by the federal government.

# Books on applying for a federal job

The federal government offers a fiercely competitive, complex, slow, and confusing hiring process for both non-professional and professional positions that is not uniform between agencies. Whole books have been written about the federal hiring process, and your author is not so presumptuous to think he has any profound advice to add.

Rather, the *Government Job Finder* explains how to find job openings in the federal government and leads you to directories that describe the activities of federal agencies and provide phone numbers and addresses for the appropriate persons to contact about jobs within those agencies. These other books focus on helping a job seeker determine which types of federal positions to seek and how to apply for them. With one exception, these books concentrate on positions for college graduates.

## Federal job overview

For an overview of federal job-seeking, see *The Complete Guide to Public Employment* (by Ronald and Caryl Krannich, Impact Publications, 1990; $15.95; 496 pages; for your convenience, available from Planning/Communications, see the catalog at the end of this book). In the first of three detailed chapters on federal hiring, the Krannichs explain the federal government's structure, its competitive and exempted services, job classifications, pay systems, job types and alternatives, strategies, and useful resources, including guides to federal job examinations.

An entire chapter is devoted to writing an effective SF–171, the standard job application form which is to the federal "government what applications and resumes are to the rest of the work world." The chapter also refers readers to a number of publications and videotapes that explain how to complete the SF–171 form.

The third chapter on federal positions explains the types of employment available with the legislative branch (40,000 employees), on Capitol Hill, and with the federal judiciary (17,000 employees).

## Technical, trades, and labor positions

While a number of books address all federal jobs, the *Guide to Federal Technical, Trades and Labor Jobs* (Resource Directories, Suite 302, 3361 Executive Parkway, Toledo, OH 43606; phones: 800/274–8515, 419/536–5353; $69.95 plus $3 shipping, 1988; new edition expected in autumn 1992) appears to be the only one to focus exclusively on the 950,000 non–professional positions that do not require a college degree, plus the U.S. Postal Service.

This volume includes job descriptions for federal Wage Grade, U.S. Postal Service, Competitive Service, and General Schedule positions. It explains the skills, education, and/or experience required for these positions as well as whether a written exam is required. The major agencies to employ non–professionals are named. The General Schedule and Wage Grade "prevailing rate" pay systems are explained as is the Postal Service's salary structure.

This hefty book also walks job seekers through the application procedures for General Schedule, Wage, and Postal Service jobs with step–by–step application instructions and sample forms and vacancy notices.

## Postal service

In his hefty *Book of $16,000–$60,000 Post Office Jobs* ($14.95, 1989, 186 pages; for your convenience, available from Planning/Communications, see the catalog at the end of this book), award–winning author and publisher Veltisezar Bautista explains the duties and salaries of, and qualifications and examinations for, all U.S. Postal Service jobs including those open to the general public and those available only to current postal employees. Nearly 300 specific job classifications are covered. It also includes a nationwide directory of the more than 370 U.S. Postal Examination Centers.

Bautista's *Book of U.S. Postal Exams* ($13.95, 1991, 264 pages, also available from Planning/Communications) explains dozens of tests the Postal Service uses, teaches techniques alleged to improve test performance, and includes realistic sample exams with answers. Also included is a national directory of the 370 plus U.S. Postal Examination Centers.

## Professional positions

One of the more detailed books on obtaining professional positions with the federal government is the *Guide to Federal Jobs* (Resource Directories, Suite 302, 3361 Executive Parkway, Toledo, OH 43606; phones: 800/274–8515, 419/536–5353; $69.95 plus $3 shipping, 1988, new edition expected in autumn 1992, 352 pages). This new edition contains profiles of federal agencies and departments with the names, addresses, and phone numbers of hiring contacts. Job descriptions, pay scales, and benefits are also identified.

For each of the 208 job descriptions of professional positions, the *Guide to Federal Jobs* presents current employment data on supervisory positions, average salary, and number of persons in each GS employment classification by sex. The locations of these jobs is also given, divided between overseas positions and domestic jobs outside D.C., and in D.C. The book also identifies the top agencies that employ people for the job described and the exact number employed by each.

Don't read more into these listings than there is. For example, the description of GS–5 Community Planners shows them employed by the Departments of Transportation, the Air Force, and the Army. However, community planners are also employed by other federal departments, particularly the Department of Housing and Urban Development, at GS–5 and other GS levels.

Step–by–step application procedures are offered for both the Competitive Service Jobs in most federal agencies (with hiring done through the Office of Personnel Management) and for Excepted Service or PAC (Professional Administrative Career) positions which are filled directly through the hiring department rather than through the Office of Personnel Management.

Detailed instructions on how to locate and apply for federal jobs are furnished as are instructions for completing the dread SF–171 form. The *Guide to Federal Jobs* explains how to use a vacancy notice to make your SF–171 job specific and examines the quality ranking factors the feds use to queue job applicants. In addition, the book identifies which positions are exempt from the standardized hiring procedures established by the Office of Personnel Management and which agencies have significant numbers of these Professional Administrative Career positions. The book concludes with employer job category indexes which enable you to relate specific jobs to specific agencies, and types of skills to specific jobs.

### All Federal positions

One of the most useful resources is *How to Get a Federal Job* (by David E. Waelde; seventh edition, 1989; $14.95; 186 pages; for your convenience, it is available from Planning/Communications; see the catalog at the end of this book). Fifteen chapters take readers step–by–step through each section of the SF–171 form; and offer advice on handling agency vacancy announcements, applying for a specific federal job, and surviving a reduction–in–force (RIF). This book closely examines the Office of Personnel Management's rules and regulations that govern the application and selection processes. The sample forms and examples are most helpful.

Another practical aid for the federal job seeker is the Krannich's *How to Get a Federal Job Fast!* ($9.95, 1990, 172 pages; just to be handy, it's available from Planning/Communications' catalog at the end of this book). While this book covers much of the same territory as Dave Waelde's volume, this one does more to debunk the myths of federal hiring and help you formulate your job search strategy. It includes a sample SF–171 form and solid advice on how to complete it most effectively.

## Completing the SF–171 application form

Patricia Wood's *The 171 Reference Book* (Workbooks, Inc., P.O. Box 4955, Timonium, MD 21093; phone: 301/561–8789) $18.95 plus $3 shipping, 1991, 120 pages; since this book is not available in many bookstores, Planning/Communications is carrying it; see the catalog at the end of this book) details how to successfully complete the SF–171 form. If you are having trouble figuring out what to write on your SF–171, this is the book for you. It teaches all the right buzzwords that get the attention of the often overworked personnel official who reviews your SF–171. If you have any doubt as to how to best complete the SF–171 form, this may be the best aid you'll ever find.

## Computer programs for the SF–171

You can complete a SF–171 form on any MS–DOS (IBM compatible) with the **SF–171 Template** ($59) for *FormWorx with Fill & File* ($149). You can print responses directly on the preprinted SF–171 form with a dot–matrix or laser printer. Responses are preserved on your computer disk so you can easily revise them without having to rewrite the entire form. Another version of this program for use with memory–hogging Microsoft Windows is *Form Publisher with Fill & File* ($195) which includes the SF–171 Template. This version allows you to use your laser printer to produce a completed form on blank paper. Both versions are available on 5.25 inch and 3.5 inch floppy disks form FormWorx Corporation (1601 Trapelo Rd., Waltham, MA 02154; phones: 800/992–0085, 617/890–4499).

There are reportedly dozens of computer programs for teh "Mac" and MS–DOS machines that help you complete the SF–171 form. We haven't tried any of them. We'd certainly appreciate hearing your experiences with them. Among these programs are:

↩ *Fedform 171 Laser* (The Arumon Group, P.O. Box 25090—CJF, Arlington, VA 22202; phone: 703/751–6549).
↩ *Quick & Easy 171's* (Data Tech Distributors, 4820 Derry St., Harrisburg, PA 17111; phone: 717/561–1335.
↩ *SF–171 Automated* (The Software Den, 103 Loudon St., SW, Historic Leesburg, VA 22075; phone: 703/771–3901).

# Chapter 5:

# Finding jobs in Canada and abroad

To avoid being labeled an "ugly American" when looking and applying for work in government outside the U.S., you will have to adapt your notions of job hunting to the cultures of the countries in which you wish to work as well as to any different hiring procedures or customs they may have.

In addition to introducing you to periodicals and directories that will facilitate your job search in Canada and overseas, this chapter presents information on a number of books that describe the different hiring procedures and customs you will encounter in other countries. If you wish to work overseas for the United States government, be sure to read Chapter 4, in addition to the job sources identified in this chapter. Also, be sure to look under "Foreign jobs" in the index of this book to identify sources of foreign positions noted in Chapters 2 and 4.

Before you begin your search for government jobs outside the United States, you should first develop a pretty good idea where you would like to work. It may help your decision to know the political, social, and economic natures of the countries you are considering for your next home. In addition, if you wish to work for a national, state, or local government in another country, you will want to know something about these governments and to whom you should apply for work, *assuming foreigners are even eligible to work for the government in that country.*

You can't go wrong if you first consult the *Worldwide Government Directory* (Belmont Publications, 1454 Belmont St., NW, Washington, DC 20009; phones: 800/562-3188, 202/232-6334; $275/softcover, $325/hardcover, shipping included; published each March; 1,000 pages). This rather thorough tome proffers detailed information on the governments of over 195 countries: full names and addresses of heads of state, ministers, department directors, cabinet members, legislative, and military personnel; complete addresses, phones, and telex numbers for national capitals, government offices and departments; proper forms of address, so you don't violate protocol; and the directors of state agencies and commercial enterprises the government operates.

In addition, the *World Government Directory* includes complete listings of each country's embassies and consulates, including United Nation's missions; addresses, phones, and officers of central banks; and basic facts on each country such as the capital city, official and business languages, religious affiliations of the population, local currency and rate of exchange against the U.S. dollar, international telephone dialing code, national holidays, and the next scheduled presidential election and political parties, if any.

This directory also furnishes information on over 100 international organizations and the United Nations. You'll find its information on Canada to be very helpful for targeting your job search.

Another similar volume is *Countries of the World and Their Leaders Yearbook 1991* (Gale Research, Inc., 835 Penobscot Bldg., Detroit, MI 48226; phone: 800/877-4253; $150/set, 1,840 pages; supplement published between editions costs $75) which includes the U.S. State Department's "Background Notes on the Countries of the World;" basic social, economic, and political data on 170 countries; current travel warnings from the State Department; and U.S. embassies and consulates and their personnel. The "Travel Notes" section describes the immigration and customs requirements of each country.

The *Handbook of the Nations* (Gale Research, Inc., 835 Penobscot Bldg., Detroit, MI 48226; phone: 800/877-4253; $95, 1991) is the re-publication of the CIA's *The World Fact Book-1990* which contains up-to-date information on the governments and economies of nearly 250 nations.

Specialty associations in foreign countries provide many of the same job services offered by associations of government professionals in the United States. Although it was practical for the *Government Job Finder* to identify only some of those associations in Canada, Great Britain, and New Zealand, you can identify professional associations outside the U.S. by using *International Organizations* (Gale Research, Inc., 835 Penobscot Bldg., Detroit, MI 48226; phone: 800/877–4253; $420/two–volume set; 1990; 1,893 pages; free supplement between editions) which lists 4,000 international and foreign national organizations outside the U.S. in 15 subject categories including government, public administration, legal, social welfare, public affairs, and health/medical.

**Where to start.** Two books by Caryl and Ronald Krannich are almost essential for starting your international job search. In *The Complete Guide to International Jobs & Careers* (Impact Publications, $13.95, 1990, 320 pages; available in bookstores, and, for your convenience, available from Planning/Communications, see the catalog at the end of this book), the Krannichs present the most effective approaches for entering the international job market and describe, in excruciating detail, each of the different sectors of the international job market including government. The book is divided into three parts: understanding and action; effective job search skills and strategies; and finding your best work setting, which examines job opportunities with government, international organizations, contractors, consultants, nonprofit organizations and volunteer opportunities, associations, foundations, and educational organizations, and business and travel industry.

Moving beyond this introduction, the Krannich's get down to the nitty gritty in *The Almanc of International Jobs & Careers* (Impact Publications, $14.95, 1991, 326 pages; available in bookstores, and, for your convenience, available from Planning/Communications, see the catalog at the end of this book), where they provide the names, addresses, and phone numbers of over 1,000 key international employers including a detailed examination of the U.S. government as well as international organizations, colleges and universities, non-profit corporations and foundations, private contractors and consultants, businesses, and education and teaching. The book goes into detail on work permit requirements, job listings, and relocation resources.

# Work permits

Restrictive work permit, visa, or immigration policies may interfere with your plans to work outside the U.S. of A. Most countries require workers from abroad to acquire a resident visa that includes a work permit. Usually, a foreigner must apply for the visa and work permit before entering the country, although a few nations allow you to apply after being in the country and obtaining a job. But generally, you've got to have an employment contract, visa, and work permit before arriving in the country.

Work permits are temporary and must be periodically renewed. The permit and visa may restrict the number of times you can enter and leave the country. Some countries invalidate the work permit if you leave the country even once. You may also be restricted as to how much local currency you can take out of the country. You must pay local taxes and special resident visa fees.

*Your best bet is to always learn about the local restrictions on foreign nationals before seeking a job in a particular country. Foreign embassies and consulates in the U.S. are good sources for information on work permits and visas.* These are listed in some of the directories identified at the beginning of this chapter and in *The Almanac of International Jobs & Careers* discussed above. Try to have your employer handle all the paperwork necessary for you to obtain a visa and work permit.

Don't try to enter a country on a tourist visa and then seek work. You'll be able to find only menial, low–paying jobs—certainly no jobs of any sort in government—and probably will not be eligible for any health benefits. So, be sure to arrange for your job; visa, if needed; and work permit before you pack up for a foreign abode.

## Canada

Although many of the periodicals described in Chapter 2 include government jobs in Canada, there are a number of Canada-based periodicals, directories, and job services that focus on jobs in Canada rather than on the "States." The most helpful of these are identified below. While some of them cover a broad area of government work, many sport a narrower focus. Unfortunately, only a few professional associations in Canada could be identified that include job listings in their periodicals or offer job services. Additional job-search aides are given for the Canadian provinces for which they could be found. Be sure to also check the index of this book under "Canadian jobs" for job sources listed elsewhere in the book that include a fair number of positions in Canada.

*In this section, prices are given first in terms of the country from which the publication or service emanates. For purposes of this chapter, U.S. citizens are the foreigners.*

---

*Payment for all periodicals and services should be made in the currency of the country in which the publisher is located. Major U.S. banks can write checks for you in the currency of nearly every foreign country.*

---

### Job openings

*The Toronto Globe and Mail* (444 Front St., West, Toronto, Ontario M5V 2S9; phone: 416/585-5000) See the classifieds section of the Saturday edition. This is probably the single best nationwide source of local and provincial government positions.

*Municipal World* (Municipal World Ltd., Box 399, St. Thomas, Ontario N5P 3V3; phone: 519/633-0031) monthly; $32/annual subscription. Most ten or so job listings under "Staff Wanted" are for Ontario Province.

*Bulletin* (Canadian Association of Municipal Administrators, 24 Clarence St., Ottawa, Ontario K1N 5P3; phone: 613/563-2590) bimonthly, available to associate members as part of salary-based dues package, and included in members' dues package. Few job ads.

*Municipal Dialogue* (Canadian Association of Municipal Administrators, 24 Clarence St., Ottawa, Ontario K1N 5P3; phone: 613/563–2590) quarterly, available to associate members as part of salary–based dues package and included in members' dues package. Few job ads.

*Civic Public Works* (Maclean Hunter Limited, 777 Bay St., Toronto, Ontario M5W 1A7; phone: 416/596–5953) monthly; $33/annual subscription (Canada), $72/foreign (includes U.S.). Jobs listed under "The Market Place."

*The Position Place* (Canadian Institute of Public Health Inspectors, P.O. Box 5367, Station F, Ottawa, Ontario K2C 3J1; phone: 613/224–7568) bimonthly, $25/annual subscription, $40/U.S. About 15 to 20 openings for public health inspector and environmental health officers fill this jobs bulletin.

*Canadian Journal of Public Health* (Canadian Public Health Association, Suite 400, 1565 Carling Ave., Ottawa, Ontario K1Z 8R1; phone: 613/725–3769) bimonthly, $51.36/annual subscription, $60/U.S., $70/elsewhere. Jobs listed under "Employment." Five to 15 job ads in a typical issue.

*Canadian Medical Association Journal* (RBW Graphics, 1749 20th St., East Owen Sound, Ontario N4K 5R2) biweekly, $85/annual subscription (U.S.), $70/Canada, $100/elsewhere. From 80 to 120 positions for physicians appear under "Classifieds" including some government positions.

*Plan Canada* (Canadian Institute of Planners, 404 – 126 York St., Ottawa, Ontario K1N 5T5; phone: 613/233–2105) bimonthly, $50/annual individual subscription, $56/U.S., $56/annual institutional subscription, $70/U.S., free to members. Small number of jobs listed.

*Canadian Institute of Planners* (404—126 York St., Ottawa, Ontario K1N 5T5; phone: 613/233-2105). CIP mails job notices directly to its members. Annual membership dues for Canadians are $100 plus provincial affiliate dues. International membership (yes, that includes the U.S.) dues are $110.

*Also see the Public Welfare Directory* listed under "Social services" in Chapter 2. It includes Canadian provincial and federal social service agencies.

*Also see the publications listed under "Legal services and court administration" in Chapter 2 for several periodicals that carry a good number of notices for law and law–related jobs outside the United States.*

*Also see the listings under "Library services" in Chapter 2 for a number of job hotlines that identify vacancies in Canadian libraries.*

## Directories

*Canadian Association of Municipal Administrators Membership Directory* (CAMA, 24 Clarence St., Ottawa, Ontario K1N 5P3; phone: 613/563–2590) available only to members, published annually.

*Associations Canada 1991* (Gale Research, Inc., 835 Penobscot Bldg., Detroit, MI 48226; phone: 800/877–4253) $160, 1991, 1,200 pages. Includes professional associations.

*Data Source for Planning in Alberta* (Alberta Department of Municipal Affairs, Research and Development, 12th Floor, City Center, 10155 102nd St., Edmonton, Alberta T5J 4L4; phone: 403/427–2225) free, published in even–numbered years. In addition to all the data on physical, social, and business conditions, this book includes the names, addresses, and phone numbers of planning and other government agencies in the province.

*Directory of Planning Agencies in Alberta* (Alberta Department of Municipal Affairs, Research and Development, 12th Floor, City Center, 10155 102nd St., Edmonton, Alberta T5J 4L4; phone: 403/427–2225) free. 30 pages.

*Canadian Environmental Directory* (Gale Research, Inc., 835 Penobscot Bldg., Detroit, MI 48226; phone: 800/877–4253) $160, 1991, 760 pages. Included federal, provincial, and municipal agencies involved with environmental issues.

## Alberta provincial jobs

*The Bulletin* (Personnel Administration, Room 1101, 620 Seventh Ave., SW, Calgary, Alberta T2P 0Y8; phones: 403/297–6427; Alberta Government Employment Office, 4th Floor, 10011 109th St., Edmonton, Alberta T5J 3S8; phone: 403/427–7891) weekly. Copies are available at government offices Canadian employment centers and post–secondary educational institutions throughout the province. Mail subscriptions are not available. Job descriptions and qualifications for about 50 positions with the provincial government appear in each issue. Includes application instructions.

*HOTLINE* for entry level clerical positions in Edmonton. For 24-hour recording of job openings with the provincial government, call 403/427-8792. Recording updated every Monday.

*rite Telephone Directory* (Alberta Public Affairs Bureau, Second Floor, 44 Capital Blvd., 10044 108th St., Edmonton, Alberta T5J 3S7; phone: 403/427-4352) updated periodically. Contact for price. Complete directory of officials in all provincial departments and agencies. Listed by agency and alphabetically by location.

## Nova Scotia provincial jobs

*Nova Scotia Civil Service Commission Employment Opportunities* (Civil Service Commission, P.O. Box 943, Halifax, Nova Scotia B3J 2V9; phone: 902/424-7660) Contact for information.

## Saskatchewan provincial and local jobs

The Public Service Commission advertises provincial jobs in the Business Section of the Saturday editions of the daily *Saskatoon Star Phoenix* (204 Fifth Avenue, N., Saskatoon, Saskatchewan S7K 2P1 Canada) and *The Leader-Post* (Box 2020, Regina, Saskatchewan S4P 3G4 Canada). Municipal jobs are advertised in local newspapers.

*The Government of Saskatchewan Directory* (Communications Director, Saskatchewan Property Management Corp., Sixth Floor, 2045 Broad St., Regina, Saskatchewan S4P 3V7 Canada; phone: 306/781-6911/6892) $7.50, price may change soon, published annually. Lists heads of provincial departments, divisions, personnel, Crown Corporations, and government agencies.

*Municipal Directory* (Communications Director, Department of Community Services, 2151 Scarth St., Regina, Saskatchewan S4P 3V7 Canada) $10. Published annually. Lists urban and rural municipal officers, elected officials, and department heads.

## Great Britain

The following items will assist the search for a government job in Great Britain. Because international currency exchange rates are so unstable, direct contact is advised to learn current prices.

*In this section, prices are given first in terms of the country from which the publication or service emanates unless otherwise noted. For purposes of this chapter, U.S. citizens are the foreigners.*

### Job openings

*New Scientist* (IPC Magazines, Ltd., Freepost 1061, Hawwards Heath, England RH16 3ZA) weekly, £110/United Kingdom annual subscription, $130 (U.S. dollars)/annual subscription via air mail to the U.S., $170 (Canadian dollars)/annual subscription via air mail to Canada. Over 100 science positions in England are listed throughout, including government jobs.

*Municipal Journal* (Municipal Journal, Ltd., 32 Vauxhall Bridge Road, London SW1V 2SS; phone: 071-973-6400). Write for details and current subscription costs.

*The Planner* (Royal Town Planning Institute, 179 King's Cross Road, London, WC1X 9BZ; phone: 071-833-9111) weekly, £35/annual subscription, free to members. Includes display ads for about 30 planning positions in government and with consulting firms.

### Job services

*National Employment Register* (Royal Town Planning Institute, 26 Portland Place, London, England W1N 4BE; phone: 071-636-9107, extension 30) available only to members, free. The job seeker completes a resume form which this service sends to potential employers who are then responsible for contacting the job candidate. This service is particularly well-suited to filling temporary positions with short notice.

*Vacation Employment Register* (Royal Town Planning Institute, 26 Portland Place, London, England W1N 4BE; phone: 071-636-9107, extension 30) available only to members, free. This service runs from April to August each year to find summer vacation employment for planning students. The job seeker completes a resume form which this service sends to potential employers who are then responsible for contacting the job candidate.

## Directories

*The Municipal YearBook and Public Services Directory* Volumes 1 and 2 (Municipal Journal, Ltd., 32 Vauxhall Bridge Road, London SW1V 2SS; phone: 071-973-6400) £94, published annually. Provides detailed information on county and district councils, and central government agencies, officials, and professional government associations.

*Planning Directory* (TPS Partnership, 13/15 Stroud Road, Glouscester, GL1 5AA) £19.95. Lists the public agencies in Great Britain concerned with town and country planning including the senior offficer contacts of local authorities and information on adotped Struture and Local Plans. Central Government departments and other organizations such as the UDCs, EZs, and National Parks are also listed.

*Annual Directory of Planning Consultants* (Royal Town Planning Institute, 26 Portland Place, London, England W1N 4BE; phone: 071-636-9107) £6, published each January.

*Directory of British Associations and Associations in Ireland* (Gale Research, Inc., 835 Penobscot Bldg., Detroit, MI 48226; phone: 800/877-4253) $180, 1991. In 548 pages, this directory lists, by subject area, over 7,000 national, local, and regional associations based in England, Wales, Scotland, and Ireland.

*Trade Association and Professional Bodies of the United Kingdom* (Gale Research, Inc., 835 Penobscot Bldg., Detroit, MI 48226; phone: 800/877-4253) $140, published in odd-numbered years. Its 575 pages give details on over 4,000 United Kingdom associations.

## New Zealand

These two items will assist the government job seeker in New Zealand. Since international currency exchange rates are so unstable, direct contact is advised to learn prices.

*In this section, prices are given first in terms of the country from which the publication or service emanates. For purposes of this chapter, U.S. citizens are the foreigners.*

## Job service

*New Zealand Planning Institute* (P.O. Box 6388, Auckland: 156 Parnell Rd., Parnell, Auckland, New Zealand) Distributes notifications of planning (and some parks and recreation) positions. Write to request to be placed on mailing list for notifications of job openings.

## Directory

*Local Government Yearbook* (Trade Publications, Ltd., P.O. Box 37-549, Parnell, Auckland, New Zealand; phone: 09/795-500) Write for price of most recent edition. Published each March.

# General notes on working overseas

Adapted from "Finding a Job Overseas," by J. Roy Saunders, Jr., originally published in Planning, July, 1980; copyright © 1980. Reprinted with permission from the American Planning Association.

The idea of working abroad is attractive to many government professionals. If you are not out to strike it rich, the public sector might be the place to start a foreign job hunt. Many public sector organizations offer internship positions for recent college graduates with limited experience. Their staffs, overall, tend to be relatively young.

Because so many qualified Americans are available, competition among Americans is stiff for positions with international lending institutions. Besides a sound knowledge of relevant skills, a government professional who wants to work for this type of agency should have some knowledge of other regions of the world as well as of a foreign language. Good research and writing skills are essential.

Some international development banks view long-range planning as a luxury since most cities in developing countries simply cannot afford it. They are looking for quick solutions to immediate problems; their survival demands this approach. So, specialists are in greater demand than generalists.

Private foundations, volunteer organizations, and nonprofit agencies also provide jobs in foreign countries. The Peace Corps deserves special mention. While it offers a personally rewarding experience, it also serves as a training ground for later overseas employment. Unlike other overseas employers, the Peace Corps does not require previous experience in foreign countries. Hence, working for the Peace Corps gets your foot in the door for other overseas employment later on.

Note also that the Peace Corps offers many white–collar professional positions and is not exclusively for the young. A typical post–Peace Corps career pattern is a training program in administration at the School for International Training and then work with an agency like CARE. There are also permanent training, supervisory, and administrative positions within the Peace Corps itself.

Private consulting firms often have work in foreign countries. Some firms operate on contracts with bilateral or multilateral public–sector aid programs; others contract directly with foreign governments.

In most cases, a graduate degree and a strong record of experience are essential. Frequently, prior overseas work and knowledge of a foreign language are required, although a demonstrated facility for languages and a willingness to undergo intensive language training may suffice.

Be forewarned about the Catch 22 of breaking into the overseas employment market. Prior overseas experience does not, by itself, indicate an ability to adapt to foreign living and working conditions, but lack of it is a serious handicap in marketing yourself. The hurdle can be cleared, but it certainly can be a serious difficulty. To the job seeker, that first overseas job is like obtaining a union card.

Adapting to life without chocolate–covered Oreos, *Star Trek: The Next Generation,* and David Letterman may be a real problem for many. Foreign employment can put substantial stress on family relationships, which can affect your performance as an employee. Some families thrive on new conditions and relish new experiences. Others wall themselves up in protective expatriate enclaves and fight boredom by complaining about the lack of conveniences. Being in a strange country, with a completely foreign language and set of cultural behaviors can be disconcerting and intimidating.

Frequently, a spouse is given a visa that prohibits employment. English language schooling is available in only a few cities. Transportation is difficult. Remote rural areas often lack western-style conveniences such as indoor plumbing, reliable electricity, telephone and mail service, but offer frequent exposure to such diseases as malaria, cholera, and hepatitis.

Insecurity is inherent in overseas consulting work. Most firms contract with people for particular projects which may last only a few months. If you relish financial security, overseas work may not be for you. Mobility is clearly an important aspect of overseas work.

## General sources of jobs abroad

Advertisements for overseas employment frequently appear in the national publications listed in Chapter 2. Look in the Index of this book under "Foreign jobs" to identify sources in other chapters. Be sure to also check the classified and business sections of the Sunday *New York Times* (229 W. 43rd St., New York, NY 10036; phone: 212/556-1234) and the *Washington Post* (1150 15th St. NW, Washington, DC 20071; phone: 202/334-6000) where overseas jobs are often advertised. Frequently, though, you will have to contact foreign government agencies directly to learn of job openings as well as to obtain a job application and information on hiring and application procedures.

If you are interested in any social service jobs, see the *Public Welfare Directory* listed under "Social services" in Chapter2. It identifies foreign social service agencies.

Each of the following publications and agencies provides some assistance to persons seeking government jobs outside the U.S. Most of these are available in public libraries. The first few publications or services are for positions with the U.S. government.

In this section, prices are for the U.S. and in U.S. dollars unless noted otherwise.

## Job openings

*Federal Job Information Center* (Room 5316, 300 Ala Moana Blvd., Honolulu, HI 96850; phone: 808/541-2784). Contact for the current listings of U.S. federal jobs overseas. Theoretically, every FJIC should have listings for all U.S. government jobs. For the nearest FJIC, see the state–by–state listings in Chapter 3.

*Peace Corps General Information Kit* (Peace Corps, Office of Public Affairs, 1990 K St., NW, Washington, DC 20526; phone: 202/606-3000) free.

*Peace Corps Professional Staff.* For professional staff positions with the Peace Corps, contact the Department of Personnel (4th Floor, 1990 K St., NW, Washington, DC 20526; phone: 202/606-3400).

*Peace Corps Volunteers.* To become a Peace Corp overseas volunteer, contact any of the Peace Corps' 16 field offices around the country (a list is available from the Washington office, call 800/424-8580, extension 93) or the Washington office (5th Floor, 1990 K St., NW, Washington, DC 20526; phone: 800/424-8580, extension 226).

*Private schools with U.S. Department of State Affiliation.* Although pretty independent of the U.S. government, these schools receive some assistance from the Department of State. Each school hires its own staff. A directory of these private and international schools is available from the Office of Overseas Schools, Room 234, SA–6, U.S. Department of State, Washington, DC 20520.

*U.S. Department of Defense Dependents Schools.* Teachers in these U.S. Military Dependents Schools work for the U.S. government. Information on employment with these schools is available in the booklet *Overseas Employment for Educators,* available free from the Office of Dependents Schools, Room 152, U.S. Department of Defense, 2461 Eisenhower Ave., Alexandria, VA 22331; phone: 202/325-0188.

*International Employment Gazette* (Global Resources Organization, Ltd., 1525 Wade Hampton Blvd., Greenville, SC 29609; phone: 800/882-9188) biweekly, $95/annual subscription (U.S.), $11/elsewhere, $35/three-month subscription (U.S,), $40/elsewhere. This tabloid contains over 400 advertisements for government and other jobs overseas.

*International Employment Hotline* (P.O. Box 6170, McLean, VA 22106; phone: 703/573–1628) monthly, $20/six–month subscription, $15/three–month subscription. Lists job descriptions (and to whom to apply) by country of assignment. Ads for jobs with foreign governments, U.S. Foreign Service, CIA, and other U.S. government overseas positions that do not require candidate to have pre–existing civil service status. Each issue is eight pages with two articles as well as job announcements. From 50 to several hundred job descriptions in a single issue, but usually towards the lower end of that range.

*International Jobs Bulletin* (Southern Illinois University Placement Center, Woody Hall, Carbondale, IL 62901; phone: 618/453–1047) biweekly, monthly, $25/20 issues, $15/ten issues, $1.50/single issue. Write for free sample issue. The typical issue contains over 75 ads for jobs in government and the private sector for accountants, physicians, computer, economists, engineers, translators, teachers, physical therapists, horticulturists, etc.

---

**Caution:** There are a number of fly–by–night operators in the overseas employment game. We feel pretty confident in the periodicals listed here. But before subscribing to any other periodical that purports to list job opportunities abroad, ask for a sample copy (free or for a single–issue price). If the publisher will not supply one, it may be prudent to be skeptical of the periodical's value.

---

*Job Opportunities Bulletin* (TransCentury Corporation, 1724 Kalorama Rd., NW, Washington, DC 20009; phone: 202/328–4400) bimonthly, $25/annual subscription (U.S., Canada, Mexico), $40/elsewhere (air mail). Lists job vacancy announcements and "Jobseekers" ads in international development, primarily for work in Third World countries. About 25 to 35 job ads, including a moderate number of government positions, appear in the typical issue. Typical positions include accountants, agriculturalists, administrators, medical personnel, teachers, refugee affairs, engineers, project managers, forestry, and environment.

*International Affairs Career Bulletin* (Jeffries & Associates, 17200 Hughes Rd., Poolesville, MD 20837; phone: 301/972-8034) bimonthly, $65/annual subscription.

*Monthly Job Vacancy Bulletin* (National Council for International Health, Suite 600, 1701 K St., NW, Washington, DC 20036; phone: 202/833-5900) monthly, write for price. Includes positions only for health care professionals.

*The International Educator* (P.O Box 103, West Bridgewater,MA 02379; phone: 508/580-1880) quarterly plus a small summer jobs issue in June, $25/annual subscription (U.S.), $35/elsewhere. Lists around 100 teaching and administrative positions in privately-owned American and International schools in English–speaking countries.

*OECD Economic Outlook* (Organization for Economic Cooperation and Development, 2001 L St., Suite 700, Washington, DC 20036; phone: 202/785-6323) semiannual, $45.70/annual subscription, $24/single issue. Exclusively positions with the OECD's Paris office. Positions include economists, data processors, econometrics, fiscal policy, nuclear engineering and physics, public administration, education policies, statistics, and urban studies.

*Internships and Careers in International Affairs* (United Nations Association of the United States of America, 485 Fifth Ave., New York, NY 10017; phone: 212/697-3232) $10/prepaid. Published in September of odd–numbered years. Lists overseas and domestic internships with U.S. government agencies, the United Nations, non–profits, and private organizations involved in international affairs. Explains the qualifications employers seek and names resources to find employment in international affairs here and abroad.

*ODN Opportunities Catalog* (Overseas Development Network, 333 Valencia St., Suite 330, San Francisco, CA 91401; phone: 415/431-4204) $7/students, $10/individuals, $15/institutions, plus $1.50 postage. Most recent revision: 1990. About 60 pages. Identifies employment and research opportunities, and internships for persons wishing to enter the international development overseas. Presents job descriptions, qualifications, names and addresses of contacts, largely with non-profits and government-related positions.

*Opportunities in International Development in New England* (Overseas Development Network, 333 Valencia St., Suite 330, San Francisco, CA 91401; phone: 415/431-4204) $5 plus $1.50 postage. Lists domestic and international internship and employment opportunities with New England-based development organizations.

## Job services

*International Placement Network* (Global Resources Organization, Ltd., 1525 Wade Hampton Blvd., Greenville, SC 29609; phone: 800/882-9188) $45/U.S., $50/elsewhere. Request an application form. In two to three weeks after submitting your completed form and check, you get a printout of foreign positions that fit your occupational interests, geographical preferences, education level, and foreign languages you speak.

*Talent Bank* (TransCentury Corporation (1724 Kalorama Rd., NW, Washington, DC 20009; phone: 202/328-4400) free. Obtain their "Professional Skills Registration Form." Submit a completed form with your resume. This service refers your resume to international employers seeking people with your background. Resumes are kept on file for two years. Typical positions include accountants, agriculturalists, administrators, medical personnel, teachers, refugee affairs, engineers, project managers, forestry, and environment.

*University Placement Service* (Southern Illinois University Placement Center, Woody Hall, Carbondale, IL 62901; phone: 618/453-1047) $30/year, $25/year SIU students. Submit 15 resumes. Resumes are given to appropriate employers who submit vacancy notices. The employer is reponsible for contacting the job seeker.

## Directories

*World Directory of Environmental Organizations* (California Institute of Public Affairs, P.O. Box 189040, Sacramento, CA 95818; phone: 916/442-2472) $35 plus 6.5 percent sales tax for California residents, foreign: $38/surface mail, $48/air mail. 175 pages.

Includes over government agencies, research institutes, and citizens' and professional associations in the U.S. and around the globe. Divided into 50 topics with index, glossary, and bibliography of related directories and databases. Most recent edition, published in 1989.

*World Guide to Environmental Issues and Organizations* Gale Research, Inc., 835 Penobscot Bldg., Detroit, MI 48226; phone: 800/877–4253) $125, 1991/ 400 pages. Includes about 250 international organizations, including national and regional government agencies and regulatory organizations, involved in solving environmental issues.

*The Peace Corps and More: 114 Ways to Work, Study, and Travel in the Third World* (Overseas Development Network, 333 Valencia St., Suite 330, San Francisco, CA 91401; phone: 415/431–4204) $6.95 plus $1.50 postage. Offers over 100 suggestions of organizations that allow you to gain Third World experience while promoting the ideas of social justice and sustainable development.

# General information on overseas work

*Work, Study, Travel Abroad: The Whole World Handbook* (Council on International Educational Exchange, 205 E. 42nd St., New York, NY 10017; phone: 212/661–1414) $12.95, published in December of odd–numbered years. 474 pages. Contains short section on applying for foreign jobs with the U.S. government. Most of the book examines foreign countries and explains how to find jobs in them.

*Careers in International Affairs* (by Linda L. Powers, Georgetown University, 1986) Hard–to–find, but well worth it. Many consider this book to offer one of the best overviews of international job opportunities. It give contacts as well as annotated descriptions of ten types of international organizations.

*Guide to Careers in World Affairs* (Foreign Policy Association, 729 Seventh Ave., New York, NY 10019, $10.95; last edition 1987, new edition in 1992. Providing an overview of alternative careers in international affairs, this book addresses careers in the federal government, international organizations, nonprofit organizations, and international business, banking, and finance.

*Looking for Employment in Foreign Countries* (World Trade Academy Press, Inc., Suite 509, 50 E. 42nd St., New York, NY 10017; phone: 212/697–4999) $16.50/paperback plus $3.50 postage, 1990. 144 pages. Profiles employment situation in 43 foreign countries, including government jobs. Sample resumes and cover letters.

*How to Get the Jobs You Want Overseas* by Arthur Lieberns (Pilot Books, 103 Cooper St., Babylon, NY 11702; phone: 516/422–2225) $4.95, 1990. Includes chapter on overseas jobs with the government.

*Evaluating an Overseas Job Opportunity* by John Williams (Pilot Books, 103 Cooper St., Babylon, NY 11702; phone: 516/422–2225) $3.95, 1990. Examine employer/employee contracts, family issues, analysis of financial factors, living overseas, taxation, and returning home.

*Strategies for Getting an Overseas Job* (Pilot Books, 103 Cooper St., Babylon, NY 11702; phone: 516/422–2225) $3.95, 1989. Identifies overseas job–finding associations, specialized employment agencies, and other foreign employment services. Special advice on resumes and interviews for jobs in foreign countries.

*Resumes for Employment in the U.S. and Overseas* (World Trade Academy Press, Inc., Suite 509, 50 E. 42nd St., New York, NY 10017; phone: 212/697–4999) $16.50/paperback plus $3.50 postage, 1990. 145 pages. Present special techniques to use when applying for foreign jobs including requirements for work permits in foreign countries.

*Construction Employment Guide in the National and International Field* (World Trade Academy Press, Inc., Suite 509, 50 E. 42nd St., New York, NY 10017; phone: 212/697–4999) $16.50/paperback plus $3.50 postage, 1990. 145 pages. Reviews government employment and how American civilians may apply for construction jobs (Standard Form 171 which is usually required for a government job is reproduced). Lists employment agencies that specialize in construction openings as well as more than 400 foreign contractors in 20 countries.

*Working in the European Communities: A Guide for Graduate Recruiters and Job–Seekers* by A.J. Rabon (Careers Research and Advisory Center) (Hobsons Limited, Cambridge, England), 1985. Presents a general review of working in Europe with chapters on Belgium, France, Germany, and the Netherlands.

# Chapter 6

# Cover letters and resumes

Even if you know how and where to find the job openings, you still have to write an effective cover letter and resume to get the job—unless you are applying for one of those government jobs which requires submission of only a specified form. However, most professional positions in local government require you to submit a resume and cover letter, some state and federal positions do as well. And even if you only have to complete a form like the federal government's SF–171, the suggestions given in this chapter will help you better organize your responses.

To take the next step in the job search process, you need to persuade your potential employer that you are worth interviewing. That's where your cover letter and resume make the difference. Once you get the interview, it's up to you to make a good enough impression to be offered the job at the salary you want.

This chapter suggests ways to write an effective application letter to accompany your resume. Then it explains how to prepare an attractive and effective resume. For the student right of out school, these guidelines take out some of the mystery from applying for jobs. For the seasoned government worker, they offer a sound refresher course and debunk many of the myths built up over the years, particularly concerning the content of a resume.

Finally, Chapter 7 reviews ways to adequately prepare for your job interview and recommends productive interview behaviors that can benefit even the most seasoned professional.

# Cover or target letters

Cover letters and resumes go hand–in–hand. A target, or cover, letter explains why you are particularly well–suited to the specific job for which you are applying. The resume outlines your professional experience, education, and other relevant accomplishments in some detail and can be used for most any job for which you apply.

The purpose of the resume is to market you to a potential employer well enough to get him to invite you to a personal interview. Because the person who does the hiring usually scours scores of applications (sometimes hundreds in today's job market), your cover letter should, in a persuasive, professional, polite, and personable manner, point out your specific qualifications for the job so well that the employer will carefully examine the resume your cover letter accompanies. As Dr. Krannich and William Banis put it in *High Impact Resumes and Letters*, ''your letter should be the sizzle accompanying the sell.'' While the resume can, and should, be mass produced, the cover letter for each job application should be individually typed and targeted to the specific job.

## Cover letter guidelines

Use your own personal stationery or blank paper and the appropriate business letter format for your cover letter. It is very bad form to use the letterhead of your current employer when applying for a job elsewhere. Use high quality white or light–colored bond paper.

If at all possible, the letter itself should be addressed to a specific person. If the advertisement or job announcement failed to name the person to whom you apply, it's usually worth a phone call to learn her name. Just ask the receptionist or secretary in the department that is doing the hiring. Sometimes you'll run into a brick wall where nobody will tell you to whom to write. One option is to consult one of directories described in chapters two or three of this book to identify the proper person. Then call the jurisdiction to confirm that the individual still works there (personnel do change after directories are published). Otherwise, make the best of it and follow the style shown in the sample cover letter for an assistant village manager position at the end of this chapter.

## Cover letter content

An effective cover letter is written with a professional tone and style and should include the following items:

cↄ *Clearly identify the job* you seek in the first paragraph or sentence.

cↄ *Indicate why you are applying* for this particular position (if you wish to state your career objective, this is the place to do it). Try to link your interests to the employer's needs.

cↄ *Describe your qualifications.* Explain why you are particularly well-suited for this specific position. Carefully review the job description or job announcement or ad to determine what skills are sought and how you meet them. In your cover letter, show how you meet these requirements. Highlight your enclosed resume and emphasize your qualifications vis-a-vis the employer's needs. In a sense, you should re-write the employer's ad around the qualifications described in it. This approach is low-keyed, but assertive while not appearing to be boastful, hyped-up, or aggressive.

cↄ *Refer the reader to the enclosed resume* for detail of your experience and education.

cↄ *Request the next step* in the hiring process: the interview, an answer to this letter, civil service exam, or a request for references (be assertive, but friendly). Make the employer an open-ended offer she can't refuse, as is done in the sample assistant village manager cover letter at the end of this chapter. This approach softens the request for an interview without putting the employer on the spot to say "yes" or "no" right away. The follow-up phone call lets you know whether or not you have any chance at all for the job. If you don't have a chance, you can move on to more promising job opportunities without waiting any longer. Conversely, the employer may find you sufficiently interesting to invite you to an in-person job interview. Either way, you get results quickly. Alternatively, you can end the letter with the conventional, "Thanks for your time and consideration. I hope to hear from you in the near future.'' Just be prepared to wait since many government employers contact only job candidates they wish to interview and never even acknowledge receiving the application of someone they don't intend to interview.

☞ *Provide any specific information* the employer asked for in his job announcement or ad. If a job ad requests references, you should give their names, addresses, and phone numbers near the end of your cover letter or on a separate sheet. As the discussion on resumes urges, do not include references in your resume. If an employer requests your salary history, include that on a separate sheet, not in the cover letter.

☞ *Thank the reader* for her time and consideration.

If you are writing a so–called ''blind'' cover letter to learn of a job opening, you will want to adjust your letter accordingly. This sort of approach letter is designed for you to gain access to an individual who will either provide you with contacts, leads, and information on job opportunities within his agency or elsewhere. Be sure to learn the correct name of the person to whom you write. The various directories of local, state, or federal officials described in the first five chapters of the *Government Job Finder* will get you their names as will a phone call to their agencies.

## Cover letter style

Your cover letter tells the employer a lot about your competency. No matter what kind of a job you seek, typographical errors suggest that you would be a careless employee. A poorly written cover letter suggests that you do not communicate effectively.

Instead, cover letters should be direct, powerful, and free of errors. Make like a good newspaper copy editor: eliminate unnecessary words; check grammar, spelling, and punctuation. Avoid using the passive voice (''should have been,'' ''it was done by me''). (It's suggestions like this one that make so many of us regret paying so little attention in high school English class.) Avoid pomposity and overly long sentences. Don't try to be cute or too aggressive like the preceding parenthetical expression did.

Keep the letter short and to the point. There's no reason to overwhelm the reader with a lengthy cover letter that repeats a lot of your resume.

Keep your letter positive. Highlight your past accomplishments and skills as well as your future value to the employer.

### References

As mentioned earlier, the ad for the job for which you are applying may have requested references. You should identify your references near the end of your letter or on another sheet of paper. *It is not desirable to list references in a resume since you might want to use different references for different jobs.* In addition, it is prudent to let your references know to which positions you have submitted an application. If you know a potential employer is likely to contact your references, you would be sagacious to send your references a copy of your cover letter and the ad for the job so they can customize their responses to better fit the job.

For each reference, be sure to give the person's correct name and title, and complete address and phone number including area code, so the reference can be contacted easily. If a reference's first name could belong to either sex (Chris, Leslie, Shelley), avoid embarrassment and use "Mr." or "Ms." before the reference's name. A fundamental principle of applying for a job is to make it as easy as possible for the potential employer to follow-up your application because some employers simply toss out an application if they are unable to reach references or obtain other relevant information about the job candidate. It's a buyer's market, and as the applicant, you are the seller.

Be certain to have permission to use these names as references. Use only references you are certain will comment favorably on your performance and ability to work with others. Be prepared to offer additional references if asked.

# The resume

Since the individual doing the hiring has to examine so many resumes, you are best off if you keep yours relatively short and sweet. Remember: your resume is both a sales pitch and a summary of your qualifications. Like it or not, those 60-second spots for political candidates nearly always have more impact than a five-minute or half-hour commercial. The same reasoning applies to resumes.

The recent college graduate isn't likely to have any problems keeping his resume down to one-page while the experienced professional may have a tough time limiting her resume to no more than four pages. The keys to making your resume stand out from the crowd—in addition to its substance—are to organize it well and produce an attractive, professional-looking document.

## Resume content

By following several general guidelines you can make the content of your resume more effective.

☐ *Include only pertinent information.* Do not include material unless it gives potential employers a reason to hire you.

   Include only information from which you can confidently expect a favorable reaction. When in doubt, leave that information out; don't gamble on adverse reactions. A resume simply is not the place to put anything negative about yourself. Remember, you are marketing yourself to the prospective employer as the best person for the job. Would the folks at Dow Chemical, so anxious to build a clean image today, advertise they manufactured the napalm used to burn and kill civilians in Viet Nam or would cigarette advertising voluntarily include warnings on the cause-and-effect relationship of smoking and cancer and other diseases?

☐ *Be scrupulously honest.* For example, in 1976, one Illinois municipality offered its village manager job to a man who appeared to have built a successful career in city government in California. Unfortunately for him, the local newspaper learned of his phony credentials when interviewing one of his past employers and exposed the rascal. It seems he failed to earn the degree from Purdue University that he claimed to possess and was ten years older than the 55 years he listed on his resume. He withdrew his name from consideration for the job before the city fathers and mothers could withdraw it for him. During the past few years, a number of high-level city employees around the country have lost their jobs, and in most cases their government careers, for misrepresenting themselves on their resumes or job applications.

Most resume fraud, however, does not become public knowledge. If a discrepancy is found during a job interview, the job simply is not offered. Fraud discovered after someone has been hired, usually results in the employer quietly asking the employee to resign with the not-so-subtle threat of dismissal hanging over his head. An executive of a credential verification service estimates that 30 percent of all resumes contain some fraudulent educational information. And with an increasing number of employers verifying this information, especially in the public sector, honesty and accuracy are essential for any resume or job application. Think about it, how could you ever trust somebody on the job if he lied to get the job?

There are a number of items of information that belong in any resume. An effective resume includes the following information in a clear, concise, and well-written style:

✑ *Applicant identification.* Your name should go at the top of the first page. If your resume is typewritten, underline your name. If produced on a word processor, place your name in a typeface and style that makes it stand out. See the sample resumes at the end of this chapter. Be sure to include your home address, home telephone number (including area code), and work phone. This is where you can indicate any preference for where you want to be contacted simply by writing: "Contact at [phone number]." You can also provide your birth date and social security number.

✑ *Education.* Identify your college degree and any advanced degrees earned. Give the names of the school that awarded your degree(s) and the years in which they were received. Include the city and state in which the school is located if that is not apparent from its name. Recent graduates may wish to list major scholarships or honors received. Also note relevant post–graduate education. Recent graduates may want to also list major extracurricular activities and organizational offices they held.

As a professional acquires more work experience, educational information becomes less important to potential employers while practical experience becomes more significant. For the recent graduate, the education section should precede the section on professional experience. The more seasoned professional will want to place the experience section of the education section. Job candidates who lack a college degree should indicate the highest level of education they have had, whether it was a high school degree, or some college or junior college education without receiving a degree.

⌒◦ *Professional experience.* Jobs in your professional field should be described under a heading such as ''Professional Experience'' or ''Work Experience.'' Jobs should be listed in reverse chronological order with the most recent first. For each position, furnish the following information:

*Job title.* Place your job title first. Use some emphasis to make it stand out: bold face, italics, borders, or boxing it if your resume is typeset or prepared on computer, underlined if prepared on a typewriter.

*Employer's name, address, and phone number.* If there is even one former employer you do not want a potential employer to call, leave out the phone numbers of all past employers. Do not give the name of your supervisor here; just give the name of the company or government agency.

*Period of employment.* If you've frequently changed jobs, like every two or three years, you don't want to advertise it. Employers like to hire people they think will stay with the agency for a long time. It costs them time and money to train a new employee. So, if you've changed jobs frequently, place the dates of employment within the heading for each job as is shown in the first sample resume at the end of this chapter. On the other hand, if you've generally held your jobs for four or more years, place the dates of employment in the left–hand margin as shown in the second sample resume at the end of this chapter.

*Responsibilities, duties, and accomplishments*. This may be the most important text in your resume. It is your opportunity to tell potential employers what you did in your former positions. Using short phrases rather than full sentences presents this information concisely without appearing to be conceit or braggadocio. Unless jobs outside the profession in which you are seeking work reflect on your ability to perform your professional tasks, this list of jobs should concentrate on the professional positions you have held.

## Doonesbury

BY GARRY TRUDEAU

*Organization memberships and honors*. Identify the professional organizations to which you belong and offices you have held in them, professional certifications or licenses you have earned, and professional honors you have been awarded. Do not use abbreviations nor acronyms. A potential employer feels pretty dumb when he doesn't recognize the acronym or abbreviation. Even if the employer is isn't too bright, why make him feel that way?

Do not include political organizations—that's not any employer's damned business, especially a government employer! You can include germane civic and community organization memberships, particularly if you are, or have been, an officer or chaired an important committee.

☞*Publications*. Clearly identify major relevant publications such as books, plans, reports, budgets, and magazine or newspaper articles so the reader can find them if she wishes. Experienced workers should not include papers or projects from college or graduate school unless they were published. List publications in chronological order with the most recent last or in reverse chronological order with the most recent first.

☞*Additional professional activities*. List other professional activities such as participation on professional conference programs, guest lectures, commission memberships, courses taught, etc.

☞*References*. As explained earlier, never identify references in your resume. At the end of your resume, insert a line like "References available upon request." If the job announcement requests references, include their names, addresses, and phone numbers in your cover letter.

## Bolstering recent graduates' resumes

For the student or recent graduate with no professional experience, it is appropriate to list nonprofessional jobs and part-time, summer, or volunteer work if you label the section something like "Work Experience." In addition, persons with little or no professional experience can list major school projects that resulted in a written product and projects they may have conducted with a citizen group or a planning commission. See the first sample resume at the end of this chapter for an example of a resume for an entry-level job candidate just graduating from school.

If you have no publications to list, you could label the publications section "Papers" and list selected papers you've written that you feel are pertinent and will generate a positive reaction from a potential employer.

Obviously, if you have no organization memberships, honors, or additional professional activities, leave these sections out of your resume.

## Correcting fallacies about resumes

Several common misconceptions about resumes continue to survive despite all the advice job counselors have given. Some items simply do not belong in a resume.

✗ *Salary*. The salaries you earned in former jobs do not belong in a resume. The purpose of your resume is to get you an interview. Don't undermine it. Past earnings could scare a prospective employer into thinking you are too high-priced even if you are willing to work for less or the same as in your current position. Even worse, listing salaries might unwittingly lead the potential employer to reduce the salary she was prepared to offer. Salary should be come up only at the end of the job interview after you've had a chance to demonstrate your value to an employer as well as learn about the worth of the position. You cannot realistically discuss, or negotiate, salary if you prematurely mention it only your resume. However, if the ad for a job requests your salary history, submit it on a separate sheet, but not in your resume. For sound advice on negotiating salary, see *Salary Success: Know What You're Worth and Get It!* ($11.95, 1990, 164 pages; for your convenience, this book is available from Planning/Communications; see the catalog at the end of this book).

✗ *Career Objectives*. If you have the insatiable urge to state your career objectives in writing, describe them in your cover letter. This approach permits an applicant to express his career objectives in terms applicable to a specific job. Do not place career objectives in your resume.

✗ *Hobbies*. Many employers do not care about an applicant's hobbies or outside interests. Frankly, a list of hobbies and outside interests only clutters your resume with irrelevant information. There is also the danger that your hobbies may scare off a potential employer. For example, one Texas planning consultant says she is reluctant to hire anyone who lists skiing or other cold-weather sports on a resume because she thinks such people would vacation a lot on weekends and be unavailable for necessary weekend work. Other employers are reluctant to hire persons with a lot of outside interests because they think it will be hard to get them to do extra work at home or work late hours. Conversely, some employers like their employees to have outside interests.

There's an old story still circulating of the job candidate who won his position over equally-qualified applicants because the agency director wanted a fourth for bridge at lunch—admittedly not a sound hiring criterion. But nobody in good conscience can state that every agency director follows sound hiring procedures. So, list hobbies and outside interests only at your own risk. If your qualifications are any good, you'll make it to an interview where the interviewer can ask about these activities if they are really important to him.

## Resume appearance and design

Although most employers are interested in the content of the resume rather than its appearance, design expectations have risen thanks to the accessibility of word processing and laser printers that have made well-designed, typeset-quality resumes today's standard. It used to cost a small fortune to produce a typeset resume. Today, typeset-quality can be produced by anyone with a word processing program and laser printer. Do not use a dot-matrix printers. The results look amateurish even in letter quality mode. Resist the urge to use them.

Today nearly everybody can have access to high-quality resume design at a reasonable cost. Many resume preparation services will convert a one- or two-page typewritten resume into a classy-looking document for fee ranging from $30 to $200. Any resume preparation service that charges $100 or more for a two-page resume should include a major editing or rewrite and redesign of your resume for that price. Resume preparation services appear in the yellow pages under "Resume Service."

There are alternatives that, although more time consuming, cost much less. If you can prepare your resume on a micro-computer, but don't have a laser printer, take a floppy disk with your resume file and word processing program on it to one of the many photocopying shops that rent time on desktop computers and laser printers. The one catch is that most of these shops use Apple micro-computers while the dominant personal computer system is the IBM-compatible, MS-DOS micro-computer, which is incompatible with Apple's computers. If you choose this approach, ask the shop what kind of personal computers it has hooked up to its laser printer. Also find out exactly what kind of laser printer it is so you can use the proper printer drivers when preparing your resume file.

On the other hand, you could just rent time on the shop's computer and prepare your resume there wit the shop's word processing and desktop publishing programs. The only difficulty comes about if you are unfamiliar with the shop's programs and computer system. But given enough time, anybody can figure out how to use nearly any word processing program.

Given the relatively high price copy shops charge for each printed page produced on a laser printer (usually around $1/page), plan to print out just one or two copies on the laser printer, and photocopy the additional copies of your resume on a photocopying machine (usually for about 6¢/page).

To assure an attractive, readable resume, type or print it neatly on 8.5 inch x 11 inch paper that is at least 20–pound weight. Unless you've got some very good reason to use bright colored paper, avoid it. Your best bet for a professional–looking resume is a conservative paper color like white, off–white, ivory, light tan, or light gray. Use a dark ink or toner such as black, navy, or dark brown. The exact format or design is up to you. Whatever you choose, keep it clean and professional looking. Two possible designs are suggested by the sample resumes that follow.

## Sample cover letters and resumes

Two resumes and cover letters that illustrate these guidelines follow. The first shows a recent graduate who is seeking an entry–level position in public administration. The second shows an experienced planner applying for a top–level position. This resume is designed to show how to present your experience when you've risen through the ranks at a single municipality so it does not look like you simply changed jobs every 18 months.

Note that the job ad for the entry–level position does not include the name of the personnel officer. However, as noted earlier, you should call the hiring agency or check an applicable directory of officials to learn the personnel officer's name so you can address your letter to her.

---

## Entry–level position in public administration

---

Assistant Village Manager Starting salary to $23,000 with fringe benefits. Require B.A.; Masters of Public Administration with 0–3 years experience preferred. Responsibilities include risk management, budget analysis and support; staffing village board committees; assistant to Village Manager. Deadline: May 1. Send resume to Personnel Officer, Riged Park Civic Center, Riged Park, Illinois 60068.

---

4321 Ocean Front Drive
Valhalla, Indiana 46208
April 15, 1992

David Murphy, Personnel Officer
Village of Riged Park
Riged Park Civic Center
Riged Park, Illinois 60068

Dear Mr. Murphy:

Your ad for an Assistant Village Manager in the March issue of <u>PA Times</u> captured my attention for several reasons. As my enclosed resume illustrates, my education, experience, and skills match the duties of the position you describe in the ad. Riged Park has a long–standing reputation for sound and effective village management. I am seeking a position with such a municipality, that not only challenges me, but fully uses my talents.

My graduate work was so practice–oriented that it effectively constitutes more than the equivalent of a year's work experience. As a management intern with the City of Valparasio, Indiana, I was charged with developing the city's preliminary 1982 fiscal year budget of $5.2 million. The City Council eventually adopted this budget, written using a custom computer program I designed. In addition, several area governments are using my masters project, Analysis of Municipal Insurance Needs for the Tri–City Area, as the basis for their joint risk management insurance program. In all, my internship and masters project have provided substantial practical experience in the field of city management certainly equivalent to at least a year of work experience.

I would appreciate more information concerning this position as well as an opportunity to meet with you to discuss our mutual interests. I will call you next week concerning any questions we both may have and to arrange an interview if, at that time, we both feel it is appropriate.

Thank you for your time and consideration. I look forward to meeting you.

Sincerely,

Diana G. Raphael

Enclosure

# Diana G. Raphael

Current address:
4321 Ocean Front Drive
Valhalla, Indiana 46208
Phone: 317/864-8335

Permanent address:
40 del Lords Lane
Lakeview, Connecticut 06566
203/456-7890

Date of Birth: November 19, 1969
Social Security Number: 350-34-9035

## Education

Master of Public Administration, University of Indiana, 1991
B. A. (Computer Science), University of Northern South Dakota at Hoople, 1987
Wahall Pembina Scholarship: 1986-89
Dean's list: 1984-85, 1988-89

## Work Experience

**Research Assistant**, School of Public Administration, University of Indiana (1426 SE Hipple, Valhalla, IN 46211; 317/353-3537) Sept. 1988-June 1989
   Developed introductory undergraduate course in public administration; identified computer applications in capital improvements programming.
**Management Intern**, City Manager's Office, City of Valparasio (1234 Bach Blvd., Valparasio, IN 46040; 317-635-8616) June 1990-Sept. 1990
   Prepared and analyzed preliminary 1989 Fiscal Year $5.2 million budget; wrote computer municipal budgeting program; staffed city council budget committee
**Program Designer**, Union City Computations (869 W. High St., Union City, IN 46301; 317-541-9119) part-time during 1987-89 school years
   Developed computer programs for financial management, investment counseling, Space Wars

## Organization Memberships

International City Management Association
American Society for Public Administration

## Major Papers and Projects

*Analysis of Municipal Insurance Needs for the Tri-City Area*, Masters Project, to be published in May 1992
*Valparasio Preliminary Budget, FY 1989*, Sept. 1990
*Computer Applications in Capital Improvements Programming*, Jan. 1989
*Systems Analysis Approach to Problem-Solving in City Government*, Nov., 1989

*References available upon request*

---

## Administrative–level position in city planning

Director of Planning. Salary range $36,312 to $44,836. Population 65,000. Responsible professional and administrative work directing technical and professional staff in planning matters related to community development, long–range master planning, and zoning. Requires degree in planning or closely related field, and considerable progressively responsible experience in the planning field. Send resume to Boris S. Goodenuff, Director of Planning, City of East Palm Beach, P.O. Box 3366, East Palm Beach, FL 33479. Application deadline: Oct. 31, 1992

---

10 E. Shuffle Street
Asbury Park, New Jersey 08002
October 12, 1992

Boris S. Goodenuff, Director of Planning
City of East Palm Beach
P.O. Box 3366
East Palm Beach, Florida 33479

Dear Mr. Goodenuff:

Your ad in JobMart for a Director of Planning immediately caught my eye as a potentially challenging and very professionally rewarding opportunity. As my enclosed resume indicates, I have been working in community development, comprehensive planning, and zoning administration for so long that I've been accused of being born to plan.

In both my present and former planning director positions, I coordinated the preparation and implementation of grant applications and community development plans. I was chief author of the innovative, award–winning policy-oriented Comprehensive Plan 1978 for Jackson Cage. Throughout my professional planning career, I have administered and written zoning provisions. As indicated by the attached resume, my experience has involved considerably increased responsibilities each step of the way.

I have enclosed a copy of the Comprehensive Plan 1978 for your examination. If you would like copies of any of my other work products or publications, please do not hesitate to ask.

I would like to learn more about this position as well as have an opportunity to meet with you to discuss our mutual interests. I will call you next Friday about any questions we may both have and to arrange an interview if, at that time, we both feel it is appropriate.

Thank you for you time and consideration. I look forward to meeting you.

Sincerely,

Bruce Fallsteen
Enclosures

# Bruce Fallsteen

10 E. Shuffle Street
Asbury Park, New Jersey 08002
Phone: 201/867–5309

Born: September 23, 1949
Social Security Number:
999–40–1987

## Professional Experience

July 1982+    Planning Director. City of Asbury Park, New Jersey (10 Freeze Out Ave., Asbury Park, NJ 08010; 201/867–5000)

> Supervise four–person planning department; manage $2.3 million community development program; write and administer land–use regulations, prepare performance zoning ordinance; provide staff assistance to Plan Commission and City Council; initiate revision of comprehensive plan and economic development studies.

Village of Jackson Cage (Village Hall, Jackson Cage, MO 65106; 314/328–8800)

Nov. 1973–
June 1982    **Community Development Director.** Aug. 1978–June 1982

> Supervised 10–person staff including divisions of planning and community relations; managed $6.8 million community development and planning program; developed village's first capital improvements program; developed and implemented integration maintenance plan.

**Chief Planner.** March 1975–Aug. 1978

> Researched and wrote innovative *Comprehensive Plan 1978*; wrote zoning ordinance revisions; reviewed zoning applications and proposed ordinances; supervised assistant planners; provided staff assistance to Plan Commission and Village Board.

**Grants Coordinator.** Nov. 1973–Feb. 1975

> Identified funding opportunities; prepared grant applications and budgets for grants totaling over $1.2 billion.

June 1972–
Sept. 1972    **Summer Intern.** Crosby, Stills, and Nash, Planning Consultants (4 Way St., Youngstown, Ohio 42351; 216/353–5555)

> Designed and completed cohort survival population projections; input–output economic analysis, *Economic Base Study of Akron, Ohio*; and origin–destination transportation studies.

## Education

Master of Urban Planning, Ohio State University, June 1973
Teaching Assistant, Sept. 1971–June 1973
B.A. (sociology), University of Chicago, June 1970
Dean's List, 1968–1970
Chairperson, Lascivious Arts Festival, 1970

## Organization Memberships and Honors

American Planning Association, 1978+
   National Award of Merit for *Comprehensive Plan 1978*
   Ohio Chapter Vice–President, 1974–76
Metropolitan Housing and Planning Council (New Jersey):
   Chairperson, Planning Committee, 1983+
Regional Finalist, White House Fellowship, 1980

## Publications

"Economic Base Studies: Whole Lotta Nothin' Goin' On?" in *Planning* magazine, April 1975, pp. 17–19.
*Comprehensive Plan 1978*, Jackson Cage, Missouri, 1978, 621 pp.
*Meeting Across the River: Integration Maintenance Plans*, Planning Advisory Service Report No. 1,749, American Society of Planning Officials, July 1979, 31 pp.
"Backstreets: The Ties That Bind – An Analysis of Urban Subculture," in *Journal of Sociology*, Oct. 1983, pp. 521–548.
"The Promised Land: Performance Zoning," in *New Jersey Planning*, May 1985, pp. 24–27.
"The River: You Can Look (But You Better Not Touch)—Time to Clean Up Our Waterways Before It's Too Late," in *Sunday New York Times*, Feb. 29, 1987, pp. 1,205–1,210.
"Government Cheese: A Lifetime of Trouble," in *Reckoning Day*, September 13, 1991, pp. 3–7.

## Additional Professional Activities

Speaker at American Planning Association National Conference:
   "Gizmo No More: Economic Base Studies" (1979)
   "New Coat of Paint: Revising the Comprehensive Plan" (1983)
Guest Lecturer: Rutgers University (New Brunswick), "Performance Zoning: A Lifetime of Trouble?" (1982)
Guest Lecturer: Rutgers University (Jersey City), "All That Heaven Will Allow: Preparing Comprehensive Policy Plans" (1983)
Guest Lecturer: Columbia University (New York), "Thundercrack: A Survival Course for Progressive Planners in Higher Education (1985)

References available on request

## Chapter 7

# Performing your best at your job interview

In government's always competitive job market, a job ad often draws over 100 responses from qualified individuals. An invitation to appear for a personal interview indicates that your cover letter and resume interested a potential employer enough to make you a serious candidate. Now it's up to you to do your best at the job interview to clinch the job. Many well–educated, intelligent, well–qualified candidates lose jobs because they are uncomfortable in interview situations or fail to prepare adequately. Others just have a natural aptitude for personal interviews. Any well–qualified job candidate can improve his performance in job interviews by following the guidelines suggested here and in books on job interviewing such as the Krannichs' *Interview for Success* (available from Planning/Communications; see the catalog at the end of this book).

Most professional positions in local and state government do not require a written examination. Instead there is an oral quasi–examination, more accurately called an interview. Some governments put you before a panel of two to four people who evaluate you. Others simply have the agency director interview you. Many small planning departments will have the most serious candidates meet with all the other professionals in the department to assure compatibility. When asked to come in for an interview, try to find out who will conduct the interview and who else will be present for it so you can be adequately prepared.

## Preparing for the interview

A personal interview not only gives your potential employer an opportunity to evaluate you in depth and you a chance to sell yourself, but it also gives you the opportunity to learn much more about the employer and the agency for which he works. You want to be able to carry on a fairly intelligent conversation with your interviewer, even if he can't. By knowing what is expected of you and by undertaking a few simple preparations, you can make a more favorable impression and minimize any nervousness you may feel.

Interviewers will size you up in terms of the following qualities:

| | |
|---|---|
| Initial impression | Fitness for the job |
| Past job performance | Maturity |
| Analytic ability | Judgment and prudence |
| Appearance and manner | Leadership |
| Motivation | Potential to grow in the job |
| Ability to communicate | Overall personality |
| Initiative | Mental alertness |
| Self–confidence | Compatibility with other staff |

Some agencies maintain a standard rating form and use a point system to rate candidates. Prior to your interview, try to obtain a copy of the rating form from the Personnel Department so you can tell exactly on what qualities you will be evaluated.

This checklist of fundamental provisions you should take before you meet your interviewer will enhance your performance at the interview:

❏ *Be certain of the exact time and place of the interview*. If you are uncertain how to get there, just ask. Write this information down and don't lose it. If you are really unsure of where the interview location is, check it out on a local street map or take a test drive there.

☐ *Arrive at the interview on time or a little early.* There is no excuse for tardiness for a job interview. Innumerable jobs have been lost because the candidate was late for the interview. If it becomes obvious you are going to be more than five minutes late, call and let the interviewer's secretary know. Try to arrive about 15 minutes early.

## SYLVIA                                        by Nicole Hollander

☐ *Know how to pronounce the interviewer's name correctly.* If in doubt, call in advance and ask her secretary how to pronounce it.

☐ *Learn all you can about your potential employer and the position for which you are applying.* If you are applying for work in local government, you want to appear reasonably knowledgeable about the community. Drive around the city. Read its most recent comprehensive plan. Ask planners at the regional planning agency, if any, about it. Find out its population and socioeconomic composition. Find out what the employing agency actually does, how it functions, who it serves, its size and budget, current issues facing the agency, with whom you will work, who your boss will be, and why there is a vacancy. Some of the directories described in chapters two through five provide details about government jurisdictions. There are also other directories available at libraries that provide census and economic information. Often a Chamber of Commerce publication will give the whitewashed version of the city.

At least try to learn enough so your potential employer won't feel you are too much of an outsider to learn the vagaries of the community in which you would be working. And by all means try to learn all you can about the person or persons who will interview you and make the hiring decision so you can present the side of you which will appeal most to their sensibilities. It is possible that other people you know in your field may be able to tell you something about your interviewer and the jurisdiction for which she works.

❏ *Make a list of points you want to be sure to make in the interview* at appropriate moments. You may have forgotten to make these points or facts about yourself at your last interview. Placing them firmly in mind before this interview should assure you don't forget them again. Even though you should never pull out such a list at the interview, the mere act of writing the list will help you remember the points.

Many interviewers will query you about your career goals. Whether or not you were once a Boy Scout, be prepared! Think this one out carefully because nearly every interviewer will hit you with this one.

❏ *Plan to bring several items to the interview*. Believe it or not, some interviewers lose a candidate's resume and cover letter just before the interview. So be sure to bring a clean copy of each with you. If requested, bring letters of reference and work samples. Students may substitute high–quality term papers or projects. Bring these materials in a folder or brief case and offer them only if asked or if they graphically illustrate a point. The interviewer's desk is probably cluttered enough as is.

## Questions interviewers ask

Be prepared to answer the questions that inevitably surface in any job interview. According to the authors of *Interview for Success*, most of the following questions about your education, work experience, career goals, and yourself tend to surface in virtually every job interview.

• Tell me about your educational background.

• Why did you choose to attend that particular college?

- What was your major, and why?
- Did you do the best you could in school? If not, why not?
- What subject did you enjoy most? ...the least? Why?
- If you started all over, what would you change about your schooling?
- Recent graduates are likely to also be asked:
- What was your grade point average? (The more work experience you have, the less likely this inquiry will be made.)
- Why were your grades so high?... so low?
- What leadership positions did you hold?
- How did you finance your education?
- What were your major accomplishments in each of your former jobs?
- Why did you leave your last position? If asked why you left any of former your jobs, give reasons that do not suggest you are a job shopper or jumper. Acceptable reasons include a return to school, better pay, new challenges, more responsibility, and a desire for a different type of work.
- What job activities do you enjoy the most? ...the least?
- What did you like about your boss? ...dislike?
- Which of your jobs did you enjoy the most? Why? ... the least? Why?
- Have you ever been fired? Why?
- Why do you want to work for us?
- Why do you think you are qualified for this position?
- Why are you looking to change jobs?
- Why do you want to make a career change?
- Why should we want to hire you?
- How can you help us?
- What would you ideally like to do?
- What is the lowest pay you would take? (Always deflect this question. See the discussion on salaries later in this chapter.)

- How much do you think you are worth in this job?
- What do you want to be doing five years from now? (Working here with a promotion or two, obviously.)
- How much do you want to be making five years from now?
- What are your short-range and long-term career goals?
- If you could choose any job and agency, where would you work?
- What other types of jobs are you considering? ... other agencies?
- When would you be able to start?
- How do you feel about relocating, travel, and spending weekends or evenings in the office?
- What attracted you to our department?
- Tell me about yourself.
- What are you major strengths?

**SYLVIA**                                                    **by Nicole Hollander**

- What are your  major weaknesses? Never say you don't have any. Turn a negative into a positive with a response like, ''I tend to get too wrapped up in my work and don't pay enough attention to my family. My wife has suggested, a couple of times, that I join Workaholics Anonymous.''
- What causes you to lose your temper?
- What do you do in your spare time? What are your hobbies?

- What types of books and magazines do you read?
- What role does your family play in your career?
- How well do you work under pressure? ... in meeting deadlines?
- Tell me about your management philosophy?
- How much initiative do you take?
- What types of people do you prefer working for and with?
- How _____ (creative, tactful, analytical, etc.) are you?
- If you could change your life, what would you do differently?
- Who are your references? (Have a printed list with names, addresses, and phone numbers to submit.)
- How would you respond to a question from a reporter about the plan commission's decision to override your recommendation? An increasing number of public sector employers are concerned with employees speaking to the press, especially on controversial issues. In developing your answer, keep in mind that when working for government, the public is your actual client and the public is represented by the people it has elected. Once the public's elected representatives, or appointed representatives such as plan commissioners, make a decision, you should not publicly criticize it, or criticize it on the record to a reporter, even if it runs counter to every sound principle of government.

## Stupid interviewer tricks: illegal questions

Unfortunately, despite great strides over the past decade, illegal questions continue to arise in job interviews, even for government work. Sexism, in particular, is alive and well in the hearts and souls of many job interviewers. While equal employment legislation makes it illegal to ask certain questions during an interview, some interviewers ask them anyway. If you are prepared, you can fend them off effectively and still score points with the interviewer. If the questions don't get asked, you've got no problem.

Illegal or inappropriate questions include:

- What's your marital status?

- How old are you?

- Do you go to church regularly?

- What is your religion?

- Do you have many debts?

- Do you own or rent your home?

- What social and political organizations do you belong to? Be wary if the interviewer steers the conversation to politics. Do not be evasive, but temper your remarks to camouflage radical or extremist views. Keep in mind that in some communities a traditionally "liberal" viewpoint is considered "radical." Your political views are really nobody's business but your own. But don't say that in an interview unless you have found an inoffensive way to express that view. Try to say no more than is necessary to answer the interviewer's broad line of questioning about politics.

- What does you spouse think about your career?

- Are you living with anyone?

- Are you practicing birth control?

- Were you ever arrested?

- How much insurance do you carry?

- How much do you weigh?

- How tall are you?

If an interviewer spouts one of these illegal questions, don't go crazy and shout "That question is illegal and I ain't gonna answer it!" You may be right, but this sort of reaction does not display any tact on your part, which may be what the interviewer is testing, albeit tactlessly. The authors of *Interview for Success* suggest that one type of response is humor. For example, if asked whether you are on the pill, you could respond, "Sure, I take three pills every day, vitamins A, B, and C, and thanks to them I haven't missed a day of work in three years."

Asked if you are divorced, you might respond, "I'd be happy to answer that question if you could perhaps first explain what bearing being divorced, or not being divorced, could have on someone's ability to perform this job?"

As you might have guessed by now, women are the main targets of these unjustifiable questions. But if you're prepared, you can neutralize them. For example, some interviewers will ask women with small children, "What if the kids get sick?" A sound response to this question goes along the lines of, "I have arranged for contingency plans. I have a sitter on standby, or my husband can take a vacation day." This sort of answer indicates to your potential employer that you are a professional (not that you should have to prove your professionalism just because you're a woman, but some "dudes" never learn) and that you've anticipated the problem.

Married women with a family often get asked, "How can you travel?" An interviewer is trying to find out if the employer will have to pay for the woman's other responsibilities. An employer may be wondering if she is going to put her family before her job. A good answer would be, "Of course I can travel if it's important to my job. I'd be happy to do it. All I have to do is make the proper arrangements."

If an interviewer learns that your spouse works for a company that likes to move its employees around every three or four years, she may ask, "What are your plans if your spouse receives orders to relocate?" That's actually a reasonable question to ask of either partner in a two-income household, but for some mysterious reason it is rarely asked of the husband. A good answer is to say, "My husband and I have discussed this issue and we've decided that my work is important for my professional growth and we will work out a plan when and if that time comes." Once a woman has been working for an employer for a while and has proven her worth, she'll have a better bargaining position if spousal relocation threatens her job.

Try to decide how you will handle illegal or inappropriate questions before you go to an interview. With a little preparation, you can turn a negative into a positive when such questions are posed. Your answers to such questions could turn out to be your strongest and most effective of the whole interview.

## Questions you should ask

Prepare questions before you go to the interview so you won't be speechless when the interviewer asks you if you have any questions. You may want to ask about the nature of the job and agency, opportunities to exercise initiative and innovation, chances for advancement, and status of the agency. Save questions about fringe benefits (health insurance, leave time, conference attendance) and salary for the end of the interview. As explained later in this chapter, you are best off if the interviewer raises these issues.

The authors of *Interview for Success* and *Careering and Re-Careering for the 1990's* and other job counselors suggest that you be prepared to ask the following questions if the interviewer has not already answered them:

- What duties and responsibilities does this position involve?

- Where does this position fit into the organization?

- Is this a new position?

- What would be the ideal person for this position? Skills required? Background? Personality? Working style?

- With whom would I work in this job?

- Can you tell me something about these people? Their strengths, weaknesses, performance expectations?

- What am I expected to accomplish during the first year?

- How will I be evaluated?

- On what performance criteria are promotions and raises based? How does this system operate?

- Is this a smoke-free office?

- What is the normal salary range for such a position (assuming it was not given in the advertisement for the job).

- Based on your experience, what types of problems would someone new in this position be likely to encounter?

- How long have you been with this agency? What are your plans for the future?

- What is particularly unique about working for this department?

- What does this agency's future look like?

## Personal appearance

Face facts: clothes and grooming certainly do not reflect on how decent or qualified a person is for a job, or how well someone will perform on the job. Just look at Albert Einstein, or, at the other extreme, most of the immaculately-groomed men who brought us Watergate or the Iran-Contra scandal. But since the interviewer does not know you personally, your appearance can greatly influence his first impression of you—and first impressions count a lot at job interviews. You will make a much better first impression if you are well-dressed and well-groomed.

As with your resume, don't take chances with appearance even if it means showing up better dressed than your interviewer. Research shows that women elicit a more favorable reaction from interviewers of either sex when they wear a dress or suit, the classic pump, nylons, and, a bra. Jeans, shorts, culottes, miniskirts, sandals, dirty or unkempt hair, an exposed middle, and flamboyant clothing evoke unfavorable responses. Carry a purse or attache case, but not both. It's hard not to look clumsy trying to handle both. If you opt for the attache case, keep a slim purse with your essentials inside the brief case.

Men should wear a suit and tie. Men make a less favorable impression with a sport coat, and a downright unfavorable one dressed in a sweater or boots. Shorts, T-shirts, jeans, or sandals turn off any interviewer. Some researchers insist that a maroon tie inspires confidence. Others have found that the shorter, more neatly trimmed the hair and beard, if any, the better the impression.

Whatever your everyday mode of dress and grooming may be, you've got to play the game when job hunting. Sometimes you will be better groomed and clothed than your interviewer, but remember that it is *your* appearance that counts. After you've landed the job, you can resume your normal work appearance if it varies from that suggested here and does not violate office standards.

For more information on how to dress for an interview, see any of dozens of books on interviewing. They'll essentially tell you what you've just read—but they'll take ten to 20 pages to do it.

## Conduct at the interview

Common sense, above all else, should govern your conduct at a job interview. For example, be punctual and, if possible, arrive a few minutes early in case there are forms to complete. It only hurts your chances to keep an interviewer waiting.

Similarly, common sense dictates that you do your best to make a good first impression since, fair or not, first impressions are quite strong and seldom change later in the interview. A friendly, warm smile helps establish a good first impression that carries throughout the entire interview. A natural smile in the right places throughout an interview can mean the difference between a favorable and unfavorable response.

Greet your interviewer(s) with a solid handshake—something a bit softer than the Hulkster might use—no matter what your sex is. Most interviewers do not like a "wet fish" handshake.

Throughout the interview try to maintain good poise and posture; sit straight and avoid leaning on your elbow or talking with your hands over your mouth. Look alert and interested throughout the interview. Demonstrate that you can be a wide awake, intelligent listener as well as a talker. If nervous, hide it. Keep your hands still in your lap; do not tap your pencil or twist your purse strap. Don't fiddle with objects on the interviewer's desk, or with your fingernails. Chewing gum, or smoking without being invited to do so, usually makes a bad impression since both are generally regarded as signs of nervousness.

Naturally, you will want to establish and maintain good eye contact. Nearly every interviewer is conscious of eye contact; it is the surest way to convince him you know what you are talking about.

Above all else, be yourself and be honest. Since most interviews follow a simple question and answer format, your ability to respond quickly and intelligently is vital. Confused and contradictory answers can cost you the job. The best preventative against contradictory answers, logically enough, is the truth. An honest answer that seems a little unflattering to you is far better than a white lie that may tangle you up in a later question. If you don't know the answer to a specific question, the best thing you can say is, ''I don't know.'' The odds are good that the interviewer knows the ''right'' answer to the question and a bad guess can only put you in a poor light.

Following several additional pointers at the interview will enhance your chances of winning the job:

☞ Follow the interviewer's lead. Most interviewers like to think they are in control. Some like to do most of the talking and judge you by your reactions. Because others believe it is your job to sell yourself, they hardly speak at all. When selling yourself, be modest about your accomplishments while getting your points across. Nobody likes, or hires, a braggart. Don't exaggerate your skills or accomplishments since most interviewers pick up on truth stretching very quickly and it hurts your chances for the job. Try to offer concrete examples of your better points.

☞ Do not take notes during the interview. A job candidate taking notes annoys and distracts some interviewers. If you must write something down, make a remark like, ''That's very interesting. Do you mind if I jot it down?'' Your best bet is to write notes of anything you have to remember after the interview.

☞ Job interviewers like candidates who are enthusiastic and responsive. Let the interviewer know you are genuinely interested in the job. If you are passive or withdrawn during the interview, the assumption can easily be made that you will behave that way on the job. Some government employers want passive employees, though. So you will have to use your judgment to determine if your interviewer wants a passive or active employee.

☛ Even if you need the job desperately, do not let the interviewer know. Candidates who call attention to their dire straits are less likely to be hired. Hiring decisions are not based on your need, but on your ability, experience, and attitude.

☛ Be as complete and concise as possible in your answers since many interviewers can give only 30 minutes to an interview. Devote more time to answering important questions that require in–depth responses than to less significant questions. Some hiring executives recommend never spending more than

## SYLVIA                                    by Nicole Hollander

one minute to answer a question. If the interviewer wants you to elaborate, he'll ask you to do so.

☛ Never denigrate a former employer. If you had difficulties, suggest that some of the blame must have rested on you.

☛ Since the last few minutes of an interview can sometimes change things, do not be discouraged if you have the impression that the interview has been going poorly and you have already been rejected in the interviewer's mind. Some interviewers who are interested in hiring you will try to discourage you just to test your reactions. Remaining confident, professional, and determined will help make a good impression.

☛ Salary is a sticky question. It is a subject best broached toward the end of an interview, preferably by the interviewer. Some experts believe an applicant should ask for as much money as possible to establish a bargaining position, and that employers offer as little as possible for the same reason. However, ads for most government jobs identify a salary range.

Others simply say, "Salary open." The interviewer may choose not to tell you the amount she has to offer and may ask how much you want. Indicate that you are more interested in a job where you can prove yourself than in a specific salary. If interested, the interviewer will usually suggest a figure. Try to find out in advance the standard or average salary for the type of position for which you are applying. The *Government Job Finder* lists several salary surveys in chapters two through five. You should also know the salary level beneath which your needs will not permit you to go. For detailed advice, see *Salary Success: Know What You're Worth and Get It!* ($11.95, 1990, 164 pages; for your convenience, this book is available from Planning/Communications; see the catalog at the end of this book).

☛ When given the opportunity, be prepared to offer a closing statement. This will be your last chance to mention any beneficial points you hadn't had a chance to bring up during the interview and to summarize the positive contribution you can make to the department.

☛ Usually no definite offer is made at the interview. The interviewer may want to discuss your application with other staff and may have other candidates to interview. Occasionally a job is offered on the spot. If absolutely certain you want it, you can accept it. However, it is best to ask for 48 hours to decide. But do not give the impression you are playing off one potential employer against another. You can easily lose both job offers that way.

☛ Since most interviews last a half hour or less, an inconspicuous glance at your watch will suggest when your time is almost up. Be alert for signs from the interviewer that the session is almost over, such as when he looks at his watch. Do not keep talking when the session appears to be ending. Summarize your thoughts and stop. Be sure to thank the interviewer for his time and consideration. Tell him to be sure to get in touch with you if he should have any further questions.

☞ With government jobs, there is usually no need to write a thank you letter after the interview. Of course, right after the interview you will note any further contact your interviewer may have suggested. Follow his instructions exactly, and don't muddy the waters by immediately sending unsolicited correspondence. If the interviewer indicated you will hear from her by a certain date and you don't, write a brief note to remind her about a week after you were supposed to hear from her. Express appreciation for the time and consideration she gave you, and briefly note your continuing interest in the position. You have little to lose at this point by refreshing her memory, and you might get a favorable response.

## SYLVIA by Nicole Hollander

### After the interview

If you don't get a flat rejection or the polite "no" that comes in the type of letter that says, "We will keep your letter and resume in our files and let you know if anything ...." keep in touch if there is still some suggestion that you should. Unless you make a nuisance of yourself, you will be able to stay in the foreground if another vacancy opens.

It's a close call as to whether you should listen to the many job counselors who encourage writing a follow–up letter right after the interview. Most conscientious government employees barely have the time to conduct interviews, much less read your post-interview letter. You will have to use your impressions of the interviewer to determine whether a follow-up letter will help or hurt you.

Following these suggestions should, at least in theory, reduce the hiring decision to one based on qualifications. Not all employers make their hiring decisions the same way. So during your interview be sensitive to hints of what criteria the interviewer will use to make his hiring decision and temper your remarks to comply with them. In general, though, following the suggestions made in this chapter will place you in good stead with a potential employer.

When accepting a job offer, you should send the employer an acceptance letter in which you clarify your assumptions about the job (salary, training, fringe benefits, responsibilities) and indicate your expected date of employment. Once an employer has decided to hire you, you can usually get the starting date changed to one more acceptable to you as long as you are reasonable. Make certain that all conditions of employment are clear and that you have a job offer in writing before you give notice to your current employer that you are leaving. Try to give one month notice if possible, but certainly no less than two weeks.

When rejecting a job offer, you should send a letter as soon as possible that declines the offer and expresses your appreciation for the employer's interest and confidence in you.

When you get rejected, but would still like to work for that employer at some future time, it doesn't hurt to send a pleasant letter thanking the interviewer for her time and expressing your disappointment at not be selected. Emphasize your interest in her department and ask to be kept in mind for future consideration. Suggest that you believe that you would work well together and that you will continue to follow the progress of her agency. Such a letter shows your continuing interest, your recognition that you were not the only qualified applicant, and your genuine desire to work for that agency. Such a thoughtfully-written, brief two- or three-paragraph letter can leave a very favorable impression and enhance your chances should you ever apply there again or encounter the interviewer in another work-related situation.

The *Government Job Finder* helps you find the type of job you want in the location you desire, and gives you a leg up on other job seekers who are unaware of the procedures and sources suggested herein. Armed with the information in this book, you can identify government job openings that most job seekers will never know existed because they limit their job search to positions discovered by word of mouth, personal contacts, and only one or two publications that carry advertisements for jobs in government.

If you are interested in the private sector or the world of non-profits, Planning/Communications offers two companion books to this volume, the *Professional's Job Finder* and *Non-Profits' Job Finder*. Both are available in book stores or through the catalog at the end of this book. These books provide the same service for job seekers in the private and non–profit sectors that this book delivers for job hunters seeking positions in government. For some specialities, a few of the sources contained the *Government Job Finder* also appear in one or both of these other two books because these sources offer jobs in two or more of these employment sectors. However, each book contains the other job sources that focus on that particular employment sector more than on the other sectors.

Even if you didn't possess these job–quest tools before, you are now prepped to prepare a convincing cover letter and a thorough, yet readable resume with which to interest an employer. Finally, you know how to prepare for that strange phenomenon called the personal interview so you can convey the best impression possible. Effective job hunting is hard work, but by using your common sense and the job–finding techniques explained in the *Government Job Finder,* your chances of finding satisfactory employment will soar even in the confusing and sometimes difficult economic times that may face us all in the last decade of the twentieth century.

# Index

## How to use this Index

As explained in Chapter 1 (remember that's the chapter that explains how to use this book, which, of course, nobody ever wants to read), this index is intended to supplement the Table of Contents. Use it to find types of government jobs that you can't find by using the Table of Contents. It will help you find job sources that are not located where you might intuitively expect them to be.

# Reader feedback form

   We'd like to make the next edition of this book even more helpful. You, our readers, are a source of valuable information and suggestions. So, please use this form to:

✍ Tell us how we can make the next edition of the Government Job Finder more helpful;

✍ Tell us about any corrections we should make; and

✍ Let us know of any useful job sources that somehow escaped our attention or appeared after this book was written.

   If you run out of space, just attach another sheet. Please send your comments to me at Planning/Communications, 7215 Oak Avenue, River Forest, IL 60305–1935.

   Thanks for your help and support.

*Daniel Lauber*

Daniel Lauber


Comments:

_____

_____

_____

_____

_____

_____

_____

_____

_____

_____

_____

_____


*Purely optional:* Clearly print your name, address, and evening phone number in case we need to reach you for more information.

## About the author

Author Daniel Lauber, AICP, worked for local and state government in Illinois as an award–winning city planner from 1972 through 1980. Since then he has served local and state government as a planning consultant and, since 1985, as a land–use attorney.

He is author of the *Professional's Job Finder, Non–Profit's Job Finder, The Compleat Guide to Finding Jobs in Government, The Compleat Guide to Jobs in Planning and Public Administration,* and *The Compleat Guide to Jobs in Planning.*

At age 35 he was elected the youngest president of the 26,000–member American Planning Association, while attending the Northwestern University School of Law full–time.

He received his Masters of Urban and Regional Planning in 1972 from the University of Illinois–Urbana, and B.A. in sociology from the University of Chicago in 1970.

He has written dozens of articles on planning and law issues in professional publications and the popular press. He created the "Condo Watch" column for the *Chicago Sun–Times* in 1979. When not immersing himself in the preparation of this book, he spends most of his time as an attorney on zoning cases and on behalf of people with disabilities who wish to live in group homes. He is also computer consultant to a number of professional offices and an editor and designer of numerous monographs and newsletters.

Unfortunately, he can't follow his own advice. He resume runs a lot longer than the four pages recommended in Chapter 6. No wonder he's a consultant.

# PLANNING/ COMMUNICATIONS

For your convenience, Planning/Communications carries these books to help you in your job quest. Several of them are noted in the text of the *Government Job Finder*. While most are available in book stores across the country, we've made them available to you by phone and mail order in case you can't find them in your local bookstore or it's simply easier or faster for you to order directly from us.

Ordering information appears on the last two pages of this catalog.

## Jobs in government

### The Complete Guide to Public Employment

*$15.95, ISBN 0–942710–23–1, 1990, 528 pages*

The perfect companion to the *Government Job Finder*, this book helps people entering government work decide what sort of government jobs to seek, and those who wish to leave government how to shift their government skills into the related worlds of trade and professional associations, contracting and consulting, foundations and research organizations, political support groups and international institutions.

Through 28 hard—hitting chapters, the Drs. Ronald and Caryl Krannich introduce a truly comprehensive concept of the public sector—an interrelated network of public and private organizations as well as domestic and international institutions. These offer thousands of rewarding job opportunities both at home and abroad for those who know how to penetrate the public sector. Moving from one set of public institutions to another, the Krannichs demonstrate a firm grasp of how the public sector operates in both theory and practice. Converting thoughtful analysis into prescriptions for action, the authors have produced the seminal "how—to" book on public employment.

## Federal government

## The Almanac of American Government Jobs and Careers

*$14.95, ISBN 0-942710-39-8, 1991, 392 pages*

In addition to describing the work of hundreds of specific federal agencies, this book provides names, addresses, and phone numbers of personnel offices and job hotlines for each. It also tells you the kind of education necessary for jobs in each agency as well as the occupational titles and whom to contact for job information in the nation's capitol and at regional offices. It also offers guidance on working for Congress, the White House, and the federal judiciary. It offers details on congressional committee staffing levels. A great companion book to the *Government Job Finder*, this directory also provides some information on local and state government—but the federal government is this book's real focus.

## How to Get a Federal Job

*$14.95, ISBN 0-917548-02-7, 1989, 186 pages*

This newest edition of David E. Waelde's best-selling federal job preparation book remains the single best source for unraveling the federal job application maze. Fifteen chapters outline how to get a federal job by using the bureaucratic application process to your advantage. Examines the role of the U.S. Office of Personnel Management's rules and regulations that govern the application and selection processes. Includes step-by-step instructions for establishing eligibility and completing each section of the federal employment application, the SF-171 form. Special chapters address advancing a federal career, handling agency vacancy announcements, locating job openings, applying for a specific federal position, and surviving a reduction in force (RIF). Includes sample forms, vacancy announcements. Essential reading for anyone planning to work for the feds.

## Find a Federal Job Fast!

*$9.95, ISBN 0-942710-36-3, 1991, 183 pages*

"A must for anyone committed to a federal job."—*Midwest Review of Books*

"A great place to start the federal job search. A well-focused book that covers, but does not overkill, the subject of how to get a federal job."—*Career Opportunities News*

Doctors Ron and Caryl Krannich reveal the secrets to quickly finding jobs in one of today's largest and most fascinating job markets. Realistic, insightful, practical, and up-to-date, this book goes beyond the rules and regulations to unveil the inside story on locating job vacancies, completing a winning SF-171 form, and marketing yourself among federal agencies.

## The SF–171 Reference Book

*$18.95, ISBN 0–913593–03–6, 1991, 162 pages*

**"Best of the best"** according to the National Education and Information Advisory Committee. If you're looking for sound, effective advice on how to write a job–winning application for federal employment, this is the definitive book for you. In addition to the standard advice common to other books, Patricia Wood explains the buzzwords that get the attention of personnel evaluators and includes a dictionary of terminology used in the federal hiring process.

## The Right SF–171 Writer
## The Complete Guide to Communicating Your Qualifications to Federal Employers

*$14.95, ISBN 0–942710–64–9, March 1992, 138 pages*

Available beginning in March 1992, this book outlines what federal hiring personnel look for on the SF–171, explains the best language to use and how to customize the form, and offers a special chapter on how to best distribute the SF–171 among federal agencies.

## Postal service

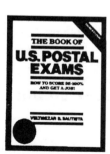

## The Book of U.S. Postal Exams

*$13.95, ISBN 0–931613–05–1, 1990, 272 pages*

Although a 70 percent score is considered passing, the Postal Service routinely selects only from among those applicants who score over 90 percent. Author Veltisezar Bautista spent eight years working for the Postal Service. His book includes exams for 13 Postal Service job classifications along with answers. These exams are unlike those you took in high school or college. They test specific skills necessary for different Postal Service positions. Bautista's tips for test taking and preparation actually do boost scores! Plus, learn the procedures that enable you to become a clerk–typist, clerk–stenographer, or letter sorting machine operator without taking the written exam.

## The Book of $16,000–$60,000 Post Office Jobs
*$14.95, ISBN 0–931613–04–3, 1989, 186 pages*

Learn where they are, what they pay, and how to get them with Veltisezar Bautista's unique guide. For each of nearly 300 specific Postal Service job classifications, Bautista provides full punctilios on grade level, salary range, who is eligible to apply, duties, and qualifications. He explains how and where to apply. You'll learn how to match your education, experience, interests, and skills with current job classifications; which jobs require exams and which don't; how to apply, whom to see, and what to say; and how to move up in the Postal Service once you're hired. A detailed index gets you to virtually every job within the Postal Service. The lengthy appendix provides the addresses and telephone numbers of over 370 U.S. Postal Service Test Centers.

# Jobs with non-profits

## Non–Profits' Job Finder
*$13.95, ISBN 0–9622019–4–4, 1992, 200 pages*

Imagine a *Government Job Finder* that focuses on the non–profit world instead of government, and you've know exactly what this book is all about. Written by Daniel Lauber, author of the *Government Job Finder*, this book provides details on hundreds of job sources for the non–profit world: specialty periodicals with job ads, job–matching services, job hotlines, directories, and salary surveys—sources that carry job vacancies you won't find in your local classifieds. Among the non–profit fields included are: all levels and types of education, social services, legal aid, the arts, advocacy, environment, religion, research, fundraising, philanthropy, foundations, media, housing, community development, public interest groups, child care, adult care, disabilities, museums, and dozens of other non–profit fields.

## Great Careers: The Fourth of July Guide to Careers, Internships, and Volunteer Opportunities in the Nonprofit Sector
*$34.95, ISBN 0–912048–74–3, 1990, 605 pages*

*Great Careers* is the grand–daddy of them all. This massive book tells you everything you ever wanted to know about working in the nonprofit sector. It's filled with details on types of jobs and some job sources for social services, legal aid, the arts, women's issues, consumer advocacy, environment, social change, research, philanthropy, foundations, disabilities, hunger and homelessness, animal rights, labor unions, children and youth, international nonprofit organizations, and many other non–profit fields.

## Jobs and Careers with Nonprofit Organizations

*$13.95, ISBN 0–931613–66–5, available Feb. 1992, 232 pages*

This book identifies the major nonprofit organizations that offer attractive job alternatives and presents job search strategies as well as contact information on hundreds of domestic and international nonprofit organizations.

## Private sector work

### Professional's Job Finder

*$15.95, ISBN 0–9622019–2–8, 1992, 450 pages*

Visualize a *Government Job Finder* for the private sector and you know exactly what this book offers: a trip to over 1,600 sources of private sector job vacancies not advertised in your local classifieds. This **one–stop shopping center** for private sector positions includes the health care, engineering, media, entertainment, financial, real estate, sales, manufacturing, science, and dozens of other private sector fields.

### Careering and Re–Careering for the 1990's: The Complete Guide for Planning Your Future

*$13.95 ISBN 0–942710–51–7, 1990, 383 pages*

One of the most important planning guides for acquiring skills, finding jobs, changing careers, and enhancing lifestyles tomorrow, this book examines each step in the career planning and job search process. Author Ronald L. Krannich begins by revealing six major developments affecting the employment futures of most Americans in the 1990's, 25 coming changes and their implications for industries and occupations in the 1990s, the 20 fastest growing occupations in the decade ahead, and the 20 best jobs in today's job market. Its 11 chapters specify how to organize a job search, communicate skills to employers, prospect and network for job leads, negotiate higher salaries, relocate to a new community, start a successful business, and take action to produce results!

*Photocopying of this catalog is welcome*

**Catalog of job-quest books**

# International jobs

## The Complete Guide to International Jobs & Careers

*$13.95, ISBN 0-942710-24-X, 1991, 320 pages*

This book proffers the best approaches for entering the international job market and describes, in excruciating detail, each of the different sectors of the international job market: government, international organizations, contractors, consultants, nonprofit organizations and volunteer opportunities, associations, foundations, research and educational organizations, business, travel industry, and starting your own international business.

"Provides **tremendous insight**...to the problem of finding work overseas. It is the most comprehensive guide we've discovered to international jobs and careers."—*International Living*

## The Almanac of International Jobs & Careers

*$14.95, ISBN 0-942710-40-1, 1991, 330 pages*

The perfect companion to *The Compleat Guide to International Jobs & Careers,* this book provides the names, addresses, and phone numbers for over 1,000 key employers in the international arena: U.S. federal government, international organizations, education and teaching, private contractors and consultants, colleges and universities, nonprofits, and businesses. Special chapters provide information on work permits, sources of job listings, and relocation resources as well as key in-country contacts for foreign embassies in the U.S., American embassies and U.S. consulates, and American chambers of commerce abroad.

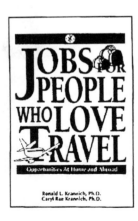

## Jobs for People Who Love to Travel: Opportunities at Home and Abroad

*$12.95, ISBN 0-942710-40-1, 1991, 241 pages*

The ideal guide for those who want to work the world before "settling down" and those who wish to put more travel into their careers and lifestyle, this new book describes hundreds of jobs in business and government, including summer jobs abroad, international careers, jobs in the travel industry, import/export opportunities, and sales and training positions. It furnishes valuable tips on how to get the right job as well as names, addresses, and telephone numbers for contacting potential employers in the U.S. and abroad.

*Order form is at the end of this catalog*

# Finding the right job for you

## Discover the Right Job for You!
*$11.95, ISBN 0–942710–33–9, 1991, 167 pages*

   One of the best books for finding the right job, this book helps you do first things first: assess skills, identify interests, and formulate a powerful job objective *before* writing resumes and letters, responding to job vacancy announcements, and interviewing for jobs. Complete with tests and self–assessment exercises, this book addresses the fundamentals central to developing an effective job search. It's an ideal job guide for folks entering the job market for the first time, people re–entering it after a lengthy absence, or anybody who intends to change jobs or careers.

## The Best Jobs for the 1990's...and into the 21st Century
*$12.95, ISBN 0–942710–61–4, 1991, 235 pages*

   The hot jobs of the 1990's and beyond differ from yesterday's top jobs. This book identifies the fastest growing jobs that also offer excellent salaries, enjoyable work settings, and job security. It names jobs on the way up and those in decline. This indispensable guide includes information on educational, training, and skill requirements; salaries, opportunities for advancement; and future job outlook along with valuable tips on how to break into the hot job fields.

## Graduating to the 9 to 5 World
*$11.95, ISBN 0–942710–50–9, 1991, 195 pages*

   It's a tough world out there on the job, especially for the first time. This book is every student's passport to the realities of the working week. Be prepared for "9 to 5 shock" by learning what it's like to working in a structured world where office politics, productivity, and performance take center stage. Learn how to use your first 90 days on the job to greatly enhance your career.

**Catalog of job–quest books**

# Applying for jobs

### High Impact Resumes and Letters: How to Communicate Your Qualifications to Employers

*$12.95, ISBN 0–942710–30–4, 1990, 257 pages*

Twice excerpted in the *National Business Employment Weekly* of the **Wall Street Journal**, this highly praised best–seller has set a new standard for resume and letter writing guides. This easy–to–follow guide walks the reader through the steps necessary to write resumes and cover letters with impact, ones that stand out from the crowd.

*"If we had money for only one book on resumes, this would be our choice."*—Career Opportunities News

### Dynamite Resumes: 101 Great Examples

*$9.95, ISBN 0–942710–52–5, 1991, 137 pages*

From the authors of *High Impact Resumes and Cover Letters* comes a unique guide for transforming ordinary resumes into outstanding ones that grab the attention of potential employers. Numerous example illustrate the key principles for revising a resume. Included are two unique chapters that critically review resume guides and computer software used specifically for resume writing.

### Dynamite Cover Letters: 101 Great Examples

*$9.95, ISBN 0–942710–53–3, 1991, 135 pages*

Many employers consider a well–crafted cover letter to be even more important than an applicant's resume. This book outlines the principles for effectively writing all the letters that are part of the job search: cover letters, blind approach letters, thank you, negotiation, rejection, and acceptance. Included are many examples of all these types of letters.

### Salary Success: Know What You're Worth and Get It!

*$11.95, ISBN 0–942710–35–5, 1990, 151 pages*

Praised by the **National Business Employment Weekly**, this book dispells myths and explains how to determine your true value, negotiate salary and employment terms, and finalize your job offer. It shows how to respond to ads that request a salary history or salary requirements and much more.

### Interview for Success: A Practical Guide to Increasing Job Interviews, Offers, and Salaries

*$11.95, ISBN 0–942710–31–2, 1990, 218 pages*

One of the most comprehensive and practical interview preparation books available today, **Interview for Success** is packed with solid advice on getting interviews and then using them to your advantage to win the job at the salary you want. The authors, Drs. Caryl and Ronald Krannich, present everything you need to know to do your best at your job interview, including handling stress, and closes with a checklist of 54 interviewing maxims.

### Dynamite Answers to Interview Questions

*$9.95, ISBN 0–942710–60–6, 1991, 163 pages*

The perfect companion volume to *Interview for Success*, this book outlines the best answers to key job interview questions. Included are sample answers to hundreds of questions interviewers are likely to spring. Learn how to turn negative responses into positive answers that can mean the difference between being hired and being rejected. If the thought of interviewing makes you nervous, this is the perfect book for you.

## Networking

### Network Your Way to Job and Career Success

*$11.95, ISBN 0–942710–11–8, 1989, 156 pages*

Pinpointing a practice often presented as merely a vague concept, this book shows you how to make the connections that get you to the jobs that aren't widely advertised. Learn to identify, link, and transform networks to gather information and obtain advice and references that lead to job interviews and offers.

**Catalog of job–quest books**

### Great Connections: Small Talk and Networking for Businesspeople

*$11.95, ISBN 0-942710-31-2, 1991, 179 pages*

Few people realize that small talk is *the* basic networking tool. The authors explain practical small talk techniques anyone can learn and quickly apply to make great connections that are vital in today's work world.

## How to order

Complete the order form on the next two pages, or call us toll-free at 800/829-5220 Mondays through Fridays, 9 a.m. to 6 p.m. Central Time. Be sure to include postage according to the formula given at the end of the order form and enclose your payment (check, money order, VISA, or MasterCard—individuals must prepay, purchase orders are accepted only from libraries, universities, bookstores, or government offices). Call or write for special quantity prices or resale prices. *Please note that prices are subject to change without notice.*

Send your payment (in U.S. funds only) to:

**PLANNING/COMMUNICATIONS**
**7215 Oak Avenue**
**River Forest, IL 60305–1935**
*or call*
**708/366–5200 or Toll–Free: 800/829–5220**
**Monday—Friday, 9 a.m.—6 p.m. Central Time**

**Purchase orders accepted only from libraries, universities, bookstores, and governments.**

## Book Title                     Price    x    #    = Total

| Book Title | Price | x | # | = Total |
|---|---|---|---|---|
| **Government Job Finder** | $14.95 x | ___ | = $___ |
| The Complete Guide to Public Employment | $15.95 x | ___ | = $___ |
| The Almanac of American Government Jobs and Careers | $14.95 x | ___ | = $___ |
| How to Get a Federal Job | $14.95 x | ___ | = $___ |
| Find a Federal Job Fast! | $ 9.95 x | ___ | = $___ |
| The SF–171 Reference Book | $18.95 x | ___ | = $___ |
| The Right SF–171 Writer [available starting March 1992] | $14.95 x | ___ | = $___ |
| The Book of U.S. Postal Exams | $13.95 x | ___ | = $___ |
| The Book of $16,000–$60,000 Post Office Jobs | $14.95 x | ___ | = $___ |
| **Non–Profits' Job Finder** | $13.95 x | ___ | = $___ |
| Great Careers: The Fourth of July Guide | $34.95 x | ___ | = $___ |
| Jobs and Careers with Nonprofit Organizations | $13.95 x | ___ | = $___ |
| [above book will be available starting February 1992] | | | |
| **Professional's Job Finder** | $15.95 x | ___ | = $___ |
| Careering and Re–Careering for the 1990's | $13.95 x | ___ | = $___ |
| The Complete Guide to International Jobs & Careers | $13.95 x | ___ | = $___ |
| The Alamanac of International Jobs & Careers | $14.95 x | ___ | = $___ |
| Jobs for People Who Love to Travel | $12.95 x | ___ | = $___ |
| Careering and Re–careering for the 1990's | $13.95 x | ___ | = $___ |
| Discover the Right Job for You! | $11.95 x | ___ | = $___ |
| The Best Jobs for the 1990's...and into the 21st Century | $12.95 X | ___ | = $___ |
| Graduating to the 9 to 5 World | $11.95 x | ___ | = $___ |
| High Impact Resumes and Letters | $12.95 x | ___ | = $___ |
| Dynamite Resumes | $ 9.95 x | ___ | = $___ |
| Dynamite Cover Letters | $ 9.95 x | ___ | = $___ |
| Salary Success: Know What Your're Worth and Get It! | $11.95 x | ___ | = $___ |
| Interview for Success | $11.95 x | ___ | = $___ |
| Dynamite Answers to Interview Questions | $ 9.95 x | ___ | = $___ |
| Network Your Way to Job and Career Success | $11.95 x | ___ | = $___ |
| Great Connections | $11.95 x | ___ | = $___ |

**Subtotal:  $___**

☛ **Illinois residents: add 7% sales tax**          +          $___

☛ **Shipping: ($3.50 for the first book plus**          +          $3.50
    **$1 for each additional book)**

☛ **Additional books:** ___ **x $1/each**          =          $___

☛ **Overseas orders: add an additional $8 per**
    **book for air mail**          +          $___

☛                          **Total enclosed:  $___**


☛ **Please continue on the other side.**

## Ship to:

Name _____

Address _____
For UPS delivery, give full street address and unit number. No post office boxes!

City–State–Zip _____

☐ Enclosed is my check or money order for $ _____ made
payable to Planning/Communications.

☐ Please charge $_____ to my (check one):

☐ VISA
☐ MasterCard

Card number: _____
Expiration date: _____
Signature:

_____
Please sign your name exactly as it appears on your charge card.

Home phone number: _____/_____

Send your order and payment (in U.S. funds only) to:

**PLANNING/
COMMUNICATIONS**
**7215 Oak Avenue**
**River Forest, IL 60305–1935**
*or call*
**708/366–5200 or Toll–Free: 800/829–5220**
**Monday—Friday, 9 a.m.—6 p.m. Central Time**